J Munser Turner.
June 1956.

CHRISTIAN WORSHIP

OXFORD
UNIVERSITY PRESS
AMEN HOUSE, E.C. 4
London Edinburgh Glasgow New York
Toronto Melbourne Capetown Bombay
Calcutta Madras
HUMPHREY MILFORD
PUBLISHER TO THE
UNIVERSITY

CHRISTIAN WORSHIP

STUDIES IN ITS
HISTORY AND MEANING

BY MEMBERS OF
MANSFIELD COLLEGE

EDITED BY
NATHANIEL MICKLEM

OXFORD
AT THE CLARENDON PRESS
1936

Doctori reverendo GULIELMO BOOTHBY SELBIE *huius libelli editores salutem in Domino.*

Quinquagesimo abhinc anno, domine, Andrean Martinum Fairbairn, virum eloquentem et eruditum, tam fidei christianae devotum quam liberi intellectus vindicem, cum benignitate et admiratione acceperunt Oxonienses. Per hos L annos Collegio de Mansfield, quod ille et fundavit et genio suo adornabat, tu imprimo discipulus, deinde praeceptor, denique principalis arcte es coniunctus. Nos igitur decet iubilaeo nunc Collegii nostri res gestas celebrantes huic opusculo, quod pignus pietatis nostrae erga Collegium proferimus, nomen tuum adscribere. Tu per haec quinque lustra ecclesiolis, ut dicitur, Independentibus fidelis et acceptus deserviisti; tu sermone et exemplo multis in Oxonio nostro fuisti pro praesidio et adiutorio fidei; tu primus Independentium in hac Universitate vicecancellarium disertissimum et facundissimum Johannem Owen ex aede Christi longo intervallo secutus vestimenta doctoris in sacrosancta theologia induisti.

Hunc libellum de cultu et religione conscriptum tibi, domine, dicare volumus, cuius vox per tot annos sive praedicantis in auribus nostris gravissime sonabat, sive orantis verbis cum simplicibus tum fervidis adsistentium preces et vota feliciter exprimebat.

FOREWORD

IN 1871 religious tests were abolished in the University of Oxford. In 1886 Andrew Martin Fairbairn came to Oxford and began his teaching. Though the buildings of Mansfield College were not completed till 1889, it is proper that the College should celebrate its Jubilee in 1936. All the contributors to this book have been associated with the College as students or as teachers; we offer our work as a contribution to its Jubilee.

Our book is a systematic study of Public Worship. While we have attempted by conference and correspondence to make our work a unity, we are not of identical opinion upon all matters here discussed, and a book on Worship that gives no consideration to the worship of the Church of England, or of the Society of Friends, or of the post-Tridentine Roman Church can make no claim to completeness. We hope, however, that our historical studies may be accepted as a serious contribution to this great subject, and that our later chapters, in particular, may serve as an interpretation, and in this sense as a vindication, of the common tradition of our Reformed Churches.

The chief burden of editorial work has been taken off my shoulders by the generous and discriminating assistance of the Rev. H. Cunliffe-Jones, B.A., B.Litt., B.D., of Witney, who has prepared the book for the press and spent much time and labour upon it. He has drawn up the index, and it is a matter of regret that it has not been possible to find space for his admirable syllabus of the whole.

Finally, we hope that our book may not merely serve

an academic purpose but may also be accepted as itself an act of praise to Him to whose glory it is written.

> Te gloriosus apostolorum chorus:
> Te prophetarum laudabilis numerus:
> Te martyrum candidatus laudat exercitus.
> Te per orbem terrarum sancta confitetur ecclesia. . . .
>   Fiat misericordia tua, Domine, super nos:
> Quemadmodum speravimus in te.

N. M.

MANSFIELD COLLEGE,
  May 1936.

CONTENTS

I

THE PHILOSOPHY OF WORSHIP

I

THE 'Holy of Holies' of human personality is the personal relation of God and man—Thou and I: man's movement towards God, because of God's movement towards man, religion receiving and responding to revelation, the divine object known and felt as no less real than the human subject. This relation is the most intimate as it is the most universal.

Speak to Him thou for He hears, and Spirit with Spirit can meet—
Closer is He than breathing, and nearer than hands and feet.
(Tennyson, *The Higher Pantheism*.)

For where the spirit of man has gone,
A-groping after the Spirit divine
Somewhere or other it touches the Throne,
And sees a light that is seen by none
But who seek Him that is sitting thereon.
(W. C. Smith, *Raban*, p. 75.)

1. This is a personal relation which must be inwardly experienced, and not merely outwardly observed; the *psychological* standpoint of observation in dealing with religion must be corrected and completed by the *psychical* standpoint of experience; and to have and to hold the experience there are individual conditions to be fulfilled, universal as the outward forms of religion may appear to be. 'Surely the Lord God will do nothing, but He revealeth His secret unto His servants the prophets' (Amos iii. 7). 'The secret of the Lord is with them that fear Him, and He will show them His covenant' (Ps. xxv. 14). 'Blessed are the pure in heart; for they shall see God' (Matt. v. 8). 'If any man willeth to do His will, he shall

know of the teaching, whether it be of God, or whether
I speak from myself' (John vii. 17). 'Now the natural
man receiveth not the things of the Spirit of God: for
they are foolishness unto him; and he cannot know them,
because they are spiritually judged' (1 Cor. ii. 14).

2. These sayings are quoted not as dogmatically
authoritative, but as historically illustrative of the general
truth that religion as an individual experience of personal
relation to God is conditioned by individual receptivity
for, and responsiveness to, the universal reality of God,
who is ever wanting to make Himself known, and give
Himself to man. While religion, in its highest stage, is
thus an individual experience of personal relation to God,
the individual is throughout its development dependent
on and affected by his social inheritance and environment. Religion is a tribal or national concern before it
becomes an individual interest. This witness of religion,
wherever it is sincere, to the reality of the revealing God,
which is the initial assumption of this essay, relieves us of
the necessity of discharging two tasks, to deal with which
would expand the essay beyond the limits of space necessarily assigned to it, namely, to show on the one hand
that the religious experience is not merely subjective, a
projection of man's wishes or ideas or ideals into the
void, as some psychologists assert, or to prove on the
other hand the reality of God by logical demonstration
from the data of experience that God exists. Only this
need here be said in regard to the first issue, that such
scepticism regarding the objectivity of man's experience
can be confined only arbitrarily to one part of that experience; and regarding the second issue, that the theistic
proofs cannot by themselves convince the unbelieving,
while they may serve for the confirmation of faith by
intelligibly and credibly relating the religious experience
to the rational, aesthetic, moral, and social interests of
man. Over against the *scepticism* which denies man's
capacity to reach and touch reality in religion, and the

rationalism which demands the satisfaction of the intellect in religion, the witness of seers, saints, and sages standeth sure. However interesting and important it may be for anthropology to trace back religion to its crude beginnings in the race, or for psychology to describe its development in the individual, it is the most mature experience in the most developed personality which discloses its true significance and its full value; and it is only as we apprehend the significance and appreciate the value of religion that the need of, and the reason for, *worship*, the subject of this volume of essays, will be understood and approved.

II

1. Many definitions of religion have been given; but for our present purpose only three of these, which, though given by great thinkers, are illustrations of an inadequate conception, need now be mentioned, as they will set us on the right way. Kant, the moralist, thinks of religion as not only subordinate, but even inferior, to morality; for those who cannot rise to the height of his conviction of the autonomy of the practical reason, moral obligations may be sanctioned as divine commands. Hegel, the philosopher, regarded the religious consciousness as an imperfect comprehension of ultimate reality of less value than the *notion* of philosophy, notably his own. Schleiermacher, who, despite his vehement detractors to-day, still holds the position of honour and influence as pioneer in the modern method of theology, as leader out of the wilderness of rationalism on the one hand, and dogmatism on the other, into the promised land of a religious approach, failed to do full justice to what religion is owing to the influence of the type of piety which had affected his early years, and of the philosophy which later he adopted. His emphasis on feeling as the psychic aspect of the subjective reference, and on dependence as the distinctive content of the objective reference is one-sided,

although it was a necessary corrective of the moralism of Kant and the rationalism of Hegel, and is nearer the heart of religion than their views.

2. It is the whole human personality, thinking, feeling, and willing, which is expressed and exercised in religion, and an exclusive moralization, rationalization, or emotionalizing is a false and wrong limitation of the range of its activity, just as dependence is only one of many elements which form the content of the personal relation of man to God. Religion, when adequately conceived, is the conservation and confirmation of all ideals and values. Its content is as varied as is human personality in all its interests, activities, and relations; and if God be 'in all, through all, and over all', ultimate cause, final purpose, realized ideal, supreme value, then nothing human, except sin, is alien to it, and all the divine which man can receive and to which he can respond is at home in it. To throw into bolder relief what is distinctive of religion as personal relation to God, we may describe religion as man's apprehension of, emotion toward, and action in regard to the reality, which is *beyond* and *above* his world and himself, and yet is *akin* to and even *within* the world and the self. There is, and must be, a recognition of divine *transcendence*, or religion would not be a distinctive relation, distinguished from all other relations, cosmic or social. There must no less be recognition of divine *immanence*, or the possibility of relation would be excluded. Hence a *pantheism* which identifies God with world and self, so far as its practice is consistent with its principle, excludes any such relation, since relation implies some difference; and a *deism*, in so far as it separates God and man, forbids the immediacy and the intimacy of the relation which alone can meet man's need of God. As we shall afterwards see, in *Worship* especially is the recognition of transcendence prominent and dominant.

3. What has been described is religion in its highest form, and not in its earliest beginnings and slow develop-

ment. There is a rationalization and moralization corresponding to the development of reason and conscience *latent* in the process from the beginning, even if it may only gradually become *patent*, since man's personality is a unity, and we cannot exclude reason and conscience as affecting the development, even when emotion is the more conspicuous feature. With this necessary *caveat*, it seems to be legitimate to describe religion as a *sentiment*, since the theory of the sentiments as presented in Shand's very valuable book on the subject, *The Foundations of Character*, does not exclude the *cognitive* or the *active*, while giving prominence to the *emotional* element in a complex expression of human personality. Religion includes creed and code on the one hand, custom and polity on the other, but what is central to it is feeling, emotion, sentiment—pain or pleasure, fear or joy, hate or love. With emotion worship is most immediately connected.

4. Otto in his book, *The Idea of the Holy*, has rendered a service in describing more definitely the kind of emotion or sentiment which is distinctive of religion, although his exposition suffers from his initial detachment of emotion from reason and conscience; this mistake makes more difficult for him the rationalization and moralization of religion which he recognizes as necessary, and offers the cover of his deserved authority to those who want to emphasize the non-rational and non-moral aspects of religion. Otto's service is the more welcome, as it corrects the exaggerated denial by James of any distinctive subjective or objective aspect of religion.[1] In the preceding pages it has been assumed that there is a specific and essential kind of religious object—the divine; and it breeds only ambiguity of language and consequent confusion of thought to extend the term of religion to man's attitude to nature or the race, as is now often done. In the following pages it will throughout be assumed that there is 'one specific and essential kind of religious act'—worship; and

[1] *Varieties of Religious Experience*, p. 28.

while morality will be recognized as the necessary practical expression of religion, 'the fruit of the Spirit', the necessity of worship as an expression of religion, not as a substitute for morality, but as complementary to it, will be insisted on. Here it may be asserted that while there may be 'no one elementary religious emotion', but a complex of varied emotions, which it might avoid misunderstanding always to call a *sentiment*, yet, as it is evoked by a distinctive object and expressed in a distinctive act, it has its own distinctive character. Otto may have reduced the complexity of the sentiment unduly to the simplicity of the emotion, but he does seem to have brought out the *distinctiveness*. He has coined the word *numinous*, from the Latin *numen*, for the object to mark this distinctiveness, and he describes the worshipper's attitude as the 'creature feeling'. The numinous object is *tremendum*, awful, and *mysterium*, baffling the intelligence—'wholly other', that is, it is transcendent, 'above and beyond'; and nevertheless it is *fascinans*, it attracts as well as repels. The word *holy* in its original sense had the same meaning, but as it has gained a distinctly moral content, the use of the word *numinous* seemed necessary to express its earlier meaning. Otto, however, retains the word *holy* in the title of his book. Man has a capacity for becoming aware, and feeling the presence, of the *Holy* (it is an *a priori* category of mind), but that capacity must be developed in experience of God. The development of religion depends on the progress of revelation. In what remains of this essay we shall be concerned with religion as a sentiment of which worship is the characteristic expression.

5. Before confining our consideration to this subject we must, however, briefly indicate other aspects of religion as an exercise of the whole personality, since all aspects find expression in worship. There is in religion *impression*, *affect*, and *expression*, as in every complete mental process. The impression is man's awareness and apprehension of

the *numinous*, followed in his intellectual progress by comprehension and explanation; myth, creed, and theology are the content of religion as thought. It is evident that the forms of worship will be affected by the way in which the object is thought, although there is not always a complete correspondence, for a ritual is usually much more conservative than a creed. Chants and hymns are sung, God is addressed in liturgical prayers that express a theology which has been superseded. In Christian worship even God is often approached as a despotic monarch rather than as the Loving Father. While some reason can be offered for maintaining, as far as possible, the continuity of worship, there seems to-day, when religious thought has undergone so far-reaching a transformation, an imperative need for making our modes of worship such that it can be said to be 'in spirit and truth' (John iv. 23). Sincerity and reality should not be sacrificed to continuity and conformity. Ritual also reacts on creed; there is a class of myths which owe their origin to the need of explaining some form of worship; in Brahmanism especially has ritual affected theology.

6. The *expression* of the religious *affect* takes two forms, worship and moral conduct. It is as the conception of the divine is moralized, as God's holiness comes to include righteousness, goodness, even love, that morality and religion are brought into close alliance; moral duties are regarded as divine commands, and conduct towards men as service of God. Moral conduct, however, is not so primary an expression as is worship; and the divorce of morality and worship is one of the *scandals* of the history of religions, the inquiry into which the necessary limitations of space in this essay forbid. It must here suffice to call attention to the teaching of the Hebrew prophets that righteousness is more important than ritual, that morality is more imperative than worship. Their warnings are all directed against a common and persistent tendency in religion to substitute the second for the first; but they are

not legitimately used to depreciate worship and the ritual which gives it form, when it accompanies in due proportion righteousness and morality. It would give an entirely false impression if this danger were to hide from our regard the influence which religion can, and does exercise in promoting morality. In Christianity religion gives to morality its commanding purpose in the nature of God Himself as holy love, its constraining motive in the love of Christ in His Cross, its attractive pattern in the grace of His perfect life, its cleansing and hallowing power in the Holy Spirit; and in so far as worship makes the reality of God as Father, Son, and Spirit more real, His revelation more intelligible, and His redemption more effective, morality owes to it an incalculable debt. But this service it can render only as the moral progress of the religion is consistently expressed in the modes of worship. The worship should be constantly subjected to a theological and an ethical scrutiny, so that creed and code may always 'make one music' with ritual, 'and vaster' as man's thoughts of God widen, and his standards of life are raised. We are now ready to pass from this general consideration of worship in relation to other elements in religion to the more specific discussion of worship itself.

III

1. The inward sentiment of which worship is the outward expression demands further consideration. Otto has called it the 'creature feeling', an inadequate description of later phases. This sentiment involves the sense of inferiority in man, the emotion of awe, which may and should persist as reverence and adoration, even when perfect love has cast out all fear (1 John iv. 18), the recognition of dependence, the impulse to submission, developing into whole-hearted and single-minded devotion and consequent complete consecration of life. Since the relation of God to man as it is realized in Christ is an

individual relation, however greatly it may be affected by social influences we cannot deal with public worship without giving some consideration to private devotion, for in the Christian community the members are all assumed to have such an individual relation to God and to contribute the gains of that individual relation to the corporate good. The public worship will be formal unless the private devotion is fervent. While society is constituted by individuals in mutual relations, the individual is completed only in these relations within society. Both will for the most part have the same content, praise, prayer, and reading of the Scriptures; while meditation on the truth in private devotion may take the place of its proclamation in public worship. The one can be more intimately individual than the other, although the common worship should aim at being as adequately representative of the thought, feeling, wish, and will of all the worshippers so joined together as is possible. In both there must be adoration, gratitude, confession of sin, acceptance of pardon, resolve of amendment, petition for individual or corporate needs, intercessions for others, both pervaded by submission to the divine will, satisfaction in the realization of God's presence, communion with Him, and reception of His goodness and grace.

2. What should distinguish worship of God from all personal relations to men is the all-pervading recognition of the absolute *worth* of God; in polytheism the worshipper may think of the gods as only *superior* to himself in whatever qualities he may assign: in *monotheism* God's *supreme* worth must be confessed: for He alone is God; the mind cannot conceive, nor the heart desire, any higher good or any other good that can be compared with Him (Pss. xvi. 2; lxxiii. 25). In the phrase 'his worship the Mayor' the word means much less; but in the Christian religion it can mean nothing less. God is the eternal and infinite reality of all man's ideals and aspirations. The conviction

of God's absolute wisdom, goodness, and grace may re-
strain a minute particularity in prayer, since Jesus gives
the assurance on the one hand, 'your heavenly Father
knoweth that ye have need of all these things' (Matt. vi.
32), and on the other, 'how much more shall your Father
which is in heaven give good things to them that ask
Him' (vii. 11); and yet the intimacy of the filial relation
to God may constrain to lay bare to His kind scrutiny all
needs, wishes, aims, and hopes. Does He not desire child-
likeness, and will He not even endure and forgive childishness, and in the discipline of prayer itself correct it?
Does not the asking develop the capacity in us for receiving what God wills to bestow, or surrendering the wish
for what He wills to withhold? Confidence in prayer
can be sustained only as there is the certainty of God's
absolute power as well as of His wisdom, goodness, and
grace.

3. This at once raises the problem whether the recognition of *the order of nature* excludes the petition for material
benefits? To deal with the solution of this problem is
here manifestly impossible, but it cannot be altogether
passed over, although it must be dealt with within the
limits which the subject of worship prescribes. The
mental, moral, and spiritual realm is no less a sphere of
order, where there is law even as in nature, and here,
too, there are limits to liberty, to *what, when,* and *how*
we can receive and God bestow. Prayer would lose its
spontaneity, its intimacy, if we were compelled to ask
anxiously what God can do and what He cannot on our
behalf. Faith will expect great things from God, and
attempt great things for God. Prayer itself, however,
should not be exempted from the scrutiny of reason and
conscience, so that we may learn to exclude unreasonable
and unlawful desires and expectations. The order of
nature is for the religious thinker the symbol of the
constancy of God, on which man as fellow-worker with
God must confidently depend. Any appearance even of

caprice in God's working would bring confusion to man's thought and life. Reverence and humility will forbid our regarding ourselves as such favourites of God that we are entitled to require Him to exempt us from the common lot of man, and work miracles on our behalf. There is a subtle, secret danger of spiritual pride in making a boast to others of our answered prayers as evidence of such favouritism. Who can, however, so define the relation of God to nature as to set limits to His freedom within the order of nature as we know it, or in ways which still lie beyond our ken? Even if our philosophy lead us to set limits to God's power, or at least to recognize that He whose will the natural order expresses has Himself set limits to its exercise, how wide is the range of possibility left open for the answer of prayer! So much at least it seemed necessary to say about private devotion as distinct from public worship.

4. The one cannot be a substitute for the other, and must seek its complement therein. For I regard the definition of religion as 'the flight of the alone to the Alone' as essentially false, because man is for philosophy social personality incomplete in himself and completed only in relations with others, and for religion generally as it has appeared in history, a member in a religious community to which he owes far more than he can give. For the Christian religion each man is one child in the human family, of which God is the universal Father. In view of some current tendencies to depreciate worship as a function of religion it seems necessary at this point to indicate the need of and reason for the personal relation to God, individual and social, of which worship is the expression. The relation of man to God and God to man must not be regarded only as a means and not an end in itself; it is of *intrinsic*, and not only *instrumental*, value. Men do not worship merely that they may obtain some earthly goods for themselves, or that they may thereby become more good morally, although the goods and the

goodness are both gifts which men seek and find at God's hands. God does not evoke the worship of man, only that He may have fitter and worthier instruments of His purpose. Man needs and finds his highest good in his communion with God, and this necessity in man as God implanted warrants us in believing that as God is love He delights in man's approach and appeal to Him. If man's relation to God in religion is the crown of all his other relations, then the expression of that relation in worship is the crown of religion, as the mutual satisfaction of God and man, the one in the other. But the crown is not the whole, and so worship must not be severed from the rest of human life, which it ought to pervade and dominate, as God is 'in all and through all and over all'. The altar should not fill the whole space of life to the exclusion of the hearth, the workshop, the study. That will be the fittest and worthiest worship which expresses a personal relation to God, in which the human personality has found its fullest exercise. The priest or the monk, the preacher or the pastor does not choose the best part, if he interprets 'the one thing needful' (Luke x. 42) in his relation to God too narrowly, and not as widely as his manhood allows, and other men need. 'All things are yours; and ye are Christ's, and Christ is God's' (1 Cor. iii. 23). 'I am become all things to all men' (ix. 22). The need of, and reason for worship as the expression of the personal relation of man to God is an end in itself, and has an *intrinsic* value for God and man; but to fulfil its end it must not be detached from, opposed to, or substituted for any of the other exercises of human personality in relation to God.

IV

1. We may now discuss in detail the constituents of worship; the manifold outward expressions of the universal sentiment. Here the history of religions may be

our guide. We are not required to imagine or invent the worship that ought to be; we must record and estimate the value of the worship which has been and is. Even in the earliest forms of religion, and what seems to us now the lowest, we find *prayer* and *gift*. The worshipper asks of his spirits or gods what he needs and wishes, and believes that they and they alone can bestow. To secure their favour or avert their displeasure he brings a gift; there is in the widest sense *propitiation*, although we must not put into the word at this stage its later content. The worshipper liked to be asked, and to get gifts, and he knew that other men did. He *anthropomorphized* in his worship as in his belief. The crudest form of prayer is petition, accompanied by flattery and bribery of the spirits or the gods.[1] As the relation to the object of worship developed, the fuller content, to which reference has already been made, would be given to prayer and its crudities would be corrected. Probably the *gift* was the earliest form of *sacrifice*; the gift might be an expression of adoration and gratitude, as well as inducement to the spirit or god to grant the petition, the motive being not solely or mainly fear of displeasure, but more generally hope for favour. We are not justified by all the facts in assuming that even at the crudest phases of religion the objects of worship were more commonly regarded as hostile than as friendly; they were not enemies to be overcome, but allies to be secured.[2] In religion there is not coercion, as in *magic*, but petition, persuasion, propitiation. From the spontaneous gestures accompanying prayer and gift a fixed ritual gradually emerged, as Marett has shown in dealing with Magic.[3]

2. When along with the moral development religion becomes moralized, both as regards the conception of the divine reality and the divine requirements of man, sin

[1] Cf. Max Müller's account of *Kathenotheism* in the Vedic literature.
[2] Cf. the classic phrases *do ut des* and Δῶρα θεοὺς πείθει.
[3] *Enc. of Religion and Ethics*, vol. viii.

is conceived as an offence against God, needing not only repentance but atonement; the divine displeasure must be averted and the divine pardon secured. However uncongenial to our modern ways of thinking the idea may be, yet there is sufficient evidence to prove that the atoning *sacrifice* was regarded, if not universally, yet very generally, as *vicarious*; there was the penal substitution of the victim for the offender.[1] Not only was the sense of social solidarity in those days so strong that the suffering of the innocent for, or along with, the guilty did not involve the problem for the moral conscience which it does for us with our strong sense of individuality, liberty, and responsibility; but also as the *contagious* variety of sympathetic magic shows, whatever belonged to a man, his name, his garment, any of his property, was so identified with him that it could take his place. There is, however, a revolt against this individualism, and recognition of solidarity for weal or woe to-day, and Paul can furnish us the words to express this tendency, 'None of us liveth unto himself, and none dieth to himself' (Rom. xiv. 7). 'Whether one member suffereth, all the members suffer with it; or one member is honoured, all the members rejoice with it' (1 Cor. xii. 26). We can accordingly be more tolerant to, and have a more sympathetic understanding of, ideas which at first may only repel us. Whether the idea of penal substitution is to be found in the Hebrew *sin* and *trespass* offering, as the older scholars maintained, or not, as the newer scholars contend, it is certain that the conception of God, revealed in Christ as Father, forbids our using that idea in the interpretation of the Cross of Christ. What we can find in that Cross is self-sacrifice, voluntary and vicarious suffering. That higher idea is anticipated in the prophet's vision of the Suffering Servant (Isa. liii).

3. That the worshipper in most sacrifices shared the

---

[1] The Greek word ἀντίψυχος and Vergil's *unum pro multis dabitur caput*, *Aeneid*, v. 815, supports this conclusion.

victim with the god has led to the *table-bond* theory of sacrifice. The common meal strengthened or renewed the fellowship and confirmed the covenant. But since among many people *flesh* is not the usual food, this theory offers no reason for its use in a meal common to god and worshipper. The late Dr. W. Robertson Smith, in his interpretation of *totemistic* practices, developed this theory into that of a *materialistic sacramental communion of the deity and his worshippers*. The animal sacrificed was one which shared a common life with the deity and worshippers; and by partaking of it, the common life was received; that common life being supernatural and not natural, the worshipper gained more than human power. Although this theory is not accepted generally in its details, it carries us over to another constituent element of worship —*sacrament*—in which a sensible channel is believed to convey a supersensible reality. In the two Christian sacraments, Baptism and the Lord's Supper, the grace of God in cleansing and nourishing the Christian life is expressed. Even if we call these ordinances *symbols*, we do not necessarily reduce them to mere *signs*, for a symbol is effective only as it also conveys what it signifies; and we can at least admit that they were *intended to convey*; and that in experience they *have conveyed* grace, even where the faith attached more to the efficacy of the sacrament, than the reality expressed; for God's goodness is not limited by theological correctitude or ecclesiastical propriety. We may, with the Reformers, however, insist that the sacraments must be subordinated to the Gospel of the grace of God, of which they are signs and seals, although they may for faith be even more. How much both sacraments meant for Paul (Rom. vi. 3–4, and 1 Cor. xi. 27–9)! Lest the word *grace* be misunderstood, as it has been, as a quasi-metaphysical entity which God communicates, and man receives through sacraments, it must be added that grace is nothing else or less than God Himself present, active, imparting Himself in His Spirit to forgive, renew, perfect, and bless. Even in pagan sacraments, however crudely, the deity offers the assurance of and the worshipper utters the aspiration after union of the divine and human, experience by man of the life of God. For Paul to live was Christ (Phil. i. 21); he was crucified and risen with Christ (Gal. ii. 20). This may be called the *mystical* tendency, and is the very core of religion, for it is this immediate contact and intimate communion which all the ordinances of worship may serve to mediate. Yet it ceases to be religious and Christian when it is absorption of man in God that is desired, or identity of man with God that is claimed. Here 'vaulting ambition o'erleaps itself', for the personal difference of man from God must remain if the personal relation to God which is religion is to be maintained, and the worship in which man recognizes God's absolute *worth* is to keep its character.

4. While religion at its highest phase consecrates all time, all space, every man; every day is the Lord's Day, every place is God's house, and every man God's child: yet man being social there must be community in worship; there are sacred seasons when and sacred places where the corporate acts of worship must take place. Without any superstition the Christian religion may recognize the spiritual value of times and spaces set apart for worship. So also not all the worshippers can take part in all the acts of worship. The service must be conducted and the sermon preached by one person, who represents the congregation in these corporate acts, for he acts not instead but on behalf of all the worshippers. There have been false prophets as well as unworthy priests; yet priesthood as mediating the approach of man to God and prophethood as mediating the approach of God to man, freed of all pretensions to exclusive validity and authority, are necessary and legitimate agencies of the community of worship. Preaching, no less than prayer and praise, is an integral part of Christian worship; the two necessary

and complementary aspects should not be exalted or depreciated in comparison with one another, in what is *the revealed religion* in which God offers *grace*, and man receives in *faith*.

5. A few words must be added, in conclusion, regarding the relation of *form* to *content*, as it is in the relation of the one to the other that the greatest differences among Christians emerge. Although all my own inclinations and tastes are to desire an approach to God with 'the thinnest human veil between' (Browning), yet I am compelled to ask myself whether this indifference to form is altogether justified. God has in wisdom, power, and goodness woven as the garment in which we see His presence and activity a material Universe with all its variety, beauty, abundance, and vastness. Man is no more a disembodied angel than a soulless beast. Even if we distinguish soul and body, and assert the superiority of soul to body, body is the one organ of man's self-expression and self-communication. As Christians we do not hold the Greek doctrine of the survival of the soul as a *shade*, but the Hebrew of the resurrection of the whole personality in a spiritual body. Man has aesthetic sense to appreciate and aesthetic talent to reproduce beauty of shape, colour, and sound. May not beauty claim a place in religion with truth and goodness? It is in worship it can most fully be expressed. The senses are not more akin to sin than to holiness; the imagination more alien to truth than the intellect. Theology is symbol even when it attempts to define. We call God 'Our Father which art in heaven'; and preaching is 'spoken symbol'; why should 'acted symbol' be so suspect? May not our worship have lost its attractiveness for many because it does not satisfy the whole man with all his varied interests? If there is ever to be a closer union of the Christian churches this question will need to be candidly and seriously considered; but meanwhile let those who dislike any ritual and those who feel their need of it learn to love one another in

Christ; and here as elsewhere love will find the way to mutual understanding and appreciation of differences in the approach to the one Father, revealed in the One Saviour and Lord, and experienced through the one Holy Spirit.

A. E. GARVIE.

PART I

BIBLICAL STUDIES

II

THE OLD TESTAMENT BACKGROUND

WORSHIP is essentially, as well as etymologically, the recognition of God's worth. It has no direct reference to the edification of the worshippers. It is an offering to God, acceptable to Him and incumbent on man. All other aspects of worship are subordinate to this primary emphasis. One of the great contributions of the Old Testament to the worship of God is that it so emphatically presents the objective worth of God as the ground of worship. The earthly temple is pre-eminently the house of praise (Pss. xxii. 3, lxxxiv. 4; Isa. lxiv. 11). In the 29th Psalm the worshippers in the heavenly courts far above the storm that rages on earth are bidden to 'Give unto the Lord the glory due unto His name'. If this worship were to cease on earth God would lose something that He values very highly; in fact, a repeated appeal to God to save man from death is because 'in death there is no remembrance of thee, in Sheol who shall give thee thanks?' At the close of Psalm cxv (cf. lxxxviii. 10) an effective contrast is made between the dead who praise not the Lord and the living who continue to worship Him (so Isa. xxxviii. 18, 19). The Jewish emphasis on worship was forcibly expressed by Simon the Just, about 200 B.C., when he said that the world rested on three pillars, namely, the Torah, the Worship, and the Bestowal of Kindnesses.

I. *The Development of Worship.* There can, of course, be no attempt here to trace the history of the development of worship in the Old Testament through a thousand years of striking change and rich variety. It is, however, important to remember that the Old Testament considered as the background of Christian worship is not a drop-curtain but a stage, with many different kinds of worship at varying distances from us. The foreground occupied by the New Testament Church and the contemporary synagogue is relatively a narrow strip of this stage. Behind it there is the elaborate cult of the temple ritual, itself the epitome of many earlier developments going back to the simple rites of Semitic nomads when they disposed of the mysterious blood of a slain animal. The analogue to these rites of the desert may be seen in 1 Samuel xiv. 33–5, when Saul, a layman, turns a great stone on his battle-field into an altar; the blood of the slain booty can here be poured out to Yahweh before the animals are eaten.

There are several remarkable features of this development which help to give to it and to its results the character which they possess. The first is the survival of primitive traits of worship (such as the disposal of blood just mentioned) into the latest ritual of the Temple. Many of the strangest features in that ritual are fossil remains from a remote past. The ordeal of jealousy, for example (Num. v. 11–31), is sheer magic, and could be paralleled from African fetish worship and other primitive beliefs. But we must not forget that the ritual of the Temple owed much of its power to its humble origin. From the beginning to the end Israel's worship was concrete; just as the prophet began to work out his oral message by symbolic acts and gestures which became part of it, so the priest and the worshippers whom he led expressed their worship in physical acts and postures, e.g. prostration to the ground or the lifting up of the suppliant's hands, as it were to receive the gift for which he asked. Worship was full of colour, noise, and movement. Its music was not harmony, but the clanging of cymbals and the blowing of horns and trumpets, whilst its highest point of achievement would be a simple melody on stringed instruments. The offerings which normally accompanied every petition, forming its basis, themselves made worship into a dramatic act, capable of a rich and noble spiritualization. This is brought out most clearly in the eloquent description of worship in ben Sirach's time (Ecclus. l. 5–21).

Another feature of great importance in the development of worship was that transference from the country high places to the central sanctuary of Jerusalem which we associate with the Deuteronomic reformation. Ancient worship, it must be remembered, was attached to fixed places, such as might have been consecrated through a theophany, or because of some remarkable tree, stone, or spring. If prayer was offered elsewhere it would usually take the form of a vow to be fulfilled at some sanctuary.[1] The effect of concentration in a single sanctuary is well known. It led to the relative purification and the great elaboration of worship. Worship celebrated in a single sanctuary could be controlled and unified. Moreover, worship inevitably became more official as a result of this elaboration. It passed more and more into the hands of experts (priests and Levites), whilst the layman's function became that of saying 'Amen' and 'Hallelujah', and of identifying himself with private offerings through 'the laying on of hands'.

One other feature of this development must be mentioned because of its great importance for the theology of the Old Testament and ultimately of the New. This is the historical interpretation of the ritual in accordance with the historical character of Israel's faith. Thus the Passover, which became the great commemoration of the Exodus, probably derives from ancient nomadic elements bare of history. The Feast of Booths, an autumn ingathering of Canaanite origin, was at a later date linked to the tradition of desert wanderings on the way to the

---

[1] Cf. W. Robertson Smith, *The Old Testament in the Jewish Church*, 2nd ed., p. 238.

promised land. By these means the ritual itself became an expression of history and pointed back to the redemptive basis of Israel's faith. This is finely expressed in the liturgy of Deuteronomy, xxvi. 1–11, where the Israelite presenting his basket of fruit at the altar looks back across it and all that it represents to those far-off days when his ancestor was a wandering Aramaean. He thanks God for the providence that has controlled the history of Israel, and his thanksgiving finds concrete expression in the basket of fruit.

II. *Worship in the Temple.* The example just given of the concurrence of word and deed is true for worship as a whole throughout its long development. As to its earlier forms we have to be satisfied with occasional glimpses given quite incidentally, such as the communion meal at a local high place (1 Sam. ix. 22–5), or the procession by night to the music of the flutes (Isa. xxx. 29; cf. *Sukkah,* v), or the water libation (1 Sam. vii. 6). The dancing of the priests of Baal around the altar on Carmel (1 Kings xviii. 22 ff.) might seem a pagan rite that did not concern us, but Psalms lxxxvii. 7, cxlix. 3, cl. 4 show us that the solemn dance was part of Israel's ritual (cf. 2 Sam. vi. 14), together with the closely related sacred processions (Pss. xxvi. 6, xlii. 4, lxviii. 25). We have no systematic account of the worship in Solomon's temple, though we can infer from Josiah's reformation of the cult that it was a very syncretistic worship containing many elements that were later regarded as pagan. Our knowledge chiefly relates to the second temple and to the form of its buildings and worship in the time of Herod. This is the more useful for our purpose since it forms the immediate background of New Testament times. The courts of the building were on ascending terraces and the profuse use of white marble and gold plates must have made the whole effect a very dazzling one. Round this outer court were elaborate colonnades. The outer space around the temple proper was accessible to Gentiles as far as a low fence with warning inscriptions. Within this and on the eastern side was a court accessible to Jewish women, beyond which they were not allowed to go. Westward of this and walled off from it was a court to the front of which male Jews were admitted. Within this, again, another enclosure marked off the court of the priests which no layman might enter except when the sacrificial ritual demanded his presence. In front of the temple porch stood the great altar, open to the sky, with a sloping ascent to it on the south side and, north of it, the tables, &c., for dealing with the sacrifices before they were placed on the altar. The temple proper had a porch projecting on both sides of the temple itself, which consisted of two parts, the Hēkāl and the Debir, the former better known to us as the Holy Place and the latter as the Holy of Holies, into which the High Priest alone might enter on the day of atonement. This, in the temple of Herod, was quite empty, whilst the Hēkāl contained on the north side the table of shewbread, in the middle the altar of incense, and on the south the seven-branched candlestick. The personnel of the temple was naturally very numerous and became highly differentiated in its later functions, matching the elaborate buildings. Besides the officiating priests and their levitical assistants (arranged in 24 rotating 'courses'), there were many other officials, such as store-keepers, temple guards, and guilds of musicians.

The central point of the whole worship was the morning burnt-offering known as the 'tamid' (Exod. xxix. 38–42), the offering being repeated in the evening. It consisted of a lamb with flour and oil and a libation of wine. The ritual began even before the break of day. In the darkness before the dawn a solitary priest entered the inner enclosure where the altar stood, to remove the ashes of the ever-burning altar fire. We are told in the *Mishnah* that 'none went in with him and he carried no lamp, but he walked in the light of the altar fire'. What a scene for a Rembrandtesque painting—the dimly seen outline of altar and building, the flickering flames lighting up that solitary figure! The ritual was apportioned by lot amongst the priests due to officiate on a particular day. Each detail, such as the removal of the ashes and the trimming of the lamps and the division of the sacrificial victim, followed a prescribed order and method. The sacrifice proper was followed by certain prayers and benedictions. The people, who were present through representatives, had no part in this except in making certain responses. The whole service was, in fact, a priestly one, performed by highly professional officials on behalf of Israel. The Levites were responsible for the music, namely, the chanting of psalms with a simple melodic accompaniment chiefly used for keeping the beats of the rhythm. Besides this daily act of worship, morning and evening, there were more elaborate services for the Sabbath and the great festivals, and at all times a large number of private offerings such as those made in fulfilment of vows.

What exactly did the sacrifice of the temple ritual mean to the worshippers? That is a difficult question to answer briefly, because the institution of sacrifices itself went through so long a development. The acts were continued, but the interpretation varied. Probably we are safest in thinking with Buchanan Gray that the Old Testament sacrifices were fundamentally conceived as a gift to God, though the blood-ritual and the communion feast preserve primitive elements themselves involving different theories. In later times the general attitude towards sacrifice would be that of the observer of a divine ordinance without much regard to its precise meaning. In certain instances, notably the sin offering and the guilt offering, these gifts would have propitiatory or expiatory value, but so indeed had the whole sacrificial system in its own degree, though it was more often eucharistic than propitiatory. We must not dismiss this ritual as being simply the *opus operatum*, a dyslogistic term somewhat overworked by Protestants. Moore[1] rightly warns us that 'while the temple was still standing the principle had been established that the efficacy of every species of expiation was morally conditioned—without repentance no rites availed'. The best evidence in support of this statement is the Book of Psalms. Many of the Psalms are directly related to the cult and show us how high a moral and spiritual meaning can be put upon the acts of the ritual. It would correct many false impressions about Old Testament worship if we accustomed ourselves to think of the Book of Leviticus and the Book of Psalms as written in parallel columns, for they were more or less contemporary productions. So central is the place of the temple and its ritual in the time of the chronicler that he can almost define Israel as the people of the true cult (2 Chron. xiii. 10, 11): 'We keep the charge of the Lord our God.' This remains true even though it is also true that, by the Maccabean period, the emphasis had been shifted from the temple to the Torah and that the Jews of the later centuries were people of a book rather than of a ritual. For Josephus, sacrifice has become a stronger form of prayer.[2]

III. *Worship according to the Psalms.* The Book of Psalms is obviously the most important part of the Old Testament for our purpose, and requires separate attention. Its direct influence upon both the Jewish and the Christian Church is illustrated by a glance at either the 'Daily Prayer Book' of the Synagogue or the Anglican 'Book of Common Prayer'. But the influence on private devotion is not less profound. If we turn over the pages of Lancelot Andrewes's *Private Prayers* in Brightman's fully documented edition we shall see what this master of prayer owed to the Psalter. He ranges over all the centuries and draws copiously from patristic, medieval, and later

---

[1] *Judaism*, i. 505.
[2] Schlatter, *Die Theologie des Judentums nach dem Bericht des Josefus*, p. 122.

sources, as well as from Scripture; but it is the Book of
Psalms that recurs most constantly in the references. If
the ordinary Christian were able to make an analysis of
his own vocabulary of prayer, he would doubtless find
this true of himself. Three reasons may be given for the
appeal of the Book of Psalms and the catholicity of the
response to it. In the first place, the Psalms are themselves
most comprehensive in the range of their material. In
the second, their language is that of an intense yet concrete simplicity. In the third, they unite in a remarkable
way the needs of individual devotion with those of a
worshipping community.

(*a*) When we look at the range of the material from
which the Psalms are drawn we may think of great con-
centric circles traced from the centre, the individual consciousness of God. The largest is that of 'Nature' (though
the quasi-independence represented by our capital letter
was foreign to Hebrew thought). The primitive cosmo-
logy and mythology were appropriated by a theistic faith
to express the glory of the Creator-God. The Nature
Psalms dwell on the majesty of the star-lit sky (viii),
or of the sun in his daily journey through the heavens
(xix. 1–6), or on the might of God heard and seen in the
thunderstorm (xxix), or on the beneficent fertility brought
by the rain (lxv. 9 ff.), or on the whole panorama of the
created heaven and earth with its animal and human
inhabitants all dependent on God, in which 'man goeth
forth to his work and to his labour until the evening'
(civ. 23). All created things are summoned to praise
their Creator (cxlviii). Within this largest circle there is
a second one of history, primarily, of course, the history
of Israel which so wonderfully exhibited God's fulfilment
of His promises to them of old (cv). In this the great
redemptive acts of the Exodus naturally held the most
prominent place, corresponding in some degree with the
centrality of the Cross in the Christian view of history
(cxxxvi); nor was the moral significance of Israel's mis-

fortunes overlooked (lxxviii and cvi). All history pointed
forward to the climax when Israel's God should in the
sight of all the nations ascend His heavenly throne and
reduce an unruly world to order; the Psalms are as full
of 'eschatology' as the Prophets, from whom indeed their
hope is largely derived (cf. xlvii and xcvi–c). A third and
closer circle is that of human society, as the Psalmists
knew it—great empires still on the horizon, if dimly seen,
small national groups in close proximity in the diversity
of that 'land of tribes', and within Israel itself the tension
of opposing political and religious parties, the conflict of
formal and intensely felt religion, the tyranny of native
or foreign rulers, the continual friction of rich and poor
living at close quarters in a relatively small community.
A fourth circle is that of the temple and its courts, to
which flowed an unceasing stream of pilgrims from the
Dispersion. The passionate phrases which describe the
devotion excited and maintained by the temple are
familiar to all; away from it the exile languishes (xlii and
xliii); the towers and bulwarks of Zion that enshrine it
are a sacramental symbol of the strength and beauty of
Israel's God (xlviii); to stand even on the threshold of
the temple is worth more than all life elsewhere (lxxxiv.
10); when it lies in ruins, its very stones and dust are
beloved (cii. 14). We have seen how rich and elaborate
the temple worship was; the Psalms are permeated with
the consciousness of the cult, even though they did not
all originate in it. Finally we come to the smallest circle
of all, the consciousness of the individual believer, ebbing
and flowing with the tides of life of the whole community,
struggling for the maintenance of his trust in God in spite
of fightings without and fears within, perplexed by the
apparent prosperity of 'the wicked', trying sometimes to
rise above the limitations of a faith that made death the
end. The 'penitential Psalms' (vi, xxxii, xxxviii, li, cii,
cxxx, cxliii) show how deep a moral consciousness was
developed in spite of the identification of forgiveness with

the recovery of health or prosperity. All these circles make their contributions to the worship of the believer as it is represented in the Psalms; all of them help him in different ways to climb in faith and prayer to Him who is over all and through all and in all. They all help to enrich the idea of God, whose loving-kindness and righteousness, majesty and mystery, are the central theme of the Psalms.

(b) The language of the Psalms owes its present fitness for universal use in worship to the very circumstance which makes it so difficult to recover the precise historical background of individual Psalms. The language of the prophets is often so much the more difficult for the modern reader because the historical references are so much more frequent. The Psalms have far fewer of these, not simply because the world of fellowship with God always tends to be timeless, but because they have been purposely adapted to the needs of a worshipping congregation, and the historical 'excrescences' have been pared away. The scholar may regret this; the devout user of the Psalms is grateful for the resultant simplicity, which deals with the universal joys and sorrows, hopes and fears, of the believer, in language to a great extent intelligible to all. Yet this simplicity is not bare and unadorned. It is concrete, because it is Hebrew. It is vivid and picturesque, because it is wedded to a developed cult and springs from the thought and life of a 'dramatic' people. It is the more intense because it is shut up to this life, and must find God *here* or not at all. This is what gives peculiar intensity to the central problem of Hebrew religion—prominent in the Psalms as well as in the Book of Job—the problem of retribution (e.g. xxxvii and lxxiii).

(c) One other important feature has helped to make the Book of Psalms a book of prayer for all men—that is the remarkable conception of 'corporate personality' which pervades it, as indeed the whole Bible, to a much greater degree than the ordinary reader realizes. There has been much dispute as to the 'I' of the Psalms; is it the worshipping individual, or is it the whole community personified? The true answer seems to be that it is neither, in any antithesis of one to the other. Our modern sharp distinction between the individual and group to which he belongs did not exist in Israel; indeed, if we go back to even more primitive thought, we find what seems to us a strange confusion of personal identity with the whole group (so, for example, amongst Australian aborigines). *We* try to create a social consciousness by moral appeal to the individual; for the Hebrew prophets and psalmists it existed already, and enabled them to make startling and unexplained transitions from one to the other (as in Ps. xxii and the Songs of the 'Servant of the Lord'). Many Psalms originate in an individual experience; yet they generally tend to show the consciousness also of a group, whether of the devout believers (cf. Isa. viii. 16; Mal. iii. 16) or of Israel as a people (cxxix). It is this fluidity that makes the Psalms so fitting for public worship, so challenging to individual devotion with its perils of a spiritually selfish isolation. Cheyne[1] aptly cites a Talmudic saying, 'In prayer a man should always unite himself with the community.' The Psalms fully observe this principle.

IV. *Worship without Temple.* Though the Book of Psalms as a whole is closely linked with the ritual of the temple, many of its elements lead us to the inner temple of the devout spirit of man. This is represented also in many non-liturgical prayers which are scattered through the pages of the Old Testament and claim attention as part of its contribution to Christian worship. The range is wide, for it extends from such a song of national praise as is the poem expanding Miriam's couplet by the Red Sea (Exod. xv. 21) to the simple petition of Abraham's servant by the well (Gen. xxiv. 12–14). The great men of the past are represented as great intercessors with God,

---

[1] *Origin of the Psalter,* p. 276.

as was Abraham pleading for mercy on the faithful few of
Sodom (Gen. xviii. 16–33) and Moses (Exod. xxxii. 31–2)
anticipating the Apostle's 'I could wish that I myself were
anathema from Christ for my brethren's sake' (Rom.
ix. 3). Job's 'oath of purgation' (xxxi) is really a prayer
of (to us) unconventional form. In the later literature
we have such profound confessions of sin as that of Dan.
ix. 3–19. The wide scope of prayer, including praise,
thanksgiving, petition, confession, and supplication, is
well illustrated by the striking passage now found as Isa.
lxiii. 7–lxiv. 12. It was the positive example of the great
prophets, and the negative influence of the exile in depriv-
ing Israel of its sanctuary, that led to the wide extension
of personal and non-liturgical prayer and became one of
the foundations of the later synagogue.

The supreme example of that direct personal approach
to God which represents the very ideal and climax of
true worship is found in the prayer-life of Jeremiah, as
set forth in his autobiographical poems. Here, indeed,
we have the model and source of much of the most
spiritual element in the Book of Psalms itself. The deep
humility with which he shrank from the call to be a
prophet, combined with the sense that he was after all
predestined by God to this work; the intense loneliness
and suffering of a task he hated, yet to which he was ever
urged by an inner compulsion too strong to be resisted;
the profound sympathy with the fate of his people, coupled
with the mission to proclaim it—these things are the
great 'tensions' of the spirit which the pioneers of religion
must always experience, and out of which the most costly
worship is born. It was from such things that Jeremiah
was made capable of advancing to the conception of a
'new covenant' of individual and inward relation to God,
a new covenant which prophesies from afar the truth of
John iv. 21–4. It was because of his worship in this inner
temple that he could preach the famous sermon denounc-
ing the external temple (vii), and like One in whom men

saw the ancient prophet returning to them, could contemplate without dismay the time when not one stone should be left upon another.

V. *The Dynamic of Worship.* As we look back on the very varied mass of material which has been no more than suggested in this brief survey, we do well to ask what is its 'projected efficiency', what are its inherent prophecies as to the true and essential character of worship? Here we are faced with the fact of certain great 'tensions' between opposing views, not of modern interpreters but of the Old Testament material itself. There is the tension between the priestly and prophetic ideals of worship, that between a nationalistic and universalistic horizon, and that between the present world-order and its manifest incompleteness.

In regard to the first, it is easy and tempting to take famous prophetic sayings about sacrifice as absolutely condemning it. 'Did ye bring unto me sacrifices and offerings in the wilderness forty years, O house of Israel?' asks Amos (v. 25), as he contrasts the present with an idealized past; his rhetorical question plainly expects the answer 'No'. Jeremiah is more explicit when he says (vii. 22): 'I spake not unto your fathers, nor commanded them in the day that I brought them out of the land of Egypt, concerning burnt offerings or sacrifices.' Obviously such passages are inconsistent with the observance in the wilderness of any such ritual as the Pentateuch ascribes to Moses; but they seem to go beyond this and to denounce sacrifice in general as a true part of worship. The prophetic emphasis falls beyond question on the moral and spiritual factors, as in that passage which best summarizes the prophetic religion: 'Wherewith shall I come before the Lord and bow myself before the high God? . . . what doth the Lord require of thee, but to do justly, and to love mercy, and to walk humbly with thy God?' (Micah vi. 6–7). Yet it is very doubtful whether we ought to make for those men the sharp antithesis that seems natural to us. They were opposing formal, extravagant, and even immoral worship in the spirit of a Puritan, but they could hardly in those days have conceived a worship without ritual of some kind. We do well to remember the balanced and restrained judgement of Buchanan Gray that 'we cannot safely conclude that all the prophets denounced sacrifice under all conditions; purged of its abuses they may have been ready enough to see the continuance of eucharistic sacrifice; it would have been much less compatible with their criticism of the popular religion to admit either the expiatory or the propitiatory validity of sacrifice'.[1] The bearing of this on the relation of Protestant and Catholic types and ideals of worship should be remembered, but the Old Testament shows that the antithesis between the prophet and the priest can be too sharply made.

The tension between nationalistic and universalistic views of religion is best seen by reading Nahum and Jonah in close succession. Both are concerned with Nineveh, actual or typical; how differently do they conceive Israel's relation to the Gentile world which Nineveh represents! Yet, again, we must not unduly exaggerate the antithesis. True as it is that the noble evangelism of Deutero-Isaiah seems to remain a voice crying in the wilderness, it is also true that there are other passages of the Old Testament that attain to a striking catholicity of outlook. One of them is Mal. i. 11, where it is said that the worship of God by Gentiles finds acceptance by the God of Israel. Another is found in Isa. xix. 24, which includes Egypt and Assyria with the privileged Israel: 'Blessed be Egypt my people, and Assyria the work of my hands, and Israel mine inheritance.' Most impressive of all is the description of the 'coronation festival' when God shall ascend His throne in Zion and lift the veil of the mourner from *all peoples* and wipe away tears from off *all faces* (xxv. 6–8). (The catholic humanitarianism of this fine passage is not nearly

---

[1] *Sacrifice*, p. 89.

as well known as it ought to be.) Naturally Israel's cause is vindicated, but that is essential for those who held that Israel worshipped the true and only God. The very fact that here and elsewhere such catholicity could be reached through an intense but spiritualized nationalism suggests that we get really nearer to each other by getting nearer to God, and that we get nearer to Him by following the particular pathway which He has revealed to ourselves, and not by compromise. The Christian ought to find no difficulty of principle in maintaining with his Master that 'Salvation is from the Jews', whilst seeking to enter into the spirit of his Master's essential universalism.

The third tension is that which springs from the high experience of seeking and finding God's 'face' in the temple when contrasted with the belief that the fellowship with Him is terminated by death. Again and again in reading the Psalms we are tempted to believe that they have overcome this limitation. Those passages which speak of deliverance from death suggest more to us than, e.g., recovery from illness, or rescue from enemies. The spiritual communion with God which finds its highest expression towards the close of the seventy-third Psalm has indeed risen from the temporal to the eternal; the psalmist seems to stand with the Apostle who said that death itself could not separate us from the love of God. Yet though the premisses would have justified the conclusion, that conclusion was not drawn in the Psalms or anywhere else in the Old Testament. What we do find there is the beginning of the hope of resurrection—a different thing from 'immortality', and one more consonant with Hebrew psychology. Even resurrection is confined to a few, and that in connexion with the apocalyptic hopes (cf. Isa. xxvi. 19; Dan. xii. 2). For the ordinary man death marked the limit of his relation to God, a belief that made his worship narrower in scope but all the more intense. God must answer his prayers in terms of this life, if at all, and the chief object of a death-bed repentance was to be saved from dying. This is one of the many lines on which Old Testament worship points forward to something beyond itself. We may say of it what Rabindranath Tagore said of the world, that if it 'remained still and became final, then it would be a prison-house of orphaned facts'.

History has demonstrated the incompleteness of the worship described in the Old Testament by the double development from it in the Synagogue and in the Church. Both can be regarded as completing in different ways the unfulfilled promises or implicit logic of their common source. Yet of both it can be said that the Old Testament worship at its height is still their teacher calling them to unrealized ideals and unfulfilled tasks. Zangwill's sonnet pictures Moses and Jesus meeting amid the 'satanic dance' of our modern world:

> Sudden from Church out rolled an organ hymn,
> From Synagogue a loudly chaunted air,
> Each with its Prophet's high acclaim instinct.
> Then for the first time met their eyes, swift-linked
> In one strange, silent, piteous gaze, and dim
> With bitter tears of agonized despair.

Agony? Yes; but not despair, at any rate for a worship and faith with the Cross at their centre. Even the Old Testament catches a glimpse of One who shall see of the travail of His soul and be satisfied, and by His own sacrifice set the supreme standard and inspiration of the highest worship of God.

H. WHEELER ROBINSON.

THE JEWISH BACKGROUND

JEWISH worship at the beginning of the Christian era was based upon two institutions, the Temple and the Synagogue. At the beginning of the Galilean ministry Jesus taught in the synagogues, and during the last week of His life He taught daily in the Temple (Mark xiv. 49). The primitive Jewish Christian community made regular use of the Temple and its services. St. Paul made the synagogues of the Dispersion a regular starting-point for his missionary work. Temple and Synagogue played a large part in the life of Judaism and the nascent Church, and it is a question of no small importance how far the Jewish worship influenced that of the early Christians. For the first disciples were Jews by birth and upbringing, and it is *a priori* probable that they would bring into the new community some at least of the religious usages to which they had long been accustomed.

There is, however, a prior question: that of the relative importance of Temple and Synagogue in the religious life of the average Jew of the period. The Temple had the prestige of antiquity, of divine institution, of metropolitan position, of imposing buildings and impressive ritual. The Synagogue was, in comparison, an innovation, an 'unofficial' institution, simple and even austere in its forms of worship. Yet the Synagogue touched the lives of more Jews and at more points than did the Temple. And this for a number of reasons.

The centralization of the Sacrificial ritual in Jerusalem was one of the first big steps in teaching Israel to do without it. The metropolitan cathedral is no substitute for the parish churches, and the Jerusalem Curia could not take the place of the local priests. It is true that the people were still kept in touch with the Temple by the rule requiring every adult male to attend the three great

annual feasts in Jerusalem; true also that the institution
of the *ma'amadoth*[1] provided for a lay representation at
the daily services; but at the best sacrificial worship could
only be an occasional thing for the Palestinian country-
folk.

Further, at the beginning of the Christian era vast
numbers of Jews were scattered over the world for whom
a visit to the Temple was something of the same kind as
the pilgrimage to Mecca—a thing that might be undertaken once in a lifetime.

Circumstances thus conspired to cut off the great
majority of Jews from the Temple worship. The development of Judaism itself tended in the same direction.
According to Simeon the Just ('*Aboth* i. 2) the Law and
the Temple service were two of the three things supporting the world. But when the regulations for the cultus
were seen as a part, and a part only, of the whole Torah,
the way was already prepared for doing without the
Temple and its ritual. For it then became natural to
regard the *raison d'être* of the cultus as obedience to the
Torah. The ritual as such ceases to have a special significance of its own apart from the Law. If God wills to
make the performance of this part of the Law possible,
well and good; if not, the pious Jew has other ways
of showing his faithfulness and obedience. The more
the Law became the centre of Jewish piety, the more the
Temple was bound to take second place, and the more
the Synagogue was bound to play the decisive part in
moulding the forms and spirit of Jewish piety.

In one respect the Synagogue could not take the place
of the Temple, in the matter of sacrifice; and the question arises how far sacrifice is, in this period, an essential

---

[1] *Ma'amad* is the name given to a group of representatives from outlying
districts, corresponding to the twenty-four 'courses of priests'. Part of them
went up to the Temple as witnesses of the offering of the sacrifices (*Ta'an.*
iv. 2), and part came together in their own town, where they held prayers
at fixed times during the day coinciding with the fixed times of sacrifice in
the Temple. Danby, *Mishnah*, p. 794.

element in Jewish worship, something which the devout Jew needed as a devout Catholic needs the Sacraments.

The answer to this question is given in principle by the considerations already advanced. For great numbers of Jews the ritual of sacrifice was something in which they could have little or no direct share. This is reflected in the fact that Jewish documents originating outside of Palestine show less enthusiasm for the Temple ritual than those of Palestinian origin. Yet the Jews of the Diaspora were devout and loyal Jews. And even in the Palestinian literature the interest in sacrifice is subordinate to the interest in the Torah as a whole. Whether the sacrificial system be regarded as among the most important provisions of the Law or be treated as secondary to more vital matters, it is still only a part of the Law; and the virtue of sacrificial worship tends to be found, not in the rites themselves, but in the fact that punctual performance of the prescribed ritual is part of that exact obedience, which ought to be given to the commandments of God. Devotion to the cultus is part of devotion to the Law. This means that there is little room left for the naïve notion that sacrifice can in some way move the divine will in the direction of man's desires: rather the punctual fulfilment of the sacrificial laws is part of the bending of man's will in obedience to God's. But only a part. The revealed will of God covers far more than the ritual of sacrifice. The business of the Synagogue was with this whole revelation as given in Scripture and tradition. That involved study of the revelation, reading and exposition of it, thanksgivings to God for it, and prayers to God for strength to be obedient to it. The worship of the Synagogue involved veneration of the whole Torah as the revealed will of God; and, when part of the Torah became impossible of fulfilment through the destruction of the Temple, the Synagogue was able to carry on. Study of the sacrificial laws was deemed an adequate substitute for the ritual which was no longer possible; and there the matter remains to this day. Other religions did not survive the overthrow of their altars: Judaism did.

This may be, in part, explained by the fact that the Synagogue did in fact model itself to some extent on the Temple. This is apparent when we consider the furniture of the synagogue: the Ark, the lamp-stands, the veil or screen in front of the Ark, and the like. The orientation of the Synagogue buildings and the posture of the worshippers in prayer as well as the separation of the sexes in worship, all probably show the same influence. The times of Synagogue worship were influenced by the times of the Temple services. Most important of all, many elements in the Synagogue liturgy were taken over from the service of the Temple, notably the names of the various daily offices, the use of certain psalms, the recitation of the Decalogue and the *Shema'*, and some of the oldest prayers (the *'Ahabah* and part at least of the *'Amidah*).

There was thus a real sense in which the Synagogue was, to use a phrase taken over by the Rabbis from Ezekiel (xi. 16), 'a smaller sanctuary', a Temple in miniature. At the same time the Synagogue had distinctive features of its own, in the formation of which the determining factors were devotion to the Torah and the type of personal piety which grew out of this devotion. Hence what is specially characteristic of the Synagogue service is the place given to the reading and exposition of Scripture and to prayer. And the articles of Synagogue furniture, which are not derived from imitation of the Temple, are just those which have to do with the reading and exposition of the sacred books. It may be noted in passing that whereas the articles borrowed from the Temple retain their Semitic names, those peculiar to the Synagogue have names borrowed from Greek—the lectern (*'ĕnālgîn* = ἀναλογεῖον), the scroll-case (*têḳ* = θήκη), the reading-platform (*bêmāh* = βῆμα), and the seat of Moses (*ḳāthedrā* = καθέδρα).

It is probably significant that where the Synoptic Gospels show Jesus taking part in the Synagogue worship, He is represented as reading Scripture or teaching, that is, sharing in the most characteristic of the Synagogue activities. Again, the liturgy of the Synagogue was enriched by the prayers of individual members; and perhaps the Lord's Prayer may be regarded in this light as a prayer made by Jesus for the use of the community of His followers. It is even possible to say that the mission of Jesus was in fact that of a Jewish Rabbi,[1] and to think of His disciples as similar to the pupils who gathered round other distinguished Rabbis. This seems to me to be an exaggeration; but it is an exaggeration of a truth. Jesus brought to His life's task, along with other and far more important qualities, a sufficiency of learning to be reckoned as a Rabbi; but the nature of His mission went far beyond the tasks of a Rabbi. Διδάσκαλος He was; but He knew, none better, that

$$\text{Διδάσκων}$$
$$\text{οὔποτε ποιήσεις τὸν κακὸν ἀνΔρ' ἀγαθόν.}$$

Devotion to the Law and the type of piety that flourished in the Synagogue produced the Ḥăbûrôth, voluntary societies of Jews who desired to maintain the highest standard of Jewish living. The members of these groups were men who took Judaism seriously and were meticulous in the observance of the minutest details of the Law and given to meeting together for devotional purposes. Again it is tempting to see in Jesus and His disciples a Ḥăbûrāh; but the analogy is not to be pressed. They certainly would not have been recognized as such by the real Ḥăbûrôth; for the things about which those societies were most particular were the very things that Jesus treated as of minor importance—ritual purity, exact tithing, and the like.

One other feature in Jewish piety in the New Testament

---

[1] Bultmann, *Jesus*, p. 56.

period remains to be noticed, that is the prominence and importance of matters independent of the Temple ritual. Such things are the rite of circumcision, the observance of the Sabbath as a day of rest, the laws of ritual purity, and the dietary laws. Of these the first place was taken by the keeping of the Sabbath. In this period Sabbath observance was *the* hall-mark of the Jew. It was obligatory on all, without distinction of age or sex, in Palestine and among the Gentiles. And it is notable that, in the 'Proselyte's Progress' sketched by Juvenal in the XIVth Satire (vv. 96–107), the mischief begins when the father starts keeping the Jewish Sabbath and abstaining from pork. The next generation are ripe for circumcision and the whole Torah. One might become a complete Jew without ever seeing the Temple or a sacrifice. Indeed it might fairly be said that the significant thing about the Jewish religion was not the fact that it had a Temple and cultus of its own, but the stubbornness and vehemence with which the Jew refused to have anything to do with the temples and cults of other people.

It is on this background that we see the beginnings of Christian worship. The earliest stage shows a little community whose worship takes place partly in private houses and partly in the Jerusalem Temple. It is curious that in the only passages in the early chapters of Acts where the Synagogue appears (Acts vi. 9; ix. 2), it is as a centre of opposition to the new movement (cf. xxii. 19; xxvi. 11). The remaining passages in Acts (from ix. 20 onwards) are almost wholly concerned with the missionary propaganda of St. Paul, and that mostly in the Synagogues of the Dispersion. On the other hand there is close contact with the Temple (Acts ii. 46; iii. 1; v. 20 ff., 42). Peter and John go up to the Temple at the hour of prayer, the ninth hour (about 3 p.m.), that is, they go up for the prayers in connexion with the afternoon sacrifice. The Temple is also used as a place for teaching and preaching the Gospel: 'And every day, in the Temple and at home, they did not cease teaching and telling the good news of the Messiah—Jesus' (Acts v. 42, Lake and Cadbury's trans.). The tumult which led up to the arrest of Paul took place when he was praying in the Temple (Acts xxii. 17). Further, according to Hegesippus,[1] this connexion with the Temple was maintained by James the Just till his death.

The missionary work of St. Paul regularly began in the Synagogues of the Dispersion and the nucleus of the Gentile churches was doubtless either converted Jews or, more frequently, converted Gentile adherents of the Synagogue. We should therefore expect the earliest Christian worship everywhere to show traces of Synagogue influence: and such traces are not wanting. The worship of the Church is akin to that of the Synagogue in the place given to the reading and exposition of the Bible,[2] in the practice of having three prayer-times in the day as in the Synagogue (Acts ii. 15; x. 9; iii. 1; *Didache* viii. 3), and in the similarities between the earliest Christian forms of prayer and the oldest prayers in the Synagogue liturgy. The most striking resemblances have been collected by Dr. Oesterley,[3] and it is not necessary to repeat them here. There is, however, one striking example that ought to be mentioned, since it affects one of the earliest and most frequently used of Christian prayers.

The Lord's Prayer has come down to us in two forms in the Gospels of Matthew and Luke. The Matthean form is the accepted liturgical form of the prayer: the Lucan (in the true text of Luke) is much shorter and simpler. The former begins Πάτερ ἡμῶν ὁ ἐν τοῖς οὐρανοῖς, the latter simply Πάτερ. There is little doubt that πάτερ is the original. It agrees with our Lord's own usage (πάτερ, Matt. xi. 25 = Luke x. 21, Q.; ἀββᾶ ὁ πατήρ, Mark xiv. 36), and with the statements of Paul (Rom. viii. 15;

---

[1] *Ap.* Eus. *H.E.* ii. xxiii.
[2] See, above all, Justin Martyr, *Apol.* i. lxvii.
[3] *The Jewish Background of the Christian Liturgy*, pp. 125-54.

Gal. iv. 6); and it has been shown by G. Kittel[1] that the use of the unqualified *'abba* in speaking of God or to God is specifically Christian, and a new thing introduced by Jesus Himself. Jewish piety shrank from addressing God simply as 'Father': Jesus did not, and He taught His disciples to follow His example. But in Matthew the original 'Father' has given place to 'Our Father who art in heaven', which is 'a common invocation in the Jewish prayer-book'.[2] The power of old associations could not be more strikingly illustrated.

The use of fasting as a religious exercise is part of the Jewish piety of New Testament times. Regular weekly fasts do not seem to have been obligatory: they were rather an additional discipline voluntarily undertaken. The Pharisee in the parable says that he fasts twice in the week (Luke xviii. 12); and it is possible that these weekly fasts are alluded to by Josephus (*c. Ap.* ii. 282). The *Didache* (viii. 1) shows us Christians also fasting twice in the week: 'Let not your fasts be with the hypocrites, for they fast on Mondays and Thursdays, but do you fast on Wednesdays and Fridays.' The alteration of the days only serves to bring out more clearly that the practice is of Jewish origin.

There remain for consideration the two central Christian rites, Baptism and the Lord's Supper. It is not possible within the limits of this essay to attempt anything like a full discussion of the problems involved: it must suffice to state what appear to the writer to be the most likely answers.

Baptism is the rite of initiation into the Christian community. It resembles the rite employed by John the Baptist, but differs from it in one important particular— it is εἰς τὸ ὄνομα τοῦ Κυρίου Ἰησοῦ. And it would appear from Acts xix. 1–7 that John's baptism was not regarded as a substitute for Christian baptism. At the same time

---

[1] *Die Religionsgeschichte und das Urchristentum*, pp. 92–5.
[2] Cf. Abrahams, *Studies in Pharisaism*, ii. 98.

it is arguable that the Christian rite is a further development along the line opened up by the Baptist. The
question then arises whether John's baptism is itself an
adaptation of Jewish liturgical practice.

The nearest Jewish analogy to John's baptism is the
ritual immersion of proselytes to Judaism; but it has been
doubted whether this Jewish rite was in existence sufficiently early to serve as a model for John's. The question
is fully discussed by Billerbeck,[1] with the result that the
chronological difficulty disappears. The Jewish proselyte-baptism is already an established institution in the
time of the Schools of Hillel and Shammai (c. A.D. 10–
80). The question under discussion between the two
Schools is not whether there should be a baptism of proselytes, but how soon it should follow after the circumcision
of a convert. We should therefore place the origin of the
rite in the pre-Christian period. The procedure at the
reception of a convert to Judaism is described by Biller-
beck.[2] The candidate is admonished concerning the seri-
ousness of the step which he is taking. If he is determined
to proceed, he is circumcised. After the healing of the
wound comes the baptism. This takes place in the day-
time and in the presence of witnesses. These witnesses
read commandments of the Law to the proselyte as he
waits in the water with the lower half of his body immersed. If he is still determined to become a Jew, he is
totally immersed. When he comes out of the water he is a
Jew in every respect.

The importance of this baptism was that it provided a
rite of reception into the Jewish community applicable
in all cases without distinction of sex. It differs from other
ritual ablutions of Judaism in that it is done once and for
all. It resembles the Christian rite in being a ceremony
of reception into full membership of the community. The
question then is whether John's baptism can be regarded

[1] *Kommentar*, i. 102–13.
[2] Op. cit., p. 110.

as the connecting link between the Jewish proselyte-
baptism and the Christian sacrament.

The records of John's ministry strongly suggest that this
question should be answered in the affirmative. For the
burden of John's preaching is the coming judgement
under the repeated figure of a consuming fire. In this
judgement it is certain for John that many who claim to
be children of Abraham—true Jews—will be revealed for
what they are—'offspring of vipers', i.e. children of Satan.
The only hope for these people is to become true children
of Abraham, by repentance and amendment of life, while
there is yet time. And just as the Gentile is received into
the Jewish community in the proselyte-baptism, so *Jews
must be received into the true Jewish community by baptism*. Those who make this new beginning will be saved
in the coming judgement, and to accept John's baptism
is to be received into the number of those who will constitute the new community in the approaching Messianic
age. If this is the correct interpretation of John's mission,
it is clear that his baptism, no less than the others, is a
rite of initiation; and it becomes possible to see that Christian baptism is a development of John's, and that both
are ultimately based on the Jewish rite. The essential
rite remains the same throughout: the significance of it
is changed, first by John's relation of it to the coming
Kingdom, and then by the Christian reference to the
Kingdom that has come in Jesus Christ.

The questions raised by the Lord's Supper are much
more difficult and complicated, because there is disagreement between the Gospels as to the date of the Last Supper. They are at one in declaring that the Supper took
place on what we should call Thursday night; but whereas
Mark holds that that Thursday night was the night on
which the Passover feast fell in that year, John is clear
that the following night was Passover night. If Mark is
right, the Last Supper was a Passover meal: if John is
right, it can hardly have been a Passover meal in the

proper sense of the word. It is true that attempts have
been made to reconcile the two accounts. Of these the
most brilliant and learned is that of Billerbeck.[1] This
theory is an elaboration of an earlier suggestion made by
Lichtenstein and favoured by Strack. It rests on the supposition that owing to a difference between the Pharisees
and the Sadducees as to the day on which the month of
Nisan began in that year, there were, in fact, two Pass-
overs, and that the Pharisees held their Passover on the
Thursday night and the Sadducees theirs on the Friday
night. On this view Jesus and his disciples kept the Passover with the Pharisees, and the Last Supper was a Passover meal according to all four Gospels. The references
in John to a Passover which is to follow the Crucifixion
are references to the Passover of the Sadducees. There
is then no contradiction between the Synoptics and John.
The conflicting data can all be explained as correct record
of a conflict between Pharisees and Sadducees. There is
nothing against this theory, except that it is pure supposition. There is no reason to think that, if there had been
such a dispute as the theory requires between Pharisees
and Sadducees, the latter would have been so broad-
minded as to permit the slaughtering of the Pharisees'
lambs to take place on what was, by Sadducean reckoning, a day too early.

Failing a convincing reconciliation of the Synoptic and
Johannine data, we have to ask what, on the supposition
that the Johannine account is correct, the Last Supper
was. The answer often given to this question is that
the Last Supper was what is known as *Kiddûsh*. This
institution is found in Judaism in connexion with the
Sabbath and Festivals. The custom was for a group of
friends (a *Hâbûrâh*) to meet on Friday afternoons for a
common meal whose culmination was reached at sunset
with the sanctification of the incoming Sabbath (the *Kiddûsh* proper). This ceremony consisted of the utterance

[1] 'Der Todestag Jesu' in his *Kommentar*, ii. 812–53.

of a blessing over a cup of wine and the passing of the cup round the company, followed by a similar blessing over the bread and its distribution. It is urged that this observance is what is described in the Lucan account of the institution of the Lord's Supper (Luke xxii. 15–19a) and in the prescriptions in the *Didache* (ch. ix).

The theory that the Last Supper was a *Ḳiddûsh* has two serious difficulties to face. Firstly, the chief witness for the *Ḳiddûsh* order of cup and loaf (Luke xxii. 15–19a) turns out on closer examination not to be so strong as could be desired. For only verses 15–18 of this passage are really independent evidence. Verse 19a is taken from Mark xiv. 22; and it is verse 19a that gives the blessing over and distribution of the bread. Luke xxii. 15–18 *is* a piece of independent tradition concerning the Last Supper; but it has nothing to say about the order in which the elements were distributed.

Secondly, whether the Last Supper be regarded as a Sabbath *Ḳiddûsh* or a Passover *Ḳiddûsh*, it falls twenty-four hours before the Sabbath and Passover (which according to John coincided in that year). This is entirely contrary to the very idea of the ceremony. For *Ḳiddûsh* is essentially the ushering in of the Sabbath or Passover, and properly takes place at the time when the Sabbath or Passover begins, not a day earlier. And to this day the Passover *Ḳiddûsh* is the first part of the Passover service. There is no evidence for a Passover *Ḳiddûsh* which takes place twenty-four hours before the feast.

These objections seem to be fatal to the theory that the Last Supper was a Passover *Ḳiddûsh*.

We thus seem to be left, by a process of elimination, with the view that the Marcan account is correct, that is, that the Last Supper was a Passover meal and that the Johannine data, which conflict with that, must be mistaken. And here may be mentioned one point which, if sound, is decisive. It is commonly suggested that the curious little incident narrated in Mark xiv. 51 f., and peculiar to that Gospel, is a bit of autobiography; that the young man who fled naked at the arrest is John Mark himself. If that supposition is well founded, the Marcan dating of the Last Supper must stand, for John Mark must have known what night it was that he escaped from the garden.

The view that the Last Supper was a Passover meal has been defended with great learning by Dalman[1] and Biller-beck.[2] Most recently the case has been stated with great clearness by J. Jeremias.[3] As a result of this discussion it can be said that some objections to the Passover theory are definitely disposed of: for example, the fact that in describing the Supper the Synoptics and Paul use the word ἄρτον where we should expect ἄζυμον or ἄζυμα. This point had already been briefly dealt with by Fiebig:[4] it is now completely demolished by Jeremias.[5] Jeremias also brings together a large number of positive reasons for identifying the Supper with the Passover: the fact that the meal took place in Jerusalem, and at night, that Jesus and the disciples reclined at the meal instead of sitting, that they drank wine with the meal, that the Supper ended with the singing of a hymn (= the Hallel psalms), and finally, that the words spoken by Jesus about the bread and the wine have their parallel in the explanatory words spoken over the elements in the Passover ritual. These reasons are not all equally convincing; but the impression remains that a strong case has been made out for the Passover.

Yet certain doubts and hesitations remain. If the Last Supper was a Passover meal pure and simple, if the institution of it arises out of the Passover ritual, certain features in the Gospels and Acts become very puzzling. In the Emmaus story in Luke the risen Jesus is recognized by two disciples 'in the breaking of bread'; but these two did not belong to the Twelve and therefore had not been

[1] *Jesus-Jeshua.*   [2] Op. cit.   [3] *Die Abendmahlsworte Jesu* (1935).
[4] *Theol. Litztg.*, 1934, col. 416.   [5] Op. cit., pp. 27–30.

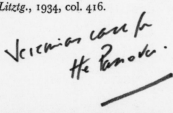

present at the Last Supper. (The same mode of expression is used in the Acts, where the 'breaking of bread' probably, though not necessarily, means the Eucharist.) Where did the two disciples learn whatever it was that was characteristic in Jesus' breaking of the bread? In other words, is the Last Supper which coincided with the Passover only the last of a series of common meals which did not coincide with the Passover?

When we raise this question we have at once to reckon with the stories of the feeding of the multitude (Mark vi. 39–44; viii. 6–8 and parallels). There there are distinct resemblances to the accounts of the Last Supper in the description of the actions of Jesus. The essential difference is that there is no cup in the feeding of the multitudes, and no words of institution. Yet the Fourth Gospel appends a eucharistic discourse to the account of the feeding. It may be that the common meal played a larger part than we usually recognize in the ministry of Jesus, and that He gave to it a special significance. This is not to say that Jesus and His disciples constituted a *Hăbúrāh* in the technical sense. The fellowship was something created by Jesus Himself, and an expression of His own purposes rather than a copy of any existing Jewish institution.

As indicating something of the nature of this fellowship we may cite the following further passages. (*a*) Mark ii. 13–17, which is to be read without bringing in the editorial modifications of Luke. If this is done, the nature of the meal appears as one in which Jesus, the 'friend of publicans and sinners', is host and the outcasts are His guests. (*b*) Mark ix. 50*b*, an obscure saying which becomes plain in the light of a passage in Robertson Smith's *Religion of the Semites* (pp. 269 f.): 'If I have eaten the smallest morsel of food with a man, I have nothing further to fear from him; "there is salt between us", and he is bound not only to do me no harm, but to help and defend me as if I were his brother.' It may be suggested that the common meal of Jesus and His followers is given by Jesus the meaning of a sacrament of brotherhood. (c) Luke xxii. 30, where the fellowship cemented by the common meal here and now is thought of as continuing in the new age. If there is anything in all this, it means that Jesus took the common Jewish figure of the Messianic banquet and gave it an anticipated realization in the present. The feast of the age to come is already in some real sense enjoyed when Jesus and His disciples sit down to share a crust of bread.

If this is the case, we have a long series of significant common meals, of which the Last Supper is in truth the last. And the Last Supper gains added significance from the fact that the death of the host is imminent. It is this approaching death that gives peculiar meaning to the cup and new meaning to the breaking of the bread. And it is to be noted that all this holds good whether the Last Supper was a Passover meal or not. If it was a Passover meal, there would be further meanings in the symbolism drawn from the associations of the rite. But they would be additional to those already involved in the meal in any case. The essential significance of the Last Supper would still be that it was the last of many fellowship-meals, the last because the death of Jesus was at hand.

We are thus brought to a somewhat strange conclusion. The question whether the Last Supper was a Passover meal or not, becomes important chiefly as a means of deciding the chronological question of the date of the Crucifixion. The deepest meaning of the Supper itself is independent of its connexion with the Passover, and must be sought in the purpose and method of the whole ministry of Jesus.

T. W. MANSON.

IV

THE WORD OF GOD IN THE NEW TESTAMENT

I

THE Word of God is His action in self-revelation. For the faith of the Old Testament history is the scene of manifestations of God, the embodiment of a Divine purpose. Something which furthers the design of the God of Israel is effected in all temporal happenings. As the result of the Divine action in the world Hebrew faith expects a consummation of history in which empirical existence will have been conformed to the intention of God. Through acts of judgement and of new creation the God of Israel, Himself exalted above history, guides it to this end. Such a belief had certainly been deeply rooted in the Jewish mind for several centuries before the time of Jesus, whether or not the earliest prophets, Amos and Hosea and Micah, spoke only of coming doom, and not at all in terms of hope for the future.

Jesus came forward with the claim that the time for the perfecting of all the long series of Divine acts had now arrived. Only this assurance explains why Jesus spoke and acted as He did. The expression commonly employed in the Synoptic Gospels to designate the realization of the purpose of God is the 'Kingdom' of God.

Jesus' conception of the Kingdom is determined by His thought of God as active will, and by the meaning of the time. Christian and Jewish scholars, as also Christian scholars themselves, do not see altogether eye to eye on the question whether the thought of Jesus about God represents anything new with respect to the Old Testament and Judaism. The discussion of this matter would gain if it were more fully recognized that the Gospels rest on a different presupposition from that of the Old Testament and later

Jewish literature, namely, that in the case of the former it is now the time of fulfilment when God acts, draws near, puts forth His innermost being as He had not done before. Thus, if pitying and forgiving love is attributed to God, as to be sure it is by Jesus and Judaism alike, it is to be expected that more will be made of this quality of His being when the belief in it is combined with a faith that 'the last things' are now becoming present. And Jesus is in fact represented, in sayings and in acts, as having conceived the Divine goodness in a way to which close analogies are not forthcoming from the Old Testament and the later Jewish sources. This is particularly the case in sayings of Jesus relating to 'sinners', to the 'lost', and in dealings with them to which He is prompted by His sense of what the Divine goodness is in the time of fulfilment: it does not simply accept the 'sinner' if he returns, but goes forth in search of him. Later Judaism, it is true, founding on prophetic announcements from Hosea onwards, kept the door wide open for repentant sinners, however far gone; those who 'returned' to God in love and obedience could count surely on His acceptance and restoration to His favour. Repentance draws down His mercy overflowingly: 'Open to me an entrance no larger than the eye of a needle and I will open to you an entrance through which tents and great timbers can pass.'[1] All reprobation ceases when it is a question of returning sinners. For Judaism and the Rabbis God is no less accessible to penitent supplication than He is in the parables of the Prodigal Son and the Ungrateful Servant. So far Jesus consoles sinners in the same way. But he does more than this. Something new comes in with Him, which was due to His assurance that God was now uniquely near. To the readiness of God joyfully to receive the repentant, He adds His active seeking for the sinner. His goodness was not exhausted in His former provisions for standing right with Him; over and above this He now takes the initiative

[1] See Moore, *Judaism*, i. 531.

again to bridge the gulf between Himself and sinners, lest they fall to His judgement. It was the time when He would hold sway, He alone. New energies of Divine love were being released correspondingly and flowing over upon the 'lost'. Jesus, commissioned to mediate these redeeming powers to the whole people of God, was specially concerned to put Himself in the way of the sinners. He would reassure them of their worth to God. The lost sheep, the lost coin—are they not sought for! And so He goes amongst them and eats with them, that is, establishes fellowship with them. He would enable them to be seized by pardoning love, which for a time, until the need for the love of God as pardoning love was over, was a manifestation of the Kingdom. There was now a forgiveness of such sort that its objects did not draw it down upon themselves by their repentance, which was conditioned rather on their side by the extremity of their case; it was unique, eschatological, an accompaniment of the turn of the Ages, a constituent element of the new exertion of the will of God which was the coming of the Kingdom. It is not that Jesus simply announced a heavenly decree to overlook sins; the present Kingdom which He was mediating was essentially Divine action directed towards men, God drawing near to make them other than they were, and this that they might be able to share with Him the bliss of His new creation.

In what has been said above, the sinners of the Gospel story have claimed attention, because in connexion with them a part of the content of Jesus' conception of the Kingdom becomes so evident: the Kingdom begins as the goodness of God which pardons and seeks so to conform its objects to His desire that they may be able to live in His presence when His Kingdom is established to the full. But the mission of Jesus was none the less national in character. It would be superfluous to discuss passages from the Gospels in evidence of this. The coming of the Kingdom of God affected the whole people. The present

had become a time of general crisis; everybody was confronted with the necessity for a decision for or against
the Kingdom in the character which belonged to it until
the present Age was over—forgiving love which sought
to make its objects 'sons of God'.

There is no necessity to press overmuch the exorcisms
and healings of Jesus as evidence that the Kingdom was
already being manifested. If what has been said about
the forgiving and seeking goodness of God is on the right
line, the present actuality of the Kingdom is evident in-
dependently of this particular kind of activity of Jesus.

The Kingdom being projected into the present Age was
of the twofold character which has now been indicated.
It was not present in the sense that those who might come
under it in obedience would be already in full possession
of the final salvation; rather, the Kingdom, as so far
manifested, is to be thought of as creating the essential
conditions of the supreme bliss and glory. It precipitated
crisis for men; a fateful 'yes' or 'no' to its gift had become
inescapable. The obedient would help to constitute a
community which God would make supremely blessed
when it stood before Him complete. On the other
hand, there is no discontinuity between the Kingdom in
the present and the Kingdom as consummated. It is the
Kingdom of God, and God is one. In the present the
character of the Kingdom is determined by the character
of the Age and its members: there is need for the Divine
forgiveness; there is need for a Divine deliverance from
evil. In the coming Age the occasion for that kind of
Divine activity would no longer exist; then God would
reign as He is in Himself, unconditioned by evil within
and without His creatures, in a sphere of being in which
everything, all who are there, had been brought into
harmony with Him.

Thus far we may conclude that Jesus meant by the
present Kingdom of God an action of God through His
own ministry. The most significant indications of the

character of this action are to be seen in Jesus' seeking of 'sinners', and in the parables of the 'Lost Sheep' and the 'Lost Coin'. The Kingdom is correlated with, and its reception made dependent upon, an ethic of entire self-offering to God through likeness to Him in His own present goodness to the 'unthankful and evil', and through complete obedience to His will in other respects.[1]

The relation in which Jesus Himself thus stands to the Kingdom prompts the reflection that whilst His preaching did indeed interpret the meaning of the Divine action, it was not in the first place interpretation; it was the action itself, a mode of its operation; the preached word was itself the Kingdom becoming present. The same essential significance attaches also to the acts of Jesus: in the search for the 'lost', the table-fellowship with 'sinners', the healings of the sick, the Kingdom was being made to arrive. The principle, 'But if I by the Spirit (Luke: finger) of God cast out devils, then is the Kingdom of God come upon you' (Matt. xii. 28; Luke xi. 20), stands alike for the whole preached word and activity of Jesus; both were God's own action in His new creative work. This amounts to the virtual identification of Jesus Himself and the Kingdom; He *was* that of which He was the bearer. Word and action of Jesus, word and action—or Kingdom—of God, and the person of Jesus merge in an inseparable unity. It is hardly worth while adding that to construe the ministry of Jesus in this way makes His Messiahship something self-evident. Israel's Messianic hope, however its content may have been filled in, was always a hope of salvation; and Jesus was bringing—the final—salvation.

The Kingdom was a gift depending on a demand, but something of the nature of the Kingdom as gift accompanied the demand. The preaching and acts of Jesus not only brought the Kingdom, they also assisted willing

---

[1] It is not possible to provide supporting reasons for this bare statement within the permitted limits of this chapter.

recipients into it; they were agencies of response to the Kingdom as well as modes of its arrival. To the Cross—which we may now bring within the scope of our theme—a similar twofold significance attached, but the demand became still more a matter of Divine provision than before.

If Jesus made His death, as surely He did, the voluntary experience of the Messiah,[1] He would not have thought of it as tragedy, nor even as mysteriously required of Him in accordance with the 'counsel and foreknowledge of God' (Acts ii. 23); nor again is it enough to see in its voluntary character Jesus' faith that His death had become the means appointed by God for the consummation of His work on earth; rather, the Cross received this value from the fact that He, the Messiah, so willed it. The Messiah brings salvation; in the time of fulfilment, when ancient hope is realized and transcended by the event, He has become Himself the Kingdom, and if He chose to make the Cross the supreme Messianic event, His death would thus bring in its perfection. There the present Kingdom would come in its greatest intensity; the forgiving and re-creative goodness of God would be put forth to its utmost reach. The earlier ministry was a bringing of the Kingdom; so, too, would be the Cross; the difference consisted in the fact that at the Cross the present Kingdom would be made perfect in that it would embrace the guilty.

It appears from such sayings as the parable of the Sower (Mark iv. 1 f.; Matt. xiii. 1 f.; Luke viii. 4 f.), the Narrow Gate (Matt. vii. 13 f.; Luke xiii. 23 f.), and the Censure of the Galilaean cities (Matt. xi. 20 f.; Luke x. 13 f.), that after a time Jesus did not expect the needful, obedient response to the Kingdom on a general scale; 'many' were thus incurring guilt. Guilt, it may be observed, in the

---

[1] The voluntary and Messianic (i.e. saving) character of the death of Jesus should be the controlling factor in the interpretation of the Agony in the Garden and the Cry of desolation from the Cross.

sense in which it existed for the beneficiaries of Jesus'
Messianic work, had a specific reference; it was guilt in
view of the Kingdom. The presence of the Kingdom
created a new and fateful possibility of guilt. It is to be
expected from the nature of the present Kingdom as
being the outpouring of the Divine compassion upon the
undeserving—and it is in fact recognized in traditional
sayings of Jesus (Mark x. 45; xiv. 24)—that guilt, in the
first instance, instead of curtailing the Divine redemptive
action, would lead to its increase. In the resolve of Jesus
to die, the task of bringing the Kingdom to the unworthy
may be seen being extended to the positively guilty; upon
them the forgiving goodness of God would overflow at
the Cross. Furthermore, in correspondence with the twofold character of all the Messianic work of Jesus, His
death would help to bring the guilty 'many' to the Kingdom, but in a more decisive way than hitherto. Unless
the Cross was to add something to Jesus' earlier work of
assisting the response to the Kingdom, the 'many' would
still remain guilty. For it is not to be supposed that in
making the Cross the extension of the Kingdom to the
guilty Jesus saw them receiving the Kingdom without
becoming in some sense radically other than they were
(cf. Mark viii. 34 f.).

The difficulty of understanding how Jesus expected
to bring the guilty into the Kingdom, whilst preserving
the necessity of the radical ethic, can be removed on
the hypothesis that with His acceptance of the Cross
He combined, whether forthwith or not, the belief that
He was passing into a solidarity-relationship with the
people of God analogous in general principle to that
presupposed in the case of the Servant of Jehovah and
the heathen nations in the fourth Servant-Song (Isa. lii.
13–liii. 12). This would mean that to that power of
aiding the response to the Kingdom which was inherent
in His preached word and flowed from His fellowship
with sinners Jesus eventually added the worth to God of

His offered life, with which the guilty 'many' would be associated in virtue of the corporate character of their relation to Him. On this view the ethic was not relaxed, in the intention of Jesus, as His Messianic work came to its climax at the Cross, but was accomplished inclusively in the completeness of His self-offering. It is certainly true—if only for the reason that the incorporation of so much obligatory ethical material in the Gospels would otherwise imply too great a misunderstanding of the mind of Jesus at the end of the ministry—that the ethic was left still in force for the beneficiaries of His consummated work, but it has the function now of authenticating their solidarity with Him in His offering. This is not to say that the 'many' remained after all in the same position as before; that which they had to become they already were before God; and from their solidarity with the Messiah proceeded new powers of attainment.

The light which is thereby thrown upon the difficulty indicated above (i.e. how the guilty 'many', the ethic being still incumbent upon them, would become acceptable to God) is a reason, to which others might be added, for believing that at the later stage of the ministry the fourth Servant-Song exercised a strong supporting influence upon Jesus—only, however, as regards a part, not the whole, of the interpretation which the Servant's suffering receives in the Song. The main lines of the interpretation may be noted. The prophet assigns a double significance to the suffering: in one aspect it is deserved suffering, penalty for sins, but for the sins of the heathen nations against God; in another it has the further purpose, other than penalty, of being the complete self-offering[1] to God which He desires from the Servant, to provide fully, on His side, for the inclusion

---

[1] Isa. lii. 13–liii. 12. For the suffering as sacrificial, and thus not penal, cf. ver. 10; as penal, vv. 4, 5, 6, 8, 11, 12—passages to which, however, from the prophet's standpoint, the thought of sacrifice also clings, the uncertainty regarding the state of the text in ver. 10 being thus offset.

of the nations in His salvation. The suffering, in the former sense, whilst being just penalty, is also imposed for a moral end, since it helps to bring about the nations' penitence; but it is the suffering as construed by the Servant in the latter sense which wipes out their guilt altogether. It is important to observe that the prophet attributes to the nations a potential solidarity-relationship with the Servant, which makes possible a kind of interchange, up to a point, of respective relations to God, the Servant thus being held to take upon himself the penalty, though not the guilt, belonging to the nations, whilst they, in turn, have secured for them the possibility of being assimilated to the guiltless Servant's life-offering to God, and of thus becoming entirely acceptable to Him. Through their penitent turning towards the God of Israel the nations would receive in actuality the Servant's access to Him. It is necessary, however, to proceed with caution in bringing the Song into connexion with Jesus' decision to die. Whilst the prophet's conception of the Servant's death as having the value of a corporate expiatory sacrifice is one which illuminates the thought of Jesus, to suppose that He was also influenced by the associated penal interpretation of the Servant's suffering would be to set His insight into the present Divine attitude to the guilty at strange variance with that which appears in his earlier mission to the 'lost', where nothing punitive can be seen in operation, only seeking, forgiving, and renewing love.

At the Last Supper the meaning which the Cross would hold potentially for 'many' may be observed being converted into fact by Jesus, in the case of a small group of disciples present with Him. With the bread and the wine was given also that which they were made to represent— the 'body' (= the self),[1] the 'blood' (= the life as wholly offered to God through death), of Jesus. He gave to the

---

[1] For the linguistic possibility of 'body' = 'gûph' = 'self', cf. Dalman, *Jesus-Jeshua*, pp. 141–3 (E.T.); Strack-Billerbeck, *Kommentar*, ii. 492.

disciples—Himself indeed, but Himself as standing to the Kingdom in a relation of virtual identity; moreover, Himself as the inclusive representative of 'many' who was about to present to God the complete self-offering necessary for the actual appropriation of the Kingdom. It would thus appear that in giving Himself to the disciples Jesus was doing two things for them: He was causing the Kingdom to reach them to the full, whilst also joining them with Him for that offering of the self to God, which death makes perfect, whereby His gift would be received.

II

In the meaning with which Jesus invested the Cross— namely, the decisive exercise of the will of God to save the guilty for His new creation—and in His anticipation, at the Last Supper, of the effect of the Cross—namely, union with the Messiah for an experience in common with Him, and so for a shared destiny—we are provided already by Jesus Himself with the primary elements of the Gospel as it appears with Paul—that is, the 'righteousness of God' and that mystical 'Body of Christ' for the fashioning of which Paul conceived that it was displayed. Any misgiving about the continuity of the Pauline Gospel with that of Jesus which might arise from the comparatively scanty reference which the Apostle makes to the 'Kingdom of God' under that designation is offset by the central position which the Divine 'righteousness' occupies in his thought. Moreover, in choosing not to repeat the public preaching of Jesus, but to ground the Gospel on 'Christ crucified' (1 Cor. i. 23; ii. 2; Gal. iii. 1), Paul only shows how surely he understood that the manifestation of the Kingdom in Jesus' preaching was taken up into, and absorbed in, that at the Cross. Again, Christians for Paul are 'Christ's body' (1 Cor. xii. 27), 'one body in Christ' (Rom. xii. 5), 'one (εἷς) in Christ Jesus' (Gal. iii. 28). With the help, in the first instance, of the reports of the Last Supper, it is not hard to understand

why Paul should have used the term 'body' to designate
the relation of believers to Christ and to one another: he
understood that when they received the 'body', or self,
of Christ at the Last Supper, the disciples present and
Christ became a joint-personality, one 'body' (see p. 58).
Already, by the eve of the death of Jesus, the mystical
'Body' had been advanced towards realization.

The earlier discussion of what Jesus meant by the present Kingdom brought by Him in His preaching and
acts, and then supremely in His Passion, has prepared us
for the recognition that Paul gave in principle the same
sense to what he called the 'righteousness of God'. He
did not intend this 'righteousness' to be understood as a
passive quality of the being of God, but as His manifested
power and—like the Gospel which reveals it (Rom. i. 16,
17)—'the power of God unto salvation'.[1] Thus the action
of God in setting forth Christ as the 'means of removing
guilt' (ἱλαστήριον) by His blood was a 'display of His
righteousness' (Rom. iii. 25). But both metaphors employed by Paul in the preceding verse (ἀπολύτρωσις,
ἀικαιοῦσθαι) contribute to the meaning of God's 'righteousness'. Similarly, the verbal form of the term, when it is
supplied with the full content which it held for Paul,
denotes the action of God the Deliverer as well as the
verdict (of innocence) of God the Judge; the latter in
consequence of the former. Thus, when Paul says out-
right that God 'justifies the ungodly' (Rom. iv. 5), the
term 'justify' will have the double sense of deliverance
and, in consequence thereof, of acquittal. He does not
mean that God acquits the ungodly as such (cf. Rom. i.
18–iii. 20); He acquits the ungodly whom He has delivered. The one 'justified' is not simply the man over
whom no 'condemnation' hangs; he is 'in Christ' (Rom.

---

[1] In so employing the term 'righteousness' with reference to God, Paul
could count on making contact with the minds of readers and hearers
acquainted with the usage in the Deutero-Isaiah and the Psalms. Cf. the
quotations and remarks in Prof. Dodd's *The Bible and the Greeks*, p. 48.

viii. 1), and thus belongs to the 'Body of Christ' (Rom.
xii. 5; 1 Cor. xii. 27), to the new creation (2 Cor. v. 17).
To make a simple equivalence of 'justification' and 'the
passing over of the sins done aforetime' (Rom. iii. 25 = 'not
reckoning unto them their trespasses', 2 Cor. v. 19) is to
miss its primary character of being the grace of God
(Rom. iii. 24), and the love of God (Rom. v. 8), as the
actual exertion of His will through Christ to deliver man
from his bondage to evil (iii. 24; vi. 7, cf. vv. 18, 22); and
also its connexion with the Pauline mysticism, to which
it is integral.

Even as the ethic of Jesus implies that the self as it is,
when confronted with the Kingdom, cannot receive it,
but only does so as it undergoes a dying which Jesus
Himself in the end effects through the corporate happening at the Cross, so, too, for Paul the 'justified' is one
whom Christ has enabled to die 'according to the flesh'.
Such a dying is 'justification', according to the fundamental Pauline usage of the term. 'He who has died (i.e.
'according to the flesh') is set free (Δεδικαίωται, Rom. vi. 7;
cf. ἐλευθερωθέντες δὲ ἀπὸ τῆς ἁμαρτίας, vv. 18, 22) from
Sin.' Since Paul often employs the term 'flesh' to mean
the self as fused with, and determined by, the great,
almost personal, evil power of 'Sin', freedom from 'Sin'
is also freedom from the 'flesh'. 'Justification' is libera-
tion from the 'flesh' and 'Sin', and then the recognition
by God of innocence before Him. From his own standpoint, the Apostle's doctrine of justification in relation to
his 'mysticism' presents no problem. The position is
simply that the Divine method of justification is to establish a relationship of solidarity between Christ and man.
Much as Paul makes of the Cross, he puts the beginning
of the exercise of God's saving power, or righteousness displayed through Christ, farther back in His sending of Christ
'in the likeness of sinful flesh' for the condemnation and
abolition of Sin and so of the 'flesh' (Rom. viii. 3). 'Flesh'
being what it was for Paul, a unity, a whole in which

all men shared, Christ to the extent that He participated
in it, was forthwith joined in solidarity with man.
Henceforth there could be no question of an individual,
isolated existence of Christ, so far as He was a bearer of
the 'flesh'; nor could the fate that He wrought for it at
the Cross have less than universal significance. The unity
of the 'flesh' made the Cross an inclusive event; and it is
clear by inference from a variety of passages that Paul
saw in the Cross the abolition of man's old evil self. Thus,
2 Cor. v. 14: from the premiss, 'one (i.e. Christ) died for
all', Paul infers the death of all. 'One died for (= 'in
the interest of') all, therefore all died' (i.e. died 'according to the flesh', the old self; cf. Rom. vi. 6). Christ dying
in the interest of all means at the same time all dying with
Him. If it is the case that, of the other passages which
come into consideration, Rom. vi. 2 f.; Col. ii. 12, are not
the only ones in which Paul is thinking of baptism as the
occasion of the dying with Christ, he is, nevertheless, extending to baptism an effect of the Cross. With Christ
Christians 'died', were 'crucified' (Gal. ii. 20; vi. 14),
'made dead' (Rom. vii. 4)—at the Cross.

Justification—the deliverance from evil through the
union with Christ in His death, and the recognition by
God of the innocence before Him which He Himself
ultimately has wrought of His grace—is not an end in
itself; God manifested His righteousness, displayed His
saving power, through Christ in order to create the mystical 'Body of Christ'; and Paul saw in justification the
first stage of its appearance. The conception, or rather,
for the faith of Paul, the simple reality, expressed by the
phrase, 'Body of Christ', is the solidarity of Christ and
the community of believers, which is logically, and in a
sense actually, that of Christ and all humanity, and this
throughout His experience of the 'flesh' of man, at the
Cross when He destroyed it, and beyond the Cross in
His resurrection-life. '*You* are *Christ's* Body' (1 Cor. xii.
27), i.e. the mystical Body is constituted by Christ and

His community together; they form a kind of joint-personality. Believers are said to be 'in Christ' in virtue of their solidarity with Him, and from this arises the possibility of regarding believers themselves as one body. 'We, who are many, are one body in Christ' (Rom. xii. 5; cf. Gal. iii. 28: 'you are all one [εἶς] in Christ Jesus'). But the latter is only arrived at by inference from the former, basic conception. In consequence of the relationship of solidarity existing within the Body of Christ, the Resurrection as well as the Death of Christ was an inclusive happening; all who with Him constitute the mystical Body died when He died, and rose with Him from the dead (Col. iii. 1, 3; cf. Eph. ii. 4–6). For the faith of the Apostle, at the moment of the resurrection of the chief member, the whole Body of Christ became for ever perfect before God; the eschatological, Divine community (the Kingdom consummated) was now a reality in heaven. But Christ alone had actual experience of those events—the Cross and the Resurrection—which marked the deliverance and perfecting of the mystical Body. He alone in this sense was as yet the Body of Christ. It is first concentrated and hidden in Himself; and then is unfolded to become actuality for all other members by renewed Divine activity—of which Paul commonly thinks in terms of the operation of the Spirit in the preached Word, in the Sacraments, and in the fulfilment of the ethical imperative: 'follow after love' (1 Cor. xiv. 1); 'mortify therefore your members which are upon the earth' (Col. iii. 5 f.; cf. Gal. v. 16 f.; Rom. vi. 12 f.; xii. 1 f.). Hence it is that Paul can regard Christians as already justified, and yet as surely look for a definitive justification (Gal. v. 5; Rom. vi. 16) when the hidden deliverance of the Body of Christ from evil, in the instance of the chief member, would be manifest reality for all others. With this realized righteousness of the whole Body would coincide its actual perfecting, its full, veritable resurrection-life with Christ (Rom. vi. 5, 8; Col. iii. 4).

III

The Word of God is God at work in self-revelation. The Fourth Evangelist has identified the person of Jesus Christ and the Word of God. Jesus, the Messiah, was the Divine Word. The Messiah is the one who brings God's final salvation. Thus blended in one with the Messiah, the Word is no longer the Word coming to a prophet, and needing to come again; the Word has now become God's culminating, ultimate Word, the Word which holds in itself the full meaning of the Word which came to prophets. Jesus was this Word of God; as such He was the Divine Life arrived amongst men. He was in person 'the Word of Life', the Word which is the Divine Life (1 John i. 1). He, the personal Word of God, was the Life (xiv. 6); here Himself, Life was here (1 John i. 2), the Life which the Father has and has granted to the Son (John v. 26). As the Word of God Jesus was the self-revelation of God in the sense of His decisive self-movement towards men, the actual presence of the Divine Life. The Word with the Fourth Evangelist was not simply the bearer of the Gospel; He was the content of the Gospel which he bore. It is not possible to detach the Johannine words of Jesus from the person whose words they are, and still to be confronted with the revelation. He *was* the Life of which He spoke, the Truth (xiv. 6) to which He bore testimony (xviii. 37). 'The time is fulfilled'—in Himself; He in His own person was the conversion of 'the last things' into fact. He—He Himself—was the realization of eschatology.

In attaching this significance to the appearance of Jesus the author of John was not giving an entirely new turn to the Christian message. The basis for it was already there within the Gospel itself for interpretative insight to use. The author has understood that the preaching of Jesus *was* the coming of the Kingdom with which it professedly had to do; that the Kingdom was becoming present in the acts of Jesus; that He dying was Himself the Kingdom—both the Divine saving action and (cf. John xvii. 19 in relation to x. 14–17; xv. 13), inclusively, the community which it creates unseen—now fully accomplished as a supra-historical reality. This is the Divine happening with which His thought is occupied. His guiding formula is the unity of the person of Jesus with the Word, rather than with the Kingdom, of God. But the Word is the Kingdom; the incarnate existence—including the Cross—of the Word is the realization of the Kingdom. It is well to observe the continuity between the Synoptic Gospels and the Fourth Gospel in this matter, for true though it remains that faith alone can affirm that 'the Word became flesh', the faith which does so is faith with a difference, if Jesus believed that He was the Kingdom in His own person.

The Word as present is not yet the Word received. Revelation is not a simple equivalent of salvation. A Divine demand is a constitutive feature of the Old Testament conception of the Word of God (e.g. Deut. iv. 12–13; x. 4); and this characteristic of it is preserved with strong emphasis in the Fourth Gospel and the first Johannine epistle. The Word is here both Life and demand. The words of Jesus in John relate to both aspects of the Word: there are words which are meant to authenticate the presence of the Word as Life; and there are words about the Word as demand, which summon to decision. With the Word as pure Life alone no direct contact is possible; the Word as Life—like the realized Kingdom, in Synoptic terminology, and the already perfected mystical Body of Christ, in the thought of Paul—is the hidden accomplishment of God, and not the immediate object of knowledge or faith in the Johannine sense of these terms, according to which to 'know' God in His revelation, the Word, to 'believe in' Christ, the Word, is to be in possession of Life. The Word as Life is communicable through the Word as demand. When it is said in John that 'he who believes has eternal life' (vi. 47; iii. 15, 36; vi. 40), that to 'know' God and Christ is eternal life (xvii. 3), faith and knowledge bear the stamp of obedience to the Word in this latter aspect. The demand with which is associated so surely the manifestation of the hidden Word of Life is the demand for love of the brethren after the pattern of the love of Christ. (It is not possible in this chapter to consider the Eucharistic words, if such they are, in John vi. 51b–8.) 'This is My commandment, that ye love one another, even as I have loved you' (xv. 12: cf. xiii. 1b; 1 John iii. 16; John xiii. 34; 1 John ii. 3–6; iii. 14, 23–4; iv. 7, 12). The departing Jesus would appear to him who has and keeps His commands (xiv. 21), which are gathered up in the one command of love (xv. 12; cf. xv. 10). Love renders fit to be on the Vine (xv. 3, 4, 5, 10, 12). Love is the Word of Life revealed within the sphere of experience.

Although revelation, the dynamic presence of the Divine Word, is not itself salvation, it comes nearer to being so than has yet been suggested. The demand for love, 'as I have loved you', is the return in the Fourth Gospel of the necessity for a self-offering to God such as He can accept, on which Jesus, as may be understood from the Synoptic Gospels, made dependent the actual reception of the Kingdom. And here, too, in John, as there, the impossible is made possible by Jesus Himself; believers, in virtue of the union with Him which the spoken Word is able to establish, yield to God the sacrifice, the self-offering, which He desires. The Word spoken 'dedicates' (John xvii. 17)—i.e. as might be shown from John x. 36–8 in relation to v. 26, x. 10b, endows with the life which it is (vi. 63), which Christ is (xiv. 6)—those who obey it (v. 24). But dedicated though they are who obey the Word, they are not yet dedicated 'in truth' (xvii. 19). This perfect dedication is too high an end for any obedience save that of Jesus Himself. For the sake, therefore, of those who have received the spoken Word

(xvii. 7, 8, 14), for His friends—His friends being those who do what He commands (xv. 14)—that these may be 'dedicated in truth', Jesus offers Himself in sacrifice to God, 'dedicates Himself' (xvii. 19) in this sense. He has joined them in union with Himself through the spoken Word; now he can, and does, accomplish their dedication 'in truth' through his own. This inclusive sacrifice, prepared for by the spoken Word, is at once their entire obedience to the Word as demand and their passage into perfected union with the Word as pure Life. Here is Divine action alone, providing the acceptable sacrifice, and fulfilling in advance of present experience the end for which the personal Word has come (x. 10b).

Christian worship is at once the Word of God and the obedient response thereto.

W. H. CADMAN.

V

THE SACRAMENT OF THE LORD'S SUPPER IN THE NEW TESTAMENT

THE most distinctive, significant, and universal rites of the Christian Church are the sacraments of Baptism and the Lord's Supper or Eucharist. Baptism, however, is an occasional and special sacrament, in which any individual may partake only once in his life. The Lord's Supper, on the other hand, is a constant and regular sacrament, in which the whole Christian fellowship unites from time to time for thanksgiving, remembrance, and communion. As such, it is the central act of Christian worship. The object of this chapter is to examine the historical origins of this sacrament as recorded in the New Testament, and to suggest a line of interpretation based upon the New Testament data.

I. *The Breaking of Bread.* According to the Acts of the Apostles, the Church observed from its earliest days a rite whose central feature was the breaking of bread accompanied by common prayers (ii. 42; cf. also xx. 7–11). This rite is distinguished as a private or domestic observance from public worship in the Temple, in which the followers of Jesus united with their fellow Jews (ii. 46). It can hardly be doubted that in this primitive observance we have at least the germ of the Sacrament of the Lord's Supper.

The Lucan work, however, was written at a date when the earliest days of the Church were already ancient history. We have no direct contemporary evidence regarding the primitive Breaking of Bread.

Our primary sources of information are three accounts of the Last Supper of our Lord and His disciples: A. Paul's account in 1 Cor. xi. 23–5, to which we should add his comments in xi. 26 and x. 16–17; B. the narrative in

Mark xiv. 22–5, reproduced with slight modifications in Matt. xxvi. 26–9; C. the narrative given in the 'Western Text' (R.V. Margin) of Luke xxii. 15–19a. In this shorter form the Lucan account seems to be substantially independent alike of Mark and of Paul. The remainder of the narrative, as found in the majority of manuscripts down to xxii. 20, has the appearance of a conflation of Mark and Paul, and cannot be treated as an independent witness.

To these we may usefully add (D.) another ancient source, namely, the eucharistic prayers contained in the *Didache*, or Teaching of the Twelve Apostles. The date of the *Didache* is uncertain, but the prayers at least must be very ancient, and may well go back to the New Testament period. In any case they are the oldest prayers of the kind that we possess. They show no trace of Pauline influence, and may be taken to represent a view of the Sacrament independent of our other early sources.

The text is as follows (*Did.* ix–x):

Concerning the Thanksgiving (Eucharist): Give thanks thus: First concerning the Cup:

We thank Thee, our Father, for the holy vine of David Thy servant, which Thou hast made known unto us through Jesus Thy servant. To Thee be glory for ever.

And concerning the Broken Bread:

We thank Thee, our Father, for the life and knowledge which Thou hast made known unto us through Jesus Thy servant. To Thee be glory for ever.

As this broken bread was scattered (as corn) over the mountains, and being gathered together became one, so may Thy church be gathered together from the ends of the earth into Thy kingdom. For Thine is the glory and the power through Jesus for ever.

And at the end of the meal give thanks thus:

We thank Thee, holy Father, for Thy holy name, which Thou hast caused to dwell in our hearts, and for the knowledge and faith and immortality which thou hast made known to us through Jesus Thy servant. Thou, almighty Lord, didst create all things for Thy name's sake. Thou didst give food and drink to men for their enjoyment, that they may give thanks unto Thee, but to us Thou hast granted spiritual food and drink and life eternal through Thy servant. Above all we thank Thee that Thou art mighty. To Thee be glory for ever.

Remember, O Lord, Thy church, to deliver her from all evil, and to perfect her in Thy love; and gather her together from the four winds, sanctified, into Thy kingdom, which Thou hast prepared for her. For Thine is the glory and the power for ever.

Let grace come and let this world pass away. Hosanna to the God of David. If any is holy, let him come; if any is not, let him repent. Marana tha (Our Lord, come)! Amen.

Among these sources it is the *Didache* alone that gives us explicit information about the form of observance, and this information is obviously incomplete, since there are no rubrics directing the action of the liturgy. We learn, however, that wine and broken bread were used, and that after these had been consecrated by prayers of thanksgiving they were consumed, before the post-communion prayers.

The Pauline account of the Supper is introduced in order to regulate the form of observance at Corinth, and we may fairly assume that some imitation, or repetition, of the words and acts of the Lord is contemplated. Explicitly we learn that the bread was broken, with thanksgiving, and the cup 'blessed', i.e. consecrated by thanksgiving.

Further, it is now generally held, and it is probably true, that the accounts of the Last Supper in the Gospels were preserved in Christian tradition in direct connexion with the observance of the Sacrament, and that the Marcan account reflects the usage of Rome, and the shorter text of Luke the usage of that church from which the Lucan special tradition came (possibly Caesarea).

Accordingly, we have four early documents, representing the Pauline churches, the Church of Rome, the Church of Caesarea (or some other), and some church in Syria (to which the *Didache* almost certainly belongs), all of which give evidence of a rite consisting of the distribution and consumption of bread and wine, accompanied by prayers of thanksgiving. That this is in fact the rite referred to in the Acts of the Apostles as 'the Breaking of Bread and the Prayers' seems fairly clear. The agreement of four independent authorities, from different parts of the Church, is enough to show that it was general and very ancient.

We may therefore make use of our four authorities to determine the ideas associated with the Sacrament in early times. Their agreements will most securely take us back to a primitive stage, while their peculiar features might be due to special local developments.

One idea which is inherent in the very form of the rite is that which is described as 'communion' (κοινωνία). The term is used in Acts, as well as in 1 Corinthians, and its meaning is indicated in Paul's words, 'We who are many are one body, for we all partake of the one bread'. In the *Didache* the idea is represented by the repeated emphasis on the unity of the Church. In the Gospel accounts of the Last Supper this idea is not made explicit; but the symbolism of the acts of the Lord and His disciples is sufficiently obvious without words.

Another idea common to all our authorities is that of thanksgiving, an act of worship by which the elements are blessed or hallowed for their use as means of communion.

Beyond these there is perhaps only one further idea which is clearly present in all four texts, and that is the eschatological reference:

A	B	C	D
'Ye proclaim the Lord's death till He come.'	'. . . until that day when I drink it new in the Kingdom of God.'	'. . . until it be fulfilled in the Kingdom of God.'	'Let grace come and let this world pass away. . . . Our Lord, come.'

The atmosphere of the Sacrament is everywhere eschato-logical. We seem justified in concluding that this aspect of it is strictly primitive.

II. *The Last Supper.* We must now consider the relation of this primitive eschatological sacrament to the actual events—the ministry and death of Jesus—out of which the Church arose.

Three out of our four sources represent the Sacrament as based upon the words and actions of Jesus at the Last Supper. Of these, A is of special importance. In actual date of writing it is the earliest. Further, Paul cites it as the account which he had given to the Corinthians when he was with them (A.D. 50–1), and as a part of the tradition which he had received—a tradition which included also the witness to the death, burial, and resurrection of the Lord (1 Cor. xv. 3–7), and doubtless other information to which he has no occasion to refer. The date at which he was instructed in this tradition must be placed, on any reasonable computation, not later than some time in the first decade after the Crucifixion, and quite possibly within the first three or four years. In the Marcan account we cannot rule out the possibility of Pauline influence, though it contains elements which are strange to Paul. The shorter text of Luke gives an account which appears to be entirely independent of Paul, and yet cor-roborates his account in essentials. We have therefore good grounds for believing that behind our documents A, B, and C there lies a true historical memory of the events of our Lord's last evening before His death.

We must now attempt to read the story of the Last Supper in the light of the eschatological reference which we have found to be a constant element in all the various accounts of the Sacrament.

The teaching of Jesus in the Gospels is expressed in terms of eschatology which has been transposed from future to present. That which was a hope has become 'good news' for the present. 'The time is fulfilled; the

Kingdom of God has drawn near: repent and believe the Gospel' (Mk. i. 15); or, more emphatically still, 'The Kingdom of God has come upon you' (Matt. xii. 28 = Luke xi. 20). This implies that whatever unrevealed glories may be still in store, the 'life of the Age to Come' (to use the Jewish phrase) is now inaugurated on earth, since God's Messiah is now here among men. To enforce this proclamation Jesus uses various forms of statement, illustration, and parable. In particular, He makes use of the traditional figure of the Messianic Banquet, and in the parable of the Great Feast He indicates that the banquet is already spread: 'Come, for things are now ready' (Luke xiv. 17; Matt. xxii. 4).

Besides parables, Jesus employed, like the prophets, symbolic action to give effect to His teaching. Such symbolism in action has been discussed by Dr. Wheeler Robinson in an important article in *Old Testament Essays* (edited by Dr. D. C. Simpson). He concludes: 'The prophetic act is itself a part of the will of Yahweh, to whose complete fulfilment it points; it brings that will nearer to its completion not only as declaring it, but in some degree as effecting it.' 'The prophet's act did not simply reveal something already achieved, but hidden; it helped to achieve something' (pp. 15–17). The symbolic act of the prophet is thus no mere illustration but a *signum efficax*. It is probably in this light that we must consider such a narrative as that of the Feeding of the Multitude. Jesus invites the crowd to a feast, surely in the sense of the parable: 'Come, for all things are now ready.' In other words, the Kingdom of God has come upon you: 'Blessed is he that shall eat bread in the Kingdom of God' (Luke xiv. 15, introducing the parable of the Great Feast). The occasion is in some sort a sacrament of the Kingdom of God, an eschatological sacrament.

The whole ministry of Jesus, then, is represented as an 'eschatological' crisis, in which the Kingdom of God comes. That crisis takes the form of a developing series

of events, but the whole series constitutes a single act of
God, in which each element is significant. Thus it is not
until the process is complete that men can in any full
sense be made sharers in all that it means. Jesus alone,
until His work is finished (cf. Luke xiii. 32), realizes in
Himself the Kingdom of God.

At the last possible moment before His work is finished,
Jesus is recorded to have performed a symbolic act, or
series of acts, of special significance, namely, that which
is described in our three reports of the Last Supper.
The similarity between these acts and those described in
the narrative of the Feeding of the Multitude is marked.
Once again we recognize a sacrament of the Kingdom of
God (to which, indeed, our accounts B and C explicitly
allude). But this time fresh elements of meaning can
enter in, because the Sacrament is now celebrated in the
presence of His finished work.

In all our accounts the central point is the blessing and
breaking of bread. Now, as before, it is the bread of the
Kingdom of God, the 'earnest' of that heavenly food by
which the 'life of the Age to Come' is sustained. But now
the symbolic act is accompanied by the words, 'This is
My body'. As we have seen, the Kingdom of God is
present in the person and the finished work of the
Messiah. In Him the life eternal is realized. In giving
the bread, therefore, He gives Himself. The day which
(on the Hebrew reckoning of days from sunset to sunset)
was begun with this meal was to see the consummation
of the symbolism in actual fact. Jesus was to give Himself over to death 'as a ransom for many' (Mark x. 45,
alluding to Is. liii. 11–12). The inward and spiritual
meaning of His death is already present in the sacrament.

On the significance of the Cup our three sources are not
in such close agreement. The words in Luke run: 'Take
this and divide it among you. For I tell you, I will not,
from now on, drink of the fruit of the vine until the Kingdom of God comes.' In Mark these words have a more

pointed form: 'I will no more drink of the fruit of the vine until that day when I drink it new in the Kingdom of God.' That is, the wine, like the bread, is a symbol of life eternal in the consummated Kingdom of God. Mark gives also the formula, 'This is My blood'. It is possible, as some critics hold, that this precise formula, which is peculiar to Mark, is not original, but due to the influence of the parallel words uttered over the bread. However that may be, the substance of the Marcan form, 'This is My blood of the covenant', is confirmed by the Pauline, 'This cup is the new covenant in My blood'. The background here is supplied partly by the Paschal associations of the Last Supper, and partly by Jeremiah's prophecy of the 'New Covenant'. The death of Christ is thought of as the sacrifice by which the new covenant of the Kingdom of God is inaugurated, and the cup is given to the disciples in token that they are made partakers in the covenant.[1] Mark's additional words, '. . . which is shed for many' (cf. Is. liii. 12), have no support in our other authorities, and add little to the meaning; while the Matthaean expansion, 'for the remission of sins', may be regarded as an allusion to the passage about the 'new covenant' in Jer. xxxi. 34.

In view of the imperfect agreement of our sources here, we cannot be quite certain of the original words used with reference to this part of the Sacrament. But the very use of the term 'cup' (which is unvarying in all references to the Sacrament in the New Testament, as well as in the liturgy of the *Didache*, the term 'wine' never occurring) is surely significant. According to Mark x. 38–9; xiv. 36; John xviii. 11, Jesus was accustomed to speak of His destiny of suffering as His 'cup'. His words, therefore, at

---

[1] It is noteworthy that at a later point Luke too introduces the idea of the covenant (xxii. 29), though this is disguised in the English version, because we have no verb to translate Διατίθεμαι, corresponding with the noun 'covenant' which translates Διαθήκη. We might render: 'I devise upon you by covenant, as My Father devised by covenant upon Me a kingdom, that you may eat and drink at My table in My kingdom.'

the Last Supper inevitably include a reference to His approaching passion. Now Mark records that when Jesus predicted for James and John a share in His sufferings, He used the words, 'You shall indeed drink of the cup of which I drink'. When, therefore, He gave a cup to His disciples at the Last Supper, can we doubt that He intended thereby to associate them with the passion which was now immediately before Him? The cup is, as Paul says, 'the communion (κοινωνία) of the blood of Christ'; that is, to use another Pauline expression, it is 'the fellowship (κοινωνία) of His sufferings'.

We conclude that in giving His disciples the broken bread and the cup, our Lord was initiating them into 'the sufferings of Christ and the glory to follow' (1 Pet. i. 11). They were thereby united with Him in the life laid down and raised in glory. The Sacrament is indeed for them still proleptic or anticipatory, for though He celebrates it in the presence of His finished work, that work is not in fact finished. His act, like the symbolic acts of the prophets, not merely declares, but helps to bring about that which God has willed. It is a *signum efficax*. The situation brings out very clearly the truth that this participation of the disciples in the life of the Kingdom of God is wholly of grace and not of merit. They are so little worthy of it that they will deny or forsake their Lord. Yet He gives them bread and cup, sealing them for that which is to come. The subsequent experience of the disciples, to which the whole New Testament bears witness, affords proof that His gift was in fact efficacious.

III. *Easter and Whitsuntide*. It is surely no accident that several of the narratives of the appearances of Christ after the Resurrection are associated with a meal (Luke xxiv. 30-5, 41-3; John xxi. 9-13). We seem justified in concluding that from an early date the breaking of bread was associated with the realized presence of the risen Lord. It is possible that we may go further and believe that historically it was this association that from the first gave a special solemnity to the common meal of the disciples. They always remembered that He was 'known to them in the breaking of bread' (Luke xxiv. 35).

The story of Pentecost signifies the moment at which the disciples realized that through the resurrection of the Lord, His work being now finished, the 'life of the Age to Come' was actually theirs. 'This', they said, 'is that which was spoken of by the prophets.' It is fulfilment. Now at last they knew what He had meant by saying 'The Kingdom of God has come upon you'.

In the Pentecostal experience, present and future are held in unity. The disciples expect the coming of the Son of Man on the clouds of heaven and the visible triumph of the Kingdom of God. That clearly is not yet; but it is for them so immediately imminent that it can be grasped in one act of spiritual apprehension with that which is already present experience—the rule of Christ through His Spirit in the Church. It was only with lapse of time that this unity of experience was dissolved, and the mood of expectancy tended to prevail over that of realization.

It is in this atmosphere that we must place the primitive Sacrament of the Breaking of Bread. Its eschatological character we have already noted: it looked forward 'till He come'. But it also expressed the conviction that Christ, risen and triumphant, was even now with His people, sharing with them the benefits of His finished work. In the *Didache* there is a prayer for the consummation. But there is also a thankful commemoration of the gifts of 'spiritual food and drink and eternal life'. There is the sense that in partaking of the bread and cup given by Christ, His followers already possess the 'life of the Age to Come'. Again, in the Revelation—the book which ends with the words, 'Yea, I come quickly. Amen; come Lord Jesus'—we meet with the remarkable passage: 'Behold I stand at the door and knock. If any man hear My voice and open the door, I will come in to him and will sup with him, and he with Me' (Rev. iii. 20). In such passages, relatively late though they are, we seem to be brought into the mood in which the Lord's Supper established itself in the life of the Church.

It is unlikely that Jesus gave instructions at the Last Supper that the Sacrament should be repeated in remembrance of Him. It is only in Paul's account that any such precept is reported. Our other two primary sources not only give no hint of it, but they indicate that the mind of the Lord was not at that moment concerned with any future history lying beyond His death and resurrection. His thought passed directly from His impending passion to the day when He should drink the 'new wine' in the Kingdom of God. Paul, however, does afford evidence that the remembrance of the Passion was early associated with the bread and cup; and this is indirectly confirmed by the emphasis laid upon the Last Supper in the Passion-narrative of the Gospels. It was, indeed, natural that a common meal which both expressed the Church's expectation of the Lord's advent and celebrated the present blessings of His reign among His people, should also carry with it the remembrance of His finished work, through which those blessings had been won, and upon which the Advent hope rested. So the Sacrament provided anchorage for the historical element in the Christian faith, along with the more mystical sense of the Lord's abiding presence, and with the hope of glory. Past and future were brought together in a present and recurrent experience.

As the too crude and literal expectation of the Advent faded, the Sacrament became the repository of all that proved permanent in the eschatology of the primitive Church. Attempts to revive the hope of a speedy Advent have, ever since the second century, had something abnormal, artificial, or fanatical about them. Yet the Church cannot rest content with the belief that the Christian life in this world, as we know it, fulfils all that

is meant by that great assurance, 'The Kingdom of God
has come upon you'. There are glories yet to be revealed,
and never fully to be revealed in this world. In the
Sacrament they are realized 'by faith, not by sight'. A
non-sacramental Christianity tends to become non-super-
natural, or else takes refuge in a mysticism which is not
distinctively Christian because it has lost the living link
with history.

IV. *Interpretation*. The Sacrament of the Lord's Supper
is in origin, as we have seen, the sacrament of a transformed eschatology. As such, it places us in the presence
of the eternal, supernatural order—the Kingdom of God.
But our approach to the eternal world is here not (as it
is apt to be with the mystics) by way of a withdrawal
from the earthly and temporal, but by a consecration of
the earthly and temporal. The eating of bread and the
drinking of wine are concrete bits of ordinary life in the
world, and they become means of access to the other
world. This mediation of the eternal through the temporal is the presupposition of the Sacrament.

With this general presupposition in mind we distinguish
two primary aspects of the Sacrament: remembrance and
communion.

1. It is of fundamental importance that here we have a
perpetual witness to the fact that our faith rests on history. It rests upon certain events that once took place,
interpreted as an act of God achieved in and through an
historical Personality. In the Sacrament there is a corporate memory of the facts, going back by an unbroken
chain of witness to a period earlier than any of our
written records. Our Lord is not one whom we found (as
John Nicholson found his God) 'in a printed book'. In
a perfectly real sense we *remember* that on the night in
which He was betrayed the Lord did this and said that.
Among other things we remember that He broke bread
and said, 'This is my body'. We remember Him, therefore, as One who gave Himself for us that we might have

life eternal. This corporate memory holds a high place among 'Christian evidences'. In face of it, it is idle to set forth as 'the Jesus of History' a figure who is no more than teacher, prophet, or leader. The words lead us directly from mere remembrance to communion.

2. As a sacrament of communion the Lord's Supper stands alongside similar rites in many religions. *Homo est quod est: man ist, was man isst.* The very act of taking food is a symbol of the fact that we live by that which we receive from the great universe beyond us. The Self is dependent on the Not-self. The acknowledgement of such dependence is the beginning of religion. Not less, the partaking of food *together* is a symbol of the fact that we share with one another the life that we derive from the universe, or the power behind it. In primitive religions people partook of the fruits of the earth in solemn feasts, as a communion with the powers of fertility which manifested themselves in the growth and ripening of crops; and in doing so, they felt themselves to be consolidating their unity with one another in the tribe.

From quite an early stage man was aware that he does not live by bread alone, but is dependent in like manner for the higher side of his life. Spiritually no less than physically he must live by that which is given to him from beyond himself, and he holds the gift on terms of sharing it with his fellows. Out of primitive fertility cults arose 'Mystery religions', whose sacraments were believed to confer a blessed immortality upon their initiates.

In any high religion it is recognized that the whole life of man, from its most rudimentary physical aspects to its most sublime and spiritual aspects, is received as a gift from God, the one Source of life and of all good. His life is, in fact, communion with God, in which he is also in communion with his fellows.

The Sacrament of the Lord's Supper expresses this truth in fitting, and indeed inevitable, symbolism. We are one body because we partake of the same bread; and that bread is to us the life of God, by which we all live. Paul pointed to an original and suggestive interpretation of the words, 'This is My body', when he spoke of the Church as the 'body' of Christ (1 Cor. xii. 27; Rom. xii. 5; Eph. iv. 12; v. 30, &c.). *Homo est quod est*: the Church, in feeding upon the bread which is the 'body' of Christ, is itself His 'body'. Its members are organically one with Him and with one another in Him. The Fourth Evangelist has suggested a similar idea in his allegory of the true Vine, which is Christ, His disciples being the branches.

The whole of Christ's Church, militant and triumphant, is present at the Table. Any individual experience that may be granted is dependent on the individual's acceptance of his place within a corporate experience, which is always richer than anything which may at the moment be present to his mind, but is always available for him. That experience is one of communion with God, of sharing in the life of God.

But here we link up communion with remembrance. The bread is the life of God; but we remember that He who gave it to us said, 'This is My body'. It is the Lord Jesus Christ who comes to us, in the virtue of His finished work. This is the teaching of the Fourth Gospel. The eternal Word was made flesh; He gives His 'flesh' to us whereby we have eternal life. The Sacrament is the guarantee of our belief in the Incarnation; for it is only Very God who can thus communicate life to our souls; and at the same time we know (we remember) that it was the man Christ Jesus who gave us this Sacrament, and in it gave Himself.

This leads us to a third aspect of the Sacrament, namely, sacrifice. The words of the Last Supper, as we have seen, indicate a self-offering of Jesus in the death He was about to suffer. Once again the Fourth Gospel interprets them for us: 'The bread which I will give is My flesh, for the life of the world': 'for their sakes I dedicate Myself' (John vi. 51; xvii. 19). The sacrifice of Christ is the dedication of His life, that it may be communicated to men. His death is the seal of this self-dedication. And whatever relation the sacramental breaking of bread at the Last Supper had to His sacrifice, with His death in prospect, that relation the breaking of the bread in the Sacrament has to His sacrifice, with His death in retrospect.

But the Fourth Gospel adds: '. . . that they also may be dedicated in truth'. As we have seen, Jesus in giving the cup to His disciples was initiating them into the fellowship of His sufferings. And so the Sacrament unites us with Christ in His sacrifice, and by virtue of that union, we, as members of His 'body', dedicate ourselves to God. This is the 'living sacrifice' for which Paul calls (Rom. xii. 1).

It is at this point that the Sacrament displays its full significance as an act of worship. We have seen that that which consecrates the elements to their use is, and was from the beginning, a prayer of thanksgiving to God for all His gifts, temporal and spiritual. Thanksgiving is itself worship; but worship at its highest involves a sacrifice, or dedication of the self. This is, however, too high an activity to be initiated by merely human effort. God Himself must give that which shall be worthy to be offered to Him. So in the Sacrament we accept that which God gives, become that which He makes of us (by grace, not by merit), and render it up to Him. Worship is here that which ideally it must be—the return to God of that which came from God.

In the Sacrament of the Lord's Supper many strains of religious belief and experience come together. Indeed, in this Sacrament the whole of what our religion means is expressed. That which otherwise we apprehend piecemeal is integrated in a rite which presents it all as the sheer gift of God. On any one occasion we may be conscious only of this or that element in the meaning; but it is all there, because God in Christ is there. In dependence on Him for everything, we render it all back to Him in thankful adoration.   C. H. DODD.

PART II

HISTORICAL STUDIES

VI

CHRISTIAN WORSHIP AS REFLECTED IN ANCIENT LITURGIES

ORIGINALLY a λειτουργία meant a public action or function performed in the service of a Greek city-state, and entrusted to a citizen as an honourable duty. From the civic sphere of representative duty it was transferred to the yet more sacred one of priestly service in the Jewish Temple; and from this the further transition was easy to its use for certain services to God and His People, proper to Christ's Gospel. In Christian worship the λειτουργία or solemn service took the form of spoken words or symbolic acts, expressive of relations between God and His special People, in and through Jesus His Christ.

At first, however, the 'enthusiastic' ('God-possessed') genius of the Church's consciousness of Salvation, alike as enjoyed in present experience and as the object of vivid hope, through Jesus its saving Lord, was the outstanding feature of such λειτουργία or sacred ministry of 'the Word'—the medium of conscious relations between God and man. Christ's folk, 'Christians' as they were soon called, were essentially an inspired people, a community raised to a new level of spiritual vision and further receptivity of like experiences. Such 'holy inspiration' (Πνεῦμα Ἅγιον, without definite article) was the distinctive mark of a Christian (Acts xix. 1 ff.). Those thus sealed with the Spirit of Sonship, and so able truly to cry 'Abba', Father, were already heirs of God, members of the People in whom His will reigned effectively, though not yet completely, pending the full consummation of His sovereign sway or 'Kingdom' in 'the Coming Age' (Eph. i. 13 f.; Heb. vi. 4 f.). This present 'foretaste' of it, however, serves to 'confirm' or 'establish' with 'full assurance' the fact of a man's filial status, and to inspire the soul further with grateful love, which overflowed in great spontaneity of utterance, particularly in the atmosphere of corporate worship.

For a time such experiences or 'Grace-gifts' (χαρίσματα) were widespread in the Church. And no account of early Christian worship and liturgies which fails to reckon with this element of inspired spontaneity, alike in 'uttering the word' and in prayer, is really true to all the historical facts of the case. It was a supreme service of St. Paul that he perceived and made clear to others the continuity and homogeneity in spiritual content and essential reasonableness underlying the 'diverse operations' of the one Spirit in both the more and the less spontaneous forms of expression. This 'holy inspiration' made Christians, as Peter also taught (1 Pet. ii. 9), 'a priesthood' fit to 'offer up spiritual sacrifices' of true worship 'acceptable to God through Jesus Christ'. This function of 'liturgy' or sacred service to God in worship, ideally open to all and for a time exercised by many, had three forms of ministry at its disposal: praise, prayer, testimony, or preaching.[1] These were all modes of the fundamental ministry of 'the Word' or revelation in the Gospel, and were all essentially 'prophetic', in the sense of being prompted by fresh, God-given insight into things Divine.

I. *The Pre-liturgic Period.* We have first to note that we possess no *complete* primitive or even early liturgy, to give us a norm by which to judge later developments. No liturgy representing primitive, that is Apostolic or even sub-Apostolic, Christian worship, ever existed. It was precluded by the fact that the New Covenant, unlike

[1] For a full and lucid account of the principles of this paragraph see Dr. A. B. Macdonald, *Christian Worship in the Primitive Church* (1934).

the Old, was essentially the religion of 'the Spirit', and so of the inspiring and guiding initiative of God within men's souls, as distinct from 'the letter' of an external Law admitting of no real flexibility or liberty in the expression of a life of loyal love. In contrast to any such statutory type of piety, the new-born Church felt that 'the Spirit of the Lord', the Spirit mediated to it through the filial personality of Jesus, its Messianic Lord, was a spirit of 'liberty'. This meant much spontaneity and variety of experiment in the sphere of worship.

The first or primitive stage of Christian worship, as of Christian thought, was one of free experiment, during which certain modes of expressing the new filial spirit of common devotion inspiring all hearts, which had been tested by experience, took shape and attained general acceptance, under the leadership of the most Spirit-gifted (πνευματικοί). These included persons whose natural gifts were of the more practical order, qualifying them for ordination to the office of supervision in the Church (presbyters or 'overseers', ἐπίσκοποι), and particularly in the orderly conduct of common worship. Even at this stage of largely free liturgic activity, when much spontaneous exercise of personal Grace-gifts (χαρίσματα) was normal and prized, there was a large element of continuity with the usages of the Jewish Synagogue, in which most Christian believers had been reared, whether Jews or proselytes of various degrees from outside. So we may assume that Christian worship was for the most part determined, as to its liturgic structure, by Jewish precedents, and included readings from the Old Testament scriptures, psalm-singing (sometimes antiphonal), exposition of Scripture and exhortations based largely on it, certain favourite synagogal prayers, more or less adapted to the new Messianic form of the worshippers' faith, as well as certain features directly inspired by this. But all that has actually reached us from this formative stage is a series of fragments, some of which will be quoted here, before we come to our earliest notice as to an 'Order of Service'.

But we must first have clear in mind the original notion of Christian worship in its essential meaning. The general idea of primitive Christian worship was the response of man's whole nature, focused in the will, to God's gracious will for his true well-being or salvation, as revealed and made incarnate in Jesus the Christ. Such self-oblation to God is described by Paul as 'the bounden service' of the 'reasonable' soul of Christian men, and as taking effect in a transformed daily life, wherein that will of God is found by the test of experience to be kind, worthy of welcome, indeed the perfect way for man (Rom. xii. 1 f.). In its more specific aspect as an act of devotional approach to its God, it is most fully and explicitly set forth in the Epistle to 'Hebrews', that is, Christians of Jewish antecedents by birth or at least training, in a way that has had deep and lasting effects on the Church's liturgies in all ages. Its great unknown writer was a son of the Jewish 'Dispersion' extending beyond the limits of the special soil and culture of Judaism, and was steeped in the best of Greek reflective or philosophic thought. His conception, then, of Christian worship is significant for the future.

To him it was the spiritual 'fulfilment' of the symbolic Old Testament cultus under the visible forms of the ritual and sacrifices of the Temple, or rather of the Mosaic Tabernacle. For it was this latter that the Jewish Dispersion, whose piety was conditioned by study of the Scriptures rather than familiarity with the actual ritual of the Temple, pictured as the *beau idéal* of Divine Worship. In terms of this, then, he gives us the first characterization of Christian worship, as the perfectly real because truly spiritual worship, that of conscious personal relationship between man and God. Such relations have been made possible, for the first time, by Jesus the Christ, unique Son of God and Son of Man, and as such, perfectly embodying the qualities common to both, since man was made 'in the likeness' of God (Ps. viii. 4 f., pointing back, as Heb. ii implies, to Gen. i. 27). Further the special glory and efficacy of the new and absolute worship lay in the fact that the privilege of direct access to communion, which the former or Old Covenant type of religion reserved for 'priests' and so made vicarious for the people, was now open to all God's people in Christ. It was their *filial* status in Christ, as historically 'the Pioneer-leader and Consummator of faith' among 'many sons' of God (xii. 2; ii. 9–18), which was the basis of the spiritually real *priesthood* conferred on all Christians as such by Jesus, as supreme Priest in this same sense. In virtue of this they were 'a holy priesthood, to offer up (the verb corresponding to the noun ἀναφορά, the Gk. equivalent of the Latin *Missa*, English 'Mass') spiritual sacrifices acceptable to God through Jesus Christ' (1 Pet. ii. 5). Such sacrifices, as Heb. xiii. 15 f. makes clear, were none other than 'the sacrifice (consisting) of praise continually to God, to wit, fruit of lips doing homage to his Name', but also of 'beneficence and sharing' God's material gifts with those in need. Similarly in the Apoc. i. 5 f. we read of 'Him who loosed us from our sins by his blood and made us priests to God and his Father', a conception expanded in the vision of worship of redeemed spirits in heaven, offered to the sacrificial Lamb, Who is associated with God as the supreme object of praise.

In the above we have as a coherent whole the essential elements of Christian worship as Divine 'Service' or homage of adoring praise in particular, whether in hymn or prayer, to the Divine Name or revealed character, as seen in his works of Creation and his redemptive acts of Grace towards men (the two are closely linked in the *Apoc.*), and particularly his chosen People, his 'Saints' or consecrated ones.

II. *Liturgical Fragments and other data.* As we have seen in Chapter V, the primitive 'Breaking of Bread' was the first distinctively Christian form of symbolic worship. Our earliest descriptions of Christian 'Eucharistic' worship are found in the traditional 'Teaching (*Didache*) of the Twelve Apostles'. This priceless relic of primitive Church life was so recognized by Bishop Lightfoot, even before criticism had had time to distinguish its secondary elements. The leading function of prophets in the Divine service of corporate worship, particularly in praise as Thanks-offering (εὐχαριστία), was already visible between the lines of 1 Cor. xiv. In the *Didache* it is stated explicitly as their special prerogative that they may lead in such prayer freely, without restrictions as regards habitual forms of words, at any corporate breaking of bread with accompanying thanks-offering.

The partially corporate or domestic type of Eucharistic worship reflected in *Did.* ix–x (quoted on p. 69 f.) was continuous with that in Acts ii. 42, 46; while this in turn was probably based on the original practice of the inner Apostolic circle at its head-quarters in the Upper Room (Acts i. 13), where the Last Supper itself may have taken place so recently. That quasi-domestic Eucharistic worship accompanied every evening 'supper' of Christians, meeting corporately as such, is most probable. At any rate it was before and after a social meal that the liturgic prayers in *Did.* ix–x were offered, with the symbolism of Cup and breaking of a Loaf which is here viewed as the figure of Church unity in Jesus (cf. 1 Cor. x. 17).

The above symbolism of Christian unity in Christ reappears in the Epistles of Ignatius (c. 110–16). He bids all assemble frequently for full corporate worship, 'breaking one loaf, which (action) is a specific for immortality, an antidote that a man die not but live in Christ Jesus for ever' (To Ephesus, xx). Ignatius was later remembered in connexion with antiphonal singing in worship, probably of psalms from the O.T. Psalter, and possibly also of fresh Christian ones in praise of Christ and thanksgiving to God for His Salvation.

All this is of a piece with the *Didache's* witness as to Eucharistic worship. But before Ignatius wrote, the *Didache* had been brought up to date touching Eucharistic worship, by a section on its fully corporate form, proper to the weekly general gathering of each local church.

'And on "the Lord's Day" of the Lord come together and break bread, and give thanks, after confessing your transgressions, that your sacrifice may be pure. Let no one that hath any dispute with his fellow come together with you, until they be reconciled, that your sacrifice may not be profaned.

'For this is that (scripture) which was spoken by the Lord (Mal. i. 11, 14): "In every place and time offer Me a pure sacrifice; for I am a great King, saith the Lord, and My name is marvelled at among the Gentiles."

'Elect, therefore (i.e. to see this rule carried out), for yourselves bishops and deacons worthy of the Lord . . . for they too minister to you the ministry (λειτουργία) of the prophets and teachers. Therefore despise them not; for they are those that are honoured of you with the prophets and teachers' (cc. xiv f.).

As we learn from the rubric at the end of the earlier section on the less formal type of Eucharistic worship already dealt with, 'prophets' were the primary leaders of the Church's worship. This was so in idea, from the very nature of the Christian stage of revealed religion, as the dispensation of the Spirit (Acts ii. 16–18, cf. 1 Cor. xii–xiv); and it remained so for more than a generation, though in decreasing frequency. This passage from the *Didache* bears witness to the moment when in N. Syria an appeal for equal honour, with prophets and other specially inspired men of 'the Word', was made for the ordinary elected Church-officers, by some leading person, while inserting in the manual of Church order in that region a fresh section on the corporate Lord's day Eucharistic worship. Such is called the Church's 'Sacrifice', the 'sacrifice of praise', as Hebrews had described it, and as Ignatius repeats, in styling the Church itself as met for worship, 'the altar area' (Eph. 5, Trall. 7). And

what is very noteworthy is that the purity, and so accep-
tability to God, of that 'Sacrifice' depends on the moral
purity of the worshippers, even of individuals among
them, in point of brotherly love, 'the bond of peace' as
Paul had called it. The central significance of this in
Christian worship was shown by the 'Kiss of Peace' (the
Pax of later liturgies), which in the earliest known usage
preceded the opening of the Church's special Eucharistic
Prayer, as distinct from certain more general intercessions
which precede this special symbol of unity.

There is another striking witness, of about the same date,
both to the idea that any breach of Christian unity in
love profaned in God's sight the Church's corporate worship, and to the division of opinion now arising as to the
respective claims of 'prophets' and ordinary Church-
officers (presbyters in this case) to offer the Eucharistic
prayer over the people's 'Gifts'. To some the former
seemed entitled to this function in virtue of their special
inspiration, otherwise recognized and honoured, and as
having exercised it in earlier and Apostolic days. To
others the latter seemed to possess prescriptive right to
this λειτουργία, as having in some cases performed it
for some time, blamelessly, and as being men installed
in their position, as the duly elected 'overseers' of the
Church's general welfare and order, by Apostles or those
so installed by them. This is what we learn from the
situation *c*. A.D. 95 in Corinth, as it is reflected in the
letter of the Roman Church to its sister there, written by
its leading presbyter Clement. He was a man of high
spiritual gifts; but he shared the strong Roman sense for
law and order. It is thus no wonder if the letter sides
strongly with the official ministry.

In an elevated passage towards the letter's close, the
Roman Church passes into formal quotation of what may
well be part of the intercessory prayer 'for all sorts and
conditions of men', running to some length, such as was
used in the pre-Eucharistic half of its corporate worship,

as Justin Martyr a generation later describes that of Christians at large. It ends with these words: 'To Thee we offer our homage through the High-Priest and Guardian of our souls, Jesus Christ, through Whom be the glory and the majesty unto Thee, both now and for all generations and for ever and ever. Amen.'

When examined closely, this prayer is seen to have much in common with the Great Prayer of the Jewish Synagogue. It was owing to the Hebraic strain of piety embodied in the Church's public worship during the primitive stage of her life, that she was able to keep as largely at bay as she finally succeeded in doing the influences of alien piety of an Hellenistic 'mystery' type. Here the affinity of religious conception and feeling between the ethical character of Hebrew piety and the Roman temper of dignified responsibility (*gravitas*) helped not a little, as appears when one compares Greek and Latin liturgies generally. Meantime let us note the conception of worship as *cultus* which characterized the Synagogue in the first century, in certain circles at least even in Palestine, much more among the Dispersion. 'One day (i.e. in the Messianic Age) all offerings will cease, only the Thank-offering will not cease: all prayers will cease, only the Thanksgiving prayer will not cease' (R. Menachem of Gallaya, citing Jer. xxxiii. 11; Ps. lvi. 13).[1] Such was the atmosphere of thought in which we should imagine primitive Christian worship.

III. *The Early Catholic Type of Service.* The first complete 'order of service' known to us is supplied by the writings of Justin, soon after A.D. 150. It consisted of:

1. Lections from the Gospels *or* the Prophets (= The Old Testament).
2. Hortatory Sermon by the presiding minister.
3. Common prayers for themselves and all men.
4. The Kiss of Peace.

---

[1] Pĕsiḥta 79ᵃ, see Strack-Billerbeck, *Kommentar*, i. 246.

5. Presentation to the president of the elements ready for use.
6. The Eucharistic Prayer over the bread and mixed Cup. (This consisted of Praise and Thanksgiving to the Father of the Universe through the Son and the Holy Spirit, both for his works in Creation and his acts in Redemption, particularly Christ's Passion. The Prayer is long and *ex tempore* in form; and the people associates itself with its offering, by the Amen.)
7. The act of Communion. (The Deacons hand round the elements for those present to partake, and convey some to those absent.)

The Collection for alms is also mentioned, but not the point in the service when it came.

The following points may be noted, in relation both to the past and to future developments. Its large agreement with Jewish worship, including the 'Sanctification' of God's name, is significant. The sacredness of Prayer as essential worship, one in spirit and kind with that of heaven (cf. Sursum Corda), is suggested by the Church's prayers being confined to the 'priestly' people, those not yet baptized not being admitted to them. The special sacredness of the Eucharistic Prayer, in keeping with what R. Menachem said touching Thanksgiving-prayer as alone to survive in the Messianic Age, is indicated by its place as climax, for which the purity of its offering 'priesthood', the whole Church, was to be safeguarded by the kiss of mutual 'peace' preceding it.

As to the place of the Sermon, which comes before what later was called 'the prayers of the Faithful', as distinct from the unbaptized inquirers (Catechumens) and outsiders generally, it seems to consist of purely practical instruction or exhortation based on 'the excellent things' for imitation in the Lections just read. That is, such ministry of 'the Word' as called for 'inspired' insight seems to have fallen largely into abeyance in

public worship. This falling out of an original element
in Christian worship as a whole was pregnant with no
little change in its conception and practice.

Another new element calls for notice, which ended in
transforming corporate Church worship far more profoundly. Thus far all has been in harmony with the
genius of biblical piety and worship. But when we come
to Justin's explanation as to the meaning of their eating
and drinking of the Bread and Cup, we are very conscious
of a changed outlook.

'We do not', says Justin, 'take these as ordinary bread and
drink; but just as by becoming made flesh through word
(= uttered command) of God, Jesus Christ our Saviour had
both flesh and blood for our salvation, so also we have been
taught that the food which through prayer of a word that comes
from Him (i.e. a sacred formula uttered in prayer, the "Words
of institution" embodied in the Eucharistic prayer itself) was
made Eucharistic—(food) from which our blood and flesh (note
the order) are by metabolism (μεταβολή) nourished—is both
flesh and blood of that flesh-made (incarnate) Jesus. For the
Apostles, in their memoirs called Gospels, so handed down that
it was enjoined on them.'

He then quotes the Words of Institution, adding: 'Which
very action the evil daemons in imitation delivered to be
enacted in the Mysteries of Mithras also.'

Here we are reminded of a very different religious
environment from that of the Synagogue, the atmosphere
of ancient pagan religions of all kinds. What was chiefly
common to most of them was the idea that Divine blessings, especially those qualifying for a happy existence in
the great Unknown World after death, were to be received by sacramental rites acting automatically upon
the frail, mortal human nature of man, and changing it
mysteriously by supernatural infusion of the Divine and
immortal nature. That some such notion is now colour-
ing the thoughts of the mass of Christians is apparent
also from other and fuller evidence of the new type of

realistic rather than symbolic conception of the effect of the Eucharistic Prayer. This made 'the body and blood', or historical human personality of Christ, not only present to the consciousness of Christian faith, but also in their real substance present in and united with the elements, by a sort of fresh or sacramental embodiment analogous to the historical incarnation. The change was due, in a single word, to the influence of non-Hebraic modes of thought upon a rite originally purely Hebraic, that is prophetico-symbolic, in nature. It had been from the first a *signum efficax*, in the sense of a symbol having efficacy for worshipping faith: it was henceforth to become largely, even where not predominantly, a symbol which also conveyed, by objective change in itself, the actual glorified substance of the body of Jesus. This is clearly taught by Justin's admiring student, Irenaeus; and in essence, though often in a less crass form, it became the idea implied in most, if not all the known Ancient Liturgies, in the texts that have reached us. But Irenaeus is a no less impressive witness to the older and more Biblical mode of thought touching the Eucharistic 'sacrifice', as distinct from the nature of Holy Communion through the act of partaking of the elements 'made Eucharistic'.

Irenaeus held that in Eucharistic *worship* man offers to God, the original Giver of all, bread and wine as his gifts of homage; that in so offering and having its oblation accepted of God, the Church is itself honoured; and that this was what Christ had in mind in instituting the Eucharist, counselling His disciples thereby to 'offer first-fruits to God from His creatures, not as to one who stands in need, but so that they themselves may be neither un-fruitful nor thankless'. He goes on to stress the idea seen already in *Did.* xiv, saying: 'Sacrifices do not sanctify a man; for God stands not in need of sacrifice: but the conscience of him who offers, if it be pure, sanctifies the sacrifice and causes God to accept it as from a friend.

Since, then, the Church offers with singleness (= purity) of heart, her gift is rightly accounted a pure sacrifice before God.' He seems to have no notion that the Eucharistic oblation has any relation to the removal of sin by propitiation.

IV. *Liturgies of the Third and Fourth Centuries.* It is not till early in the third century that we first get knowledge of the actual text of a Liturgy; and even so, it is only the central portion or 'canon' of the Eucharistic service, the ἀναφορά or prayer of 'sending up' (= Latin *missa* = *missio*) of the Sacrifice of thanksgiving, when at its climax. It is the form used apparently by Hippolytus of Rome, a younger contemporary of Irenaeus; but it reaches us only through the use made of it in late fourth-century liturgies. What most concerns us is the conception of the Church's own act of worship, on the basis of the example of its Head in His self-oblation.

'In memory, then, of His Death and Resurrection, we offer to Thee bread and the cup, giving thanks to Thee in that Thou hast held us worthy to stand before Thee and do sacred ministry to Thee; and we beseech Thee to send Thy Holy Spirit on the oblation of the holy Church. *Joining them together into one*, grant to all saints who partake, that it may serve to fill them with holy Spirit, unto confirmation of faith in truth; that we may praise and glorify Thee through Thy Child Jesus Christ, through whom be to Thee praise and honour in thy holy Church, for ever and ever. Amen.'

One early authority[1] shows no trace of an invocation (ἐπίκλησις) of God's holy Spirit on the elements, but only that the worshippers themselves may be made one, so as to be filled with (the) Holy Spirit, so as to be confirmed in faith, that they may (thereby be fitted habitually to) praise and glorify God. It may be, then, that this formal invocation, which becomes a characteristic difference between Eastern and Western liturgies of the Roman type, was not originally in the Hippolytean form of

---

[1] *Test. Domini*, i. 23.

consecration prayer. This would bring it into closer accord with the normal Roman Eucharistic tradition. The words italicized above are an interesting trace of continuity with another idea already seen to be characteristic of the primitive Christian Eucharistic Sacrifice, viz. the Spiritual unity of those offering it, and themselves in and through it, to God and His service in life.

We will pass now to the fully official Roman Liturgy of the latter part of the fourth century, as being that which has most importance for the communion service in the West, as it is in essentials the Roman Mass of later ages also.

'Make for us this oblation accredited, ratified, spiritual (with allusion to Rom. xii. 1), acceptable, since it is a *figure* of the body and blood of our Lord Jesus Christ, Who (after instituting the holy Supper of Fellowship on the basis of His Passion) said, "As oft as ye shall do this, so oft ye shall make commemoration of Me, until I come again".

'Therefore in memory of His most glorious Passion and Resurrection from Hades and Ascension to heaven, we offer to Thee this spotless sacrifice (*hostiam*, as in Rom. xii. 1), a spiritual sacrifice, a bloodless sacrifice, this holy bread and cup of eternal life: and we beg and pray that Thou mayest receive this oblation on Thine altar on high by the hand of Thine angels, even as Thou didst deign to receive the *gifts* of Thy righteous servant Abel, and the sacrifice of our *forefather* (patriarcha) Abraham, and that which the high priest Melchizedek offered to Thee.'

In the above form of the Roman type of 'Canon' or central part of the Eucharistic prayer of Consecration, *c.* 400, we may note a few points. The absence of any ἐπίκλησις, usual in the East, where in some circles the idea of 'transubstantiation' of the elements into 'the body and blood of Christ' first arose: the comparison of 'the bloodless sacrifice' of the Church to the 'Gifts' of Abel, Abraham 'our patriarch' (a phrase perhaps due to the early Jewish-Christian basis of this paragraph), and Melchizedek, which, along with a petition for its similar acceptance, and its transference to God's 'altar on high', suggests the idea of simple Thank-offerings such as Irenaeus speaks of and Clement's epistle had already described as the Church's 'gifts' to God; also the styling of the oblation, at the opening, a 'figure' of the body and blood of Christ, i.e. something analogous rather than identical with these as a sacrifice, though offered on the basis of the latter (which has given Christians their priestly status). This clause is significantly absent from the Roman Mass as known to us from later sources: it may have been felt a compromising expression, in view of the theory of the Eucharistic oblation which soon came to prevail so strongly as not to tolerate the other and older view side by side with it. Yet it is really implicit in the reference to the Old Testament analogies still left standing in the present Roman liturgy. The fact is that this contains inconsistent strains, shown by dislocations as compared with other liturgies generally, like the place of the *Pax*, and by rudimentary rubrics like 'Let us pray' (*Oremus*), early in the service, with no prayer following. These all help to swell the chorus of witness to the older non-propitiatory and more Evangelic conception of the Christian Sacrifice of the Church's praise and self-obla-tion, set forth from the first, and to the idea of Christian worship with which it is most congruous.

Conclusion. In Chapter V it was said of the Lord's Supper that 'in this Sacrament the whole of what our religion means is expressed. That which otherwise we apprehend piecemeal is integrated in a rite which presents it all as the sheer gift of God' (p. 82). This is true of the Last Supper, steeped as it was in the associations of the Passover as redemption from the bondage of Egypt ('the world' of Sin), into liberty of life devoted to God as His special People (His 'Kingdom'), through the sacrificial blood of God's lamb. There the 'implicit Eschatology' of the historical setting of such redemption, in the time-and-space ministry of Jesus the Christ, is transformed into terms of the eternal order of religious fellowship between the Divine and human, symbolized by the Messianic Feast in the Kingdom of God. The adoring sense of these ideas of Redemption and Communion inspired 'the sacrifice of praise' which was the essence of Christian 'Eucharistic' worship in the New Testament.

These same themes continued to pervade the liturgies of the ancient Church, and last on through the worship of the Medieval and the Reformed types of piety in the Church, down to our own times. But of the 'many strains of religious belief and experience' which were 'integrated' in the central rite of the sacrament of the Lord's Supper as alluded to in the New Testament, not all survived, as we have seen, unimpaired in such ancient liturgies as have reached us. There appeared too not a few *motifs* of alien type and origin, due to religious experience and thought falling back on earlier forms, derived partly from out-of-date Old Testament strains, but partly also to unconscious alien influences from racial training and cultural environment. Certainly the conception of the 'Eucharistic' Sacrifice as propitiatory, which gradually crept into the Liturgies, both the East and the West, is wholly unknown to the New Testament idea of Christian worship. So also is the notion of objective change in the elements themselves, as the result of their consecration to the spiritual use of Christian faith. By this the idea of the 'real presence' of Christ was changed, in emphasis at least, from the sphere of immediate or mystic religious experience, in the only sense proper to Biblical religion, to that of doubtful metaphysical theory.

Such are some of the losses involved in the developments which necessarily took place in adapting the wording of a symbolic rite to the current forms of language most helpful to varied and changing human mental receptivity. Certain gains in outward, immediate impressiveness for all sorts and conditions of humanity, there doubtless were. Beyond this, there was the gain of safeguarding a large comprehensiveness in the aspects of the sacrament, corresponding to the many moods of human experience and need. For it was out of these that the several prayers forming the total liturgy had sprung through the 'prophetic' utterances of the Church's inspired ministry. But, be the gains what they may, the loss in primitive simplicity and truth, both in emphasis and in actual conception of the authentic Christian revelation of God in Christ, and of His saving Passion implicit in the symbolism of the Last Supper—as stamped by the creative thought of the Master's own mind—was certainly great and grievous. For it thereby had ceased to be an undistorting reflector of the Gospel, with its note of personal experience.

J. V. BARTLET.

VII

CHRISTIAN WORSHIP IN THE MIDDLE AGES

I

IT is now generally recognized that the primitive
Christian act of worship was a Eucharist, which was
very early organized on a double basis. There was first
a service of prayer and praise together with instruction;
and this was followed by the celebration of the rite of the
Lord's Supper. The former part was a continuation of
the worship of the Jewish synagogue; the latter was the
special addition made to this by the Christian Church.
Out of this combination arose the original form of worship proper to Christianity, and out of it also rise all the
special problems of Christian worship, which are still
with us and insistently call for solution. The purpose of
the present essay is to consider what the Middle Ages did
to solve these problems; or, alternatively, how far they
increased them and made them more difficult for subsequent times, including our own. Here, however, the first
point to be observed is that the Middle Ages were in the
main more a period of appropriation from the past than
of creation of what was new. This was certainly the case
in the matter of Christian worship. Medieval Christianity inherited from the Ancient Church both its scheme
and its interpretation of worship. Thus both the practice
and the theory of medieval worship can only be studied
properly as developments of the practice and the theory
of the worship of the Ancient Church. Already in the
Church of the fourth century the simple worship of the
primitive Eucharist had grown up into an imposing structure of ritual, in which the daily office may be regarded
as an extension of the first part of the Eucharistic service;
while the various occasional offices which also formed a
part of the structure connect themselves more with the

rite of the Lord's Supper. In other words, the whole of Christian worship took the form of synagogue-worship enriched by various rites of a sacramental character. It should also be noted that at the same time when this great system of worship had reached a relative degree of completion in the Ancient Church, two other important features had established themselves as characteristic of it. One was that except for the homily which formed part of the instruction in the first part of the Eucharist the whole worship had taken a definite liturgical shape. The other was that this liturgical shape included a variation of the praises and prayers, and also of the Scriptural lections which formed part of the instruction, all in accordance with times and seasons. The Divine office was distributed over the different hours of the day and night, each part with its own proper liturgical form; while the whole worship including the Eucharist was diversified in accordance with the festivals and fasts of the Church year, in which were commemorated not only the great facts of the history of redemption through Christ, but also the saints of the Church from the Apostles onwards. In the present essay attention will be fixed on the Eucharist as the central act of Christian worship in the above scheme, and next in order on the regular worship of the daily office. The scope of the essay will not allow any discussion of the occasional offices.

II

We begin accordingly with the Eucharist. What did the Middle Ages here inherit from antiquity? For a fuller answer to this question the reader is referred to the previous chapter; but a résumé of the main points is necessary for our present purposes. The first part of the Eucharistic service, which is often spoken of as the Liturgy of the Catechumens, consisted of prayers, psalms from the Old Testament or sometimes Christian hymns, Scriptural lections and a homily. The essential items of the

second part, which correspondingly gets the name of the
Liturgy of the Faithful, were the oblation of the Eucharistic elements of bread and wine, the special Eucharistic
prayer of consecration over them including the words of
Institution, and the actual communion in the elements.
An important addition to the earliest form of Eucharistic
worship was the saying of the Creed: this was originally
and properly part of the Liturgy of the Faithful, and only
later in the West was introduced into the Liturgy of
the Catechumens after the sharp distinction in the service
had disappeared. It is necessary to note that the Agape
or congregational supper, which was originally celebrated
together with the Eucharist proper, was early separated
from the latter. In thinking of the problems presented by
the Eucharist it is relevant to remember that the primitive Christian oblation consisted not only of the Eucharistic elements but also of other gifts of food to be shared
by the community.

If we now ask what changes were introduced by the
Medieval Church into the Eucharistic ritual, the answer
is that both in East and West there was a movement towards a greater uniformity of type, while in the East
especially there was also a continual enrichment of the
service through a multiplication of parts. While in the
Ancient Oriental Church there were various collateral
types of ritual, in the Medieval Greek Orthodox Church
(apart from the heretical sects) one particular Liturgy
became dominant. This was the Liturgy of Constanti-
nople or, as it is usually called, the Byzantine Liturgy.
Even this rite, however, existed in three different but
related forms, which go by the names of the Liturgy of
St. John Chrysostom, the Liturgy of St. Basil, and the
Liturgy of the Presanctified: of these the Liturgy of St.
John Chrysostom was the staple form of Eucharistic worship, the other rites being used only on special occasions.
All three Liturgies are contained in the Barberini MS.
of (probably) the ninth century, which is our ultimate

authority for the medieval Byzantine rite: its contents, however, require to be supplemented from other sources which serve to rubricate them. These sources also bear witness to the development of the Byzantine rite, both before and after the ninth century. The later expansion of the Liturgy right up to its modern form has not substantially altered the character of the worship, but has merely further complicated it with more prayers and ceremonies, all adding to that richness of symbolism which is so marked a characteristic of the Greek rite.

Just as the Byzantine Liturgy ultimately superseded other types in the East, so in the West the Roman Liturgy or Mass ultimately superseded other parallel forms. These, the Mozarabic and Gallican rites, stood nearer to the Eastern Liturgy than did the Roman Mass: thus the final result was a more complete differentiation of Eastern and Western usage. Nevertheless, the fixing of the difference did not take place until the Roman Mass had itself accepted considerable infusions which brought it somewhat nearer to the Eastern rite. By the eleventh century the Roman ritual in this final form was practically universal in the West; though local variations within the common type still continued. Familiar examples of such variations are the uses of Salisbury, Hereford, York, Bangor, and Lincoln, mentioned in the Preface to the Anglican Book of Common Prayer. It is in general sufficient to refer to the modern Roman Missal for all the fundamental features of the Western rite, which continue to-day just as they were in the later Middle Ages.

The first noteworthy difference between the Byzantine and the Roman ritual is that the former has transferred the preparation of the elements to the beginning of the worship, thus introducing a special service of Prothesis or setting-forth which took place in a side-chapel with special prayers and many symbolic observances. This symbolism was more and more added to during the Middle Ages: the final result was the present highly

complicated Greek Orthodox rite of Prothesis, where the
general idea of the symbolism is the imitation of the
details of the Passion. The Roman Mass has no Prothesis,
but maintains the original order of the service, beginning
directly with the Liturgy of the Catechumens. In both
East and West this part of the worship retains still unchanged in the Middle Ages its form of prayers, chants,
and lections, but the details are often very different in the
two rites. An important feature of the Byzantine liturgy
is the 'Little Entrance', where the celebrant enters the
Sanctuary in procession from the nave with a deacon
bearing the book of the Gospels, while the anthem 'Trisa-
gion' is sung. In the Roman rite the entrance of the priest
is marked by the chanting of a special psalm (the *Introit*),
after which follows a rudimentary litany (*Kyrie Eleison*)
and an anthem of praise (*Gloria in excelsis*): this anthem
having first been used on Christmas Day had gradually
established itself as a fixed part of the Mass. In the West
as in the East the preliminary prayers end with a prayer
for the people.

In both rites the lections now follow: viz. an Epistle
and a Gospel. Between these was a chant taken from the
Psalter. After the Gospel was the place in the Eastern
Liturgy for the homily which expounded it. In the Roman Mass the creed was first said before the sermon: the
creed is here regarded as part of the instruction in which
all may share. At the end of the Liturgy of the Catechumens in the Byzantine rite there is still found the dismissal of the catechumens and the closing of the doors
before the Liturgy of the Faithful. This had been a real
thing in the Ancient Church, but in the Middle Ages it
became a dead letter even in the East: in the Roman rite
it has disappeared altogether.

In the Liturgy of the Faithful the order of East and West
exhibits great differences. The Byzantine Liturgy begins
with the Prayers of the Faithful, after which the sacred
elements already prepared in the Prothesis are brought

in at the 'Great Entrance', while an anthem, the 'Cheru-
bic Hymn', is sung. Here in the Eastern rite is the place
of the Creed, not as in the West in the earlier part of the
service. The Creed thus retains in the East its proper
meaning of a confession of faith rather than a law of belief.

The Roman form of the Liturgy of the Faithful begins
with a suggestion of the Prayers of the Faithful, when the
priest says, *Oremus*; but the actual prayers are wanting.
The sacred elements are prepared and offered to God in
prayer: there is at this point an anticipatory prayer for a
blessing upon them before the actual consecration.

In both rites there now follow the noble and familiar
words of the Preface, with the *Sursum Corda*, *Sanctus*, and
Hosanna. But after thus coming together in a passage the
germ of which is as old as the Canon of Hippolytus in
the early third century, East and West divide again. The
Greek Liturgy continues with the Eucharistic prayer,
culminating in the recitation of the words of Institution
and directly followed by the oblation of the 'reasonable
and unbloody sacrifice' of the Eucharistic gifts and the
Invocation of the Holy Spirit upon them for their consecration. In the Roman Mass there is no Invocation of the
Spirit at this stage: the consecration takes place simply
through the recitation of the words of the Saviour: it is
followed by prayers asking that the sacrifice of the consecrated elements may be acceptable to God for the living
and the dead. In both East and West there is now an act
of intercession on behalf of various persons named. Then
in the Byzantine rite all present join in the Lord's Prayer,
after which the priest elevates the bread, saying 'Holy
Things for Holy Persons'. In the Roman ritual cup and
bread are elevated, and the saying of the Lord's Prayer
follows. The actual communion is preceded in the East by
praise:

> 'There is One Holy, One Lord Jesus Christ,
>   To the glory of God the Father,
>   To the fullness of Holy Spirit.'

In the Roman Mass the communion takes place upon the note of supplication:

> 'Lamb of God, that takest away the sins of the world,
> Have mercy upon us.'

The communion itself is much the same in both cases, though the words are different. It begins with the celebrant and may end with the people.[1] In both instances it is followed by a Thanksgiving and the dismissal of the people.

One important difference between the medieval liturgies of East and West was that the former, even if it was archaistic in language, was still such as could be 'understanded of the people', while the latter, continuing to be said in Latin after the fall of the Roman Empire, was intelligible only to the learned, which is practically tantamount to saying, to the clergy. During the later Middle Ages some attempt was made to remedy this defect by the introduction of a vernacular office attached to the sermon at High Mass on Sundays and festivals: this was called the Prone. Its content was not definitely fixed; but it normally included such items as intercession, a general confession and absolution, the Creed, the Lord's Prayer, and the Decalogue with hortatory expositions.

Only a small space can be given here to the Daily Office, interesting and important as that is. The Middle Ages inherited this worship in a high state of completion from the Ancient Church, where growing up out of the regulation of private prayers together with the custom of observing vigils before the celebration of the Eucharist, it had finally taken shape as a public office, and largely under monastic influences had been fixed in the seven hours which gradually became universal. In the Middle Ages the prayers, chants, and lections, of which the service was composed, were collected into a breviary or order of

---

[1] In both East and West simple attendance at the Liturgy with infrequent communion on the part of the Laity became customary in the Middle Ages.

service for the entire year: of this, however, there were variant forms. The present Roman office is a revision of the Franciscan reformed breviary of 1241. Theoretically the Daily Office was the common prayer of the Church. Unfortunately it did not properly fulfil this purpose in the Middle Ages. It was in general regarded as a service said on behalf of the Church by the secular and regular clergy. In the West, moreover, like the Mass, it was removed from the full participation of the laity by being said in Latin. The layman's needs were met in England by the Prymer, an important part of which was a translation of special devotions to the Virgin Mary.

III

The Middle Ages inherited from the Ancient Church not only a great system of worship, but also certain interpretations of its meaning. Already in the earliest form of Christian worship, with its combination of Jewish liturgy and New Testament rite, there presented themselves to the reflective mind the fundamental questions: What constitutes Christian worship? What is its essential nature? How does it differ from worship in general? To these questions as early as Justin Martyr three different answers begin to show themselves.

1. In the first view emphasis is put upon what Christianity inherits from the synagogue, while there is at the same time a definite rejection of the sacrifices offered at heathen altars, and for the matter of that also in the Jewish temple. Here we have the conception of worship frequently described in the Ancient Church by the name of 'reasonable service' (Rom. xii. 1), or 'sacrifice of praise' (Ps. l. 23 [LXX and Vulg.]). Justin speaks of Christ as the great Teacher of this spiritual worship, born into the world for this very purpose (Apol. i, c. 13).

2. Another view assimilates Christianity in its proper essence not with the religion of the synagogue, but rather

with that of the mystery-cults, whose characteristic mode was that of a dramatic presentation of Divine saving acts, manifesting the Divine grace in the sphere of sense and thus bringing it near to the individual, that by a corresponding sensuous reception he might participate in it. This view of worship is plainly seen in Justin, when he says that the food which is consecrated (*Eucharistized*) by the prayer of the Word from Jesus Christ, and from which our blood and flesh are nourished by transmutation, is the blood and flesh of that Jesus Who was made flesh (Apol. i, c. 66).

3. There is a third view which is maintained in spite of, or at least as a supplement to, the conception of Christian worship as a 'sacrifice of praise' in which all altar sacrifice is done away. This last view is that Christian worship all the same has an altar and a sacrifice of its own. Justin leads the way, when he refers to the text Mal. i. 10–12, and says that God speaks through the prophet 'of those Gentiles, namely us, who in every place offer sacrifices to Him, i.e. the bread of the Eucharist and the cup of the Eucharist'.[1]

These three different theories of Christian worship continued to exist side by side in the Ancient Church. They were not indeed always kept sharply separated from one another. On the contrary, they enter into combination and modify one another, so that there are many different shades and complications of meaning. The second view can be subordinated to the first by the notion that the sensuous manifestation is mere symbolism: on the other hand the 'reasonable service', as it takes definite liturgical form, can itself be filled with mysterious meaning, every act and word coming to possess a theurgic significance. Again, the first and the third views can be comprehended under the common head of 'offering', in spite of the difference of what is offered; while finally the idea of oblation, as applied to the Eucharistic elements, whether before or

[1] Dialogue with Trypho, c. 41.

after consecration, is naturally enhanced by their symbolical meaning, in virtue of which they possess a mysterious character which gives potency to the offering. Further possibilities of combination also exist, and are actually realized; nevertheless, when all is done, the three types of interpretation stand out distinct and clear. It has been a chief problem of the Christian Church ever since early times to come to a settlement about their relative importance and value. The question rises whether any of them alone, or all of them together, can give us a true conception of Christian worship, or whether alternatively some further idea altogether is required.

There is no need now to go farther in considering the legacy of interpretation which the Ancient Church left to Medieval Christianity in the matter of worship. What has been said primarily concerns the Eucharist; but we started from the position that the Daily Office may be regarded as an extension of the synagogue-worship part of the Eucharist, while the occasional offices extend its specifically sacramental part. Thus in settling the meaning of the Eucharist we are implicitly fixing the meaning of Christian worship as a whole. In discussing medieval worship we shall accordingly keep the Eucharist steadily in view, and bring in other types of worship as occasion arises. In fact, the very first point to be observed about Medieval Christianity both in East and West is that the Eucharist remains as it was in the Ancient Church the fundamental and central Christian service, to which everything else leads up and in relation to which all else is to be interpreted. In the Eucharist the medieval conception of worship is focused at a single burning centre: the rest of the worship of the Church spreads out the same conception into its subordinate parts. At the same time it is to be observed that the focusing of all the elements of worship into one point is felt to raise the worship to a higher level: we have illustrated here the well-known principle that the whole is more than the sum of the parts. If worship is in general communion with God, that communion is understood to rise to a higher point in the Eucharist than in any other form of worship, other sacraments included. Although he puts the point in terms of Latin theology, St. Thomas Aquinas is representative of the whole of Medieval Christianity when he says that all the sacraments contain grace, but the Eucharist contains Christ Himself, Who is received under the forms of the bread and the wine.[1]

It is from this affirmation of the supremacy of the special rite of the Eucharist that we can best approach the question, how Medieval Christianity dealt with the traditional interpretations of worship received from the Ancient Church.

1. It is natural that the simple service of prayer, praise, and Scripture reading (with or without exposition) takes altogether a lower place in the scheme of worship. It is conceived to be rudimentary and preparatory in character, leading on to what is above and beyond it. Nevertheless this preliminary worship has its independent importance. St. Thomas brings out the medieval philosophy of it when, in explaining the order of the Mass, he says that there must be a preparation for the celebration of the mystery proper, which preparation rightly consists of praise, prayer, and instruction.[2] On the first point he quotes Ps. l. 23: *sacrificium laudis honorificabit me.* As to prayer, he says that the priest offers it for the people that they may be judged worthy of mysteries so great. The instruction is begun from the doctrine of prophets and apostles and ends with that of Christ Himself in the reading of the Gospel.

It is essentially the same elements of prayer, praise, and instruction which compose the Daily Office; but as Heiler well shows from the rule of St. Benedict the separation of

---

[1] S. Th. III. lxv. 3.
[2] S. Th. III. lxxxiii. 4.

the office from the Eucharist can give it an independent value of its own. Heiler says:[1]

'The Hellenistic and primitive Christian idea that the offering of praise and thanksgiving is the true sacrifice, the λογικὴ θυσία, has maintained itself in the monastic prayer of the hours even to the present day. . . . Here, as nowhere else the monk experiences God's gracious presence. *Ubique credimus divinam esse praesentiam . . . maxime hoc sine aliqua dubitatione credamus, cum ad opus divinum adsistimus* (Reg. St. Ben. 19).'

If this conception of worship were to be followed up, the worship of prayer, praise, and instruction in the Eucharist also would have to be reckoned as having more than a merely preparatory worth. The conception of 'reasonable service' might then be so extended so as to take up into itself without changing its character even the special institution of the Eucharist:[2] this would lead to the interpretation of the sacramental rite as a simple repetition by way of memorial of the significant acts of Our Lord on the night on which He was betrayed. As a matter of fact, this interpretation of the rite was never wanting either in East or West: it is present in both forms of the Medieval Eucharist. The Liturgy of St. John Chrysostom follows up the recitation of the Institution with the words:

'Remembering therefore this commandment of the Saviour and all that has been done for our sake . . . we offer to Thee of Thine own what is Thine own in all and for all, and we praise Thee, we bless Thee and give thanks to Thee, O Lord, our God.

The Roman Mass has a parallel passage at the same point:

'Wherefore, O Lord, both we Thy servants and also Thy holy people, remembering the blessed Passion of the same Christ, Thy Son, our Lord, and His Resurrection from hell and His glorious Ascension into heaven, offer to Thee of Thine own gifts.'

[1] *Der Katholizismus*, 1923, p. 452.
[2] In the Liturgy of St. John Chrysostom the offering of the gifts to receive consecration is actually called 'this reasonable and bloodless service'; while in the Roman Mass the oblation (before consecration) is called *sacrificium laudis* in the intercession beginning *Memento, Domine*.

Certainly the notion of memorial is but one strand among others in the texture of medieval worship; but it is not to be overlooked or lightly accounted. St. Bonaventura names the remembrance of the Death of Christ as one of the principal intentions to be cherished by the celebrant.[1]

2. Nevertheless, we should be wrong if we overstressed the importance of the idea of memorial in connexion with the Medieval Eucharist. The Middle Ages did not stop at the simple notions of praise and memorial, but preferred in general to interpret the Eucharist by the ideas of mystery and sacrifice. In the East the notion of mystery is dominant, and tends more and more to absorb the whole worship into itself. Pseudo-Dionysius[2] first views the preliminary part of the Eucharist, including the psalms and lections, as a revelation of God in symbolic form: what is all Scripture but a revelation through symbols? He is thus able to regard the special words of institution just in the same way, as a showing forth of the work of redemption by which Christ united humanity to Himself and purged it from its stains. The root-idea in such a conception of the Eucharist is that the dramatic repetition of the Divine saving acts has in itself saving power for those who experience its virtue by the illumination of their minds and the participation of the sacred elements. Here different shades of thought are possible: in fact, the whole notion of 'mystery' is one of half-lights and dissolving views. There can be a more spiritualistic or a more realistic conception of the mystery; though indeed the line between them is fluctuating and uncertain. Thus the Liturgy of St. Basil prays that the Holy Spirit may descend upon the offered gifts, and bless and sanctify them, and 'show' them to be the body and blood of the Lord; while the Liturgy of St. John Chrysostom asks that the Spirit may 'change' the elements, and 'make' them Christ's body and blood. It is practically the same difference that we have in the West between the Augustinian spiritual-

---

[1] *De praeparatione ad missam*, c. xi.   [2] *De Ecclesiastica Hierarchia*, c. iii.

istic doctrine of the sacrament, and the Ambrosian realistic doctrine which issued finally in the Medieval dogma of transubstantiation. It would be wrong to make too much of this difference, which was more metaphysical than strictly religious. But it may be observed that the 'showing' links up the mystery-idea with the simpler service of prayer, praise, and instruction, so that the term 'reasonable service' can still be used without any sense of incongruity for the Eucharist conceived as a mystery: on the other hand, the word 'make' prepares the way for an easy transition from the conception of the Eucharist as representation (fresh showing forth) of Christ's sacrifice to us on God's part, to that of the sacrament as a re-presentation (fresh offering) of the sacrifice to God by us, which is the dominant motive of the Western rite. Before, however, we pass on to this third point of view, we must note that the Eucharist is still held to be a mystery in the West. This was natural enough; since the central rite is itself dramatic in character and tells again the story of redemption. But, what is more, we even find Western attempts to bring the preliminary service under the general notion of mystery. Alexander of Hales sees in the worship of prayer, praise, and lections a renewal of the preparation made in the history of Israel for Our Lord's advent in the flesh: it is meet that His spiritual advent in the sacrament should be prepared for by such a repetition.[1] The earlier Amalarius of Metz goes still farther in the inclusion of the preparatory service in the mystery. He regards the first part of the Mass as symbolizing the history of Christ before the Passion, while the Canon of the Mass symbolizes the Passion itself with the events leading up to it and those immediately following it.[2] This type of interpretation was very popular in the Middle Ages: it attached itself rather to the incidents of the ceremonial than to the actual text of the Liturgy, but all the more effected the purpose of

[1] S. Univ. Th., Pars. iv, qu. xxxvii.
[2] Brilioth, *Eucharistic Faith and Practice, Evangelical and Catholic,* 1930, p. 83.

dramatizing the service. Batiffol has pointed out that a similar instinct was at work in the selection of the chants (responds and antiphons) of the Daily Office in order to illustrate the Church Year, which in its course furnished another way besides the Eucharist of dramatizing the historical preparation for Christ and the events of His life on earth.

3. Yet after all the idea of mystery was not the dominant note of worship in the West. St. Thomas Aquinas says of the Eucharist (loc. cit.): 'It is both offered as a sacrifice, and is consecrated, and is received as a sacrament.' It has been mentioned already that the oblation offered in the Eucharist was originally of gifts, partly intended for the poor, partly for the service of the rite itself. But when in the third century the offering of gifts for the poor became separated from that of the Eucharistic gifts, a change began to take place in the meaning attached to the offering of the bread and wine: instead of, or at least along with, the notion of their being offered for consecration there soon appears that of the offering of them as already consecrated and mystically transformed into the body and blood of Christ. Here is the basis of the characteristic Western conception of the Eucharist as a sacrifice, which is the new presentation of Christ's sacrifice on Calvary and acts as a propitiation for the sins of the world. In the Byzantine Liturgy the older interpretation of the Eucharistic sacrifice as an oblation of the gifts of the Church is still uppermost; but in the Roman Mass the newer idea is presented with unmistakable force and clarity. There is indeed an oblation of the gifts before their consecration, but it is overshadowed by the subsequent offering of the consecrated elements, as follows:

'We offer to Thy most glorious Majesty of Thine own gifts, a victim pure, a victim holy, a victim immaculate, the holy bread of life eternal and the cup of perpetual salvation: upon which be pleased to look with a propitious and serene countenance and to accept.'

The offering of this prayer is further intensified by the *Agnus Dei*, said in preparation for the reception of the sacrament, and striking a very different note from the Εἰς ἅγιος, which occupies a parallel position in the Byzantine rite. It is true that in the Byzantine Liturgy, just as in the Roman Mass, mention is made of those for whom the Eucharistic worship is offered; but that does not alter the fact that in the Eastern rite what is offered is the gifts of the worshippers to be consecrated by the Spirit for sacramental use, whereas in the Mass it is the body and blood of Christ that are offered as a sacrifice after the consecration has taken place. As the Middle Ages drew to a close, the supremacy of the view of the Eucharist as a propitiatory sacrifice continually increased in the Western Church; as is particularly evidenced by the institution of the 'low mass', which was said as a rite of propitiation rather than as a service of communion. The low mass never obtained in the Eastern Church, which kept consistently to the primitive idea of the Eucharist as an act of communion.

IV

In conclusion, we ask how far the Middle Ages solved the problem of Christian worship. Did they, or did they not, come to a right understanding of its nature? The question is important to-day, when medieval ideas of worship are influencing even the Evangelical Free Churches, which in the past have broken farthest away from this type of service. If loyalty to tradition is the test, then unquestionably the Middle Ages behaved well in the matter of Christian worship. They zealously maintained both the ritual handed down from the past and the traditional interpretations of it: all that they did was more fully to organize the worship and more fully to work out the interpretations. But was this enough? It has been truly said that the rule of prayer (*lex orandi*) is the same thing as the rule of faith (*lex credendi*): the meaning is, that as man prays, so he believes. But the converse is also true: as man believes, so he prays. *The problem of Christian worship is really a theological problem.* How we are to worship God as Christians depends upon how we think of God and of salvation through Christ. The Ancient Church and the Middle Ages had a natural theology or rational doctrine of God, upon which was superimposed a doctrine of redemption, which the East conceived essentially as the sanctification and deification of humanity through the Incarnation, while the West thought mainly of a propitiation offered to God by Christ. Medieval worship is definitely organized in agreement with these ideas. The 'reasonable service' of prayer, praise, and instruction is regarded as only of a preliminary character: its value is best expressed in the Old Testament phrase *sacrificium laudis*: it was a service undertaken for the Divine honour, in which man paid his due to his Maker. The highest interest, however, is concentrated upon the sacramental rite. The view of it as a mystery or as a conveyance of Divine grace through sensuous media corresponds to the doctrine of sanctification and deification through the Incarnation; while the doctrine of salvation through the propitiatory sacrifice offered on the Cross finds a development in the conception that the sacrifice is ever newly presented in the forms of bread and wine upon the altars of the Church.

The Reformation, by returning to the original sources of the Christian religion in the Scriptures brought about a better understanding of God and of His relation to man and of salvation through Christ: the result of this was a theology different from that of the Middle Ages and equally a new conception of worship, which presently took shape either in the reform of the ancient ritual or in the abandonment of it altogether. The central doctrine of the Reformation was that of God's grace as free favour shown to man in Christ and accepted in faith or trust. Such an apprehension of God was bound to transform worship, even where old forms were retained. There was no longer room for the distinction of a preliminary worship of prayer, praise, and instruction from the more perfect worship of the sacramental rite: nor, again, was the conception of Eucharistic worship either as mystery or as propitiatory sacrifice any longer tenable. Evangelical worship in all its parts is communion with a God already known to be gracious. If the Eucharistic rite with its memorial of the Passion proclaims the grace of God, that same grace is the basis of the whole worship. In particular the sermon which preaches it afresh comes to have an importance quite beyond that accorded it in the Middle Ages:[1] to call it 'instruction' is altogether to minimize its value as a proclamation of the Gospel. Evangelical practice no doubt has not always come up to Evangelical principles; for the force of tradition is strong. To discuss Protestant worship, ideal and actual, in any detail would be to go beyond the scope of this essay: it must end here with the recognition of the ultimate incompatibility of medieval worship and Evangelical faith.

[1] Preaching generally declined in the Middle Ages both in East and West; so that the Liturgy could be and was celebrated without a sermon. In the West, however, attempts were made from time to time to revive preaching.

A Comparative Table of the orders of the Byzantine Liturgy in the ninth century and of the Roman Mass in the later Middle Ages (principal items only included).

THE BYZANTINE LITURGY	THE ROMAN MASS
Prothesis	

(The Liturgy of the Catechumens)

The Little Entrance with Prayers and Trisagion	Introit, Kyrie, Gloria, and Collect

Lections, Chants, and Prayers

Dismissal of the Catechumens with Prayer	The Creed

(The Liturgy of the Faithful)

The Prayers of the Faithful	
The Great Entrance with prayer and the Cherubic Hymn	Oblation of the elements for consecration
The Creed	

Sursum corda

Preface, Sanctus, and Hosanna

Prayer of Consecration including the words of Institution and the oblation of the elements with Invocation of the Spirit: Intercession	Renewed oblation of the unconsecrated elements with Intercession: the words of Institution: Offering of the consecrated elements with Intercession

The Lord's Prayer

Εἷς ἅγιος	Agnus Dei

Communion with Thanksgiving: Dismissal.

R. S. FRANKS.

anti-liturgical. He certainly objected to 'liturgies' in the
Latin sense of the term, as rites which were supposed to
mediate God as the Word could not do, within a supernatural mechanism operated by priests. For him the
preached Word seemed to reveal the Lord fully and to
posit faith as the one response needful; everything in the
service was secondary to the Word; it was for the Church
to sit like Mary at the feet of the Lord, listening to His
Voice. In moments of exaltation he would sometimes
ask, 'Is this not enough for the faithful?' Indeed, are they
not better without external rites, for rites tend to divert
attention from what is essential and spiritual? And then
they become not merely formal but statutory, an inva-
sion of Christian freedom and an inroad upon the rights
of conscience. Do real Christians require any forms of
worship? Or, if they do, cannot they be left to improvise
a few simple rules and habits of the devotional life for
themselves? Let there be true Christians, and there will
be true worship!

This phase of detachment from rites and forms is not
unintelligible. In his many-sided nature there was a
vein of serene indifference to such outward details, partly
due to his own experience—had he not found his way
to God through the Word, and not through breviaries
and missals?—and partly due to a superb confidence in
the Word, which also made him less interested than
Calvin was in the polity of the Church. If only the Word
was preached and received, what did it matter about
forms of worship? It is this, no less than a natural conservatism and an instinct for continuity in worship, that
made him not only less definite and decided in breaking
away from medieval ceremonies than from papalism and
ascetic penances but also slow at first to admit the need
of drawing up any positive equivalent in the shape of
worship for evangelical Christians. He had a prophetic
consciousness that God can work even without forms and
formulas of the conventional type, an inward quietism

which was accentuated by the widespread feeling that, as the end of the world was near, all that could or should be done was to preach the Gospel to as many as possible in the brief, dark interval before the close.

Fortunately his reluctance was overborne by practical experience of the deplorable condition of religion in Germany. Particularly after the visitation of electoral Saxony, it became plain to him, as it had become already to responsible leaders of the re-formed movement, that if they were not to be content with founding a new sect, the principles and praxis of worship must be faced. For it was in worship that the great body of the people held and expressed their faith. The theurgic sacrifice of Latin piety was embodied in the canon of the Mass. If the Latin Mass was sub-Christian or, as Luther bluntly declared, anti-Christian, surely something had to be done with it in the interest of the Gospel. The care of the churches now involved for Luther some constructive interest in public worship; even spiritually minded Christians required training and guidance in this matter, for, as he was reminded, apart from the large body of the ignorant and superstitious, devout worshippers would be generally the better for a common cultus which should be an equivalent for the Mass, were it only to exorcise the self-centred individualism which besets the spiritual venture and to escape the vague religiosity which is apt to haunt any rise to a higher level of inner devotion.

Even as he undertook to speak his mind on worship, however, the quietistic tendency moved him for a time. He was so impressed by the need for instruction among young and uneducated people in religion that he stressed in a one-sided fashion the educational aspect of worship. The Word preached and taught in prayer-meetings, with calls to repentance and appeals to the unconverted, with elementary instruction in belief and morals—this was to be the chief form of worship, little more than revivalist or mission services, intended for those who were either not

yet Christians or immature Christians. Regular attendance at church on Sundays and stated seasons was
for untrained laity at the best. Once people became true
Christians, why should they not be able to dispense with
such elementary aids to the spiritual life, which after all
corresponded to the function of 'the way for the Lord',
prepared by John the Baptist. They were not the way of
the Lord. They acted as the 'schoolmaster to bring us to
Christ'; once real faith was reached, the spiritual *élite* no
longer needed any such provisions and practices for worship in the spirit. This conception was diametrically
opposed to his larger mind on worship. It would have
reduced the aim of worship to the objects of a school or a
synagogue, and presented Christianity as a sect instead
of as a Church. It would have resulted in the creation of
a special body of believers who could worship God anywhere, apart from any participation in forms which the
lower rank and file required. But is the Church a lecture-
room or a sermon-house? It was all very well to insist
that the whole Christian life should be a worship of God,
and not simply attendance on rites, or that personal
religion was not confined to churchy customs made by
hands. It was one thing to claim that people required
to learn how religion made demands upon their practical
life in the first instance, demands for regular training
and moral instruction. But the preoccupation with these
aspects led to results which were far from helpful to devotion, even after Luther had moved to his fuller position.
In desiring to make worship educative, for example,
he still gave directions or made suggestions which were
not always for good. Like Wesley he was interested in
national education on account of his zeal for the better
knowledge of God in life, and this controlled his projects
for translating the Bible and for catechetical instruction
as well as for encouraging the preaching of the Word (as
opposed to the mere saying of the Mass) in season and out
of season. But his zeal was not according to knowledge,

when, for example, in his book on the *German Mass* (1526), he inserted in the service an exhortation to communicants, which practically superseded the noble Preface, and, for the sake of edification, not only paraphrased the Lord's Prayer but transferred it to a place before the exhortation. Nor was it an improvement when he sought to make praise a lesson-book by versifying the Nicene Creed, the *Sanctus*, and even the *Te Deum*. A didactic interest[1] spoiled these productions as well as some of his own hymns. Luther rightly wanted worshippers to learn as well as to listen. So serious was the ignorance and the apathy of the masses around him, that it was a timely service to religion in the circumstances to set instruction within worship as definitely as he did. This counteracted the superstitious idea of worship. But a directly didactic aim dries up real devotion; and, again, the more one becomes a Christian, the more, not the less, does one realize the need of common worship and fellowship. All this was present to the mind of Luther, when he allowed the full implications of the function of the Word to develop. The narrowly didactic interest proved to be no more than a dark line in the spectrum of his shining counsels on the essence and the expression of worship according to the Word within the Church.

II

As Luther eventually set himself with pastoral concern to show how much the corporate worship of the Church meant to Christians one by one, in the fellowship of the Sacraments and at other services, as he laboured to make

---

[1] A remarkable instance occurs in his admission (preface to the *German Mass*) that 'if I could manage it, and if Greek and Hebrew were as familiar as Latin, we should celebrate the mass and sing and read in all four languages, German, Latin, Greek, and Hebrew, one Sunday after another'. Wittenberg being a university centre, Latin was not exactly a foreign tongue, it must be remembered. But he would have liked Latin instead of the vernacular, for the sake of its educational value.

worshippers vividly conscious of their responsibilities and privileges, his position is surprising, and that on two accounts. (*a*) Instead of deriving from the Word authoritative regulations for worship, as Calvin did, Luther steadily refused to standardize the praxis of worship, even upon biblical lines. Hence, while the *Institutio* contains Calvin's definite views of proper worship, Luther's are more fluid and flexible, so far as details are concerned. There is no liturgy of Luther, strictly speaking, only some programmes or rubrics which, he modestly admitted, were open to criticism and change; they were provisional and might be altered or dropped, as indeed some of them were, in many of the churches which adhered to his conception of the Gospel. His view of the Word did not involve any fixed or explicit form of worship. Nor would he exercise any *jus liturgicum.* So long as the heart of the Word was soundly preserved, he cared comparatively little how the faithful in his own communion expressed their devotion, though he pled for a reasonable uniformity. As he respected Christian freedom, he refused on principle to be the lord of any one's faith, since that would reintroduce a legalism into worship. Also, he did not regard 'the Word within the Word' as a source of any such regulation, beyond the injunctions upon baptism and the eucharist; indeed he derided those who thought that the Church of Christ possessed a book of Leviticus. His liberal attitude was due to the conviction that unless the Word explicitly forbade a form of devotion, i.e. unless an existing form of worship was plainly inconsistent with the Word of the gospel, there was no obligation to surrender it. Within such limits he freely recognized that varieties of temperament and tradition might find manifold methods of worshipping the same God. He would welcome all aids to worship. In the preface to his *Booklet of Spiritual Hymns* (1524) he protested, 'Gladly would I see all the arts, especially music, in the service of Him who gives them, as He created them.' 'I condemn no ceremonies,' he told Wilhelm Pravest, a preacher in Kiel (March 14th, 1528), 'except such as are opposed to the gospel; all the rest I retain intact within our Church. . . . I hate none so heartily as the people who upset free and harmless ceremonies.' He had always an imperfect sympathy with evangelicals who looked on the entire Latin liturgy as a 'damnosa haereditas'. By precept and example he showed how important it is to conserve the continuity of religion in the sphere of worship, and to avoid indulging in a wanton love of novelties at the expense of deep-seated convictions and customs shared by the faithful during centuries behind us. He desired worship to be reformed when it was needful, not to be flung aside petulantly in favour of novel improvisations. For spontaneous and fresh forms of worship he was willing and eager to make room, but he had sufficient psychological insight to realize that the worship which is to stir and satisfy the new needs of men in any generation must be careful to draw upon prayers and praise and sacred rites from the far past, with their wealth of associations and their glow of inspiration. It was by this wisdom that he was prompted to secure his churches against merely negative or eccentric plans of worship, whether or not they claimed to be scriptural. His tendency to retain as much as possible of the old service was at its best derived from the deep principle that worship must be in the genuine sense of the term 'conservative', even, nay especially, at the moment when it is impelled by the Spirit to be also creative.

(b) In refusing to allow worship to be cramped by biblicism, Luther appealed to the Word, nevertheless, for his philosophy of worship. The second surprising feature is the principle which he sought and found in Scripture, viz. that true worship, underneath any form, more or less liturgical, is fixed by the sovereign will of God, who is to be worshipped as He chooses, not otherwise. The sanctions and standards of worship are ultimately grounded in the early commandments of the decalogue, interpreted but not superseded by the Word as the redeeming revelation of God's good will. That is, the appeal is to the Word as embodying the Will of God. When one recollects how Luther found the sum of practical religion within the scope of the first commandment, it is less paradoxical that he has more to say about worship in connexion with that commandment than with the fourth (his third). 'Thou shalt have none other gods but Me' excludes negatively the false worship or idolatry which is still possible in Christendom, wherever the one true God is wrongly worshipped in order selfishly and nervously to accumulate merits, instead of with whole-hearted confidence in His gifts and goodness. Positively the command exhibits a God who requires nothing except faith, and who makes an absolute response to such faith. To view worship as an *officium* instead of a *beneficium*, to calculate upon winning the favour of heaven for oneself or for others by charitable foundations, by saying or paying for masses, &c., as though these were needed to please or satisfy the Most High, was for Luther no more than specious modern idolatry, a violation of the first commandment. To understand this commandment and to live by it, he would say, is worship itself. His controlling belief in the divine will led him to insist that from the first God had thus laid down specific regulations about the nature of the worship which was due to Him. Ours to obey, not to argue, much less to modify or abrogate them. The first Divine Word on worship is therefore 'thou shalt'. The human instinct of worship must obey Him who says 'I am', if it is not to run to seed. Now between monks and mystics worship had suffered sorely, in Luther's view. It had been either narrowed to fasting and ecclesiastical observances (mere will-worship!), as if these, even when performed painfully instead of perfunctorily, amounted to a true Christian cultus, or set aside because men preferred abstractions or mystical reveries, objecting to water in Baptism, for instance, or to the elements in the Eucharist. Had not God chosen such sacramental methods of revelation? Did not the Word prove that He had been pleased so to manifest His saving purpose—thus and not otherwise? For Luther worship is not a contrivance of men, even of earnest men, to honour God, much less to devise pleasant ways of securing His favour; it is a means of intercourse with Himself, the one access to religious reality, which is presented to men by God. Fellowship with Him is only to be enjoyed upon His own terms. Why, he boldly asks, in his preface to the version of the Old Testament, why does Moses fill the book of Deuteronomy with such explicit details about worship? 'To leave human reason no room to invent worship of its own!' Sectaries who claimed that they could dispense with all or nearly all worship-forms were as objectionable to him as those who had turned the Mass into a propitiatory sacrifice or who sought to placate God by self-imposed penances and pilgrimages, instead of seeking His presence through the appointed Word. It was not that God's Word had a static objective authority, as in the Roman system; the Word was dynamic, and as the *verbum internum* or living Voice of the Lord it was heard only by faith. God had not fixed certain sacramental forms which mediated His power and presence by their very existence or celebration. Indeed the Word could act sacramentally even apart from sacraments, as it was conditioned by the personal faith of those who listened and obeyed. Nevertheless the Word was *there*; it was God's chosen method and organ for the revelation of His will or eternal truth in this world of time. What Luther is eager to maintain, in this connexion, is that only where the will of God is recognized, as revealed by His commanding Word, can true worship be offered. Union with the high and holy God means communion, and communion implies the humble, reverent, thankful use of His sacramental provision for man's need of Him as laid down in the Word, culminating in the Word as the Gospel of the New Testament. The essence of the latter is God giving and forgiving, but upon His own terms.

III

These terms are sacramental, as they have always been. We poor mortals, Luther once remarked, live in our five senses! It is the will and kindness of God to reach us through some 'sensible' sign of His Word, that we may see and cling to the invisible Order of His grace. Between the 'Sacraments' of the Old Testament and those of the New there is a difference of degree rather than of kind. In expounding Exodus xv. 16, 17 he points out that God of old would be sought and found at His appointed place, the tabernacle, the temple, and so forth. 'But this has always been His way. Thus He has also built a temple for us Christians, where He will dwell, that is, the spoken Word, baptism and the Lord's supper, which are actually existent' (*leibliche Ding*). What endangered the pure Word in the contemporary Church was either the secularization of the Sacraments by the Latin hierarchy or the disparagement of sacramental worship by votaries of the inner light who decried not only rites but even the Word as being non-essential to fellowship with the Lord. Hence Luther's spiritual realism led him to reiterate afresh the Catholic truth that in the religion of the Incarnation sacraments of the Church, enshrining the Word as read and preached, were vital, and being vital were objective.

The determining factor in worship, therefore, is no longer the Church and the Sacraments, as it had been in Latin medievalism, but the Word and the Sacraments, and both with a new contour and colour. Indeed, the Word is restored to its original sacramental efficacy. For Luther the Word represents the revelation through scripture of redeeming Love, an authoritative declaration of

God's saving will, lying in the whole of the Bible (for prophets and psalmists predict Christ) but with its beating heart in epistles like St. Paul's, especially in Romans and Galatians, as well as in the Gospel of John; these in presenting the life and death of the living Lord become not a mere record but a means of revelation, and so of communion. The Word, the Spirit, and the Church form an organic unity, for the Word is charged with the Spirit, and neither can be isolated from the Church or from one another. Normally the Spirit works in and through the Word; such is God's will. 'This Word is the bridge and the path by which the holy Spirit comes to us,' he observes in a sermon on 1 Tim. i. 8–11 (March 18th, 1525). Or again, in the *Larger Catechism*: 'Why, the whole gospel and article of the Creed about "I believe in the one holy catholic Church, in the forgiveness of sins, &c."—all this is embodied in the sacrament by the Word and revealed to us.' The Word does not mean the New Testament read without the presuppositions of the Church. From start to finish the experience of the individual Christian, including his worship, is conditioned by the corporate Church, in which Word and Spirit operate. 'I believe in the holy Spirit' (he continues) means that 'the holy Spirit carries out our sanctification through the Community of the saints, that is, the Christian Church, through the forgiveness of sins, the resurrection of the body, and the life everlasting; that is, as He leads us into the holy Community and lays us upon the bosom of the Church. Thus is it that He teaches us and brings us to Christ.'

This synthesis means that in worship the Word fulfils two functions. Through the Word the glory and grace of the Lord are set before the worshippers, as testimony is borne to the living Christ; also the Lord is present, applying His Word to the soul, eliciting and developing the faith of the congregation. Through the Word, thus alive with the Spirit, the Lord is directly revealed to the heart of worshippers in the Church; it is not ideas about Him nor memories of His life, but He Himself, not even as the mere object of faith but 'living and working in us, not by way of speculation but in reality, most directly and powerfully' (*realiter, praesentissime et efficacissime*). Few things are more thrilling in Luther than his testimonies to the presence of the Lord in worship and the Word. He can even say (on Ps. lxxxix. 49), 'the Lord's proper and mystical Body is the Church and the Gospel'. The last three words are significant. It was when he undertook to find a theological rationale for this intuition that trouble began.

The Word has a sacramental efficacy therefore, independent of church services. It was a lasting contribution of Luther to vital Christianity that he counteracted the isolation of the Mass from daily life by restoring God's Word as a constant revelation of His presence, since it sets the Lord before the spirit of faith, prayer, and dutiful love anywhere; real communion with Him may be enjoyed apart from the Sacraments, for private devotions and personal religion draw upon the Spirit's power within the Word. By reading or hearing the Word prayerfully, one comes into direct touch with the living God. This is *the* means of grace. Or, to put it otherwise, this vital truth enters into all the means of grace. For what makes the Communion service or the Sacrifice of the Altar itself a valid sacrament is the Divine Promise or Word of consecration. Instead of arguing about the metaphysics and theology, 'Why not fling aside these curious speculations and adhere simply to the words of Christ, willing to be ignorant of what takes place in this Sacrament, and well content to know that the real Body of Christ is present in it by virtue of the words of consecration?' It is a Word of promise, promise not only made but fulfilled at Communion. Luther stressed the term 'promise', in his desire to remove any notion of propitiatory or meritorious sacrifice such as the Latin Mass implied. We

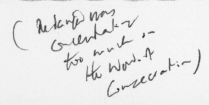
(Luther was careful not too much of the Word of Consecration)

worship, he insisted, to receive God's promised gift, not to offer Him a bloodless sacrifice for the sake of winning His favour. Hence he used the Latin term *promissio*. Admittedly 'promise' carries the suggestion of something in the future; at first sight it does not indicate the immediate presence of the Lord, and it does not occur in the New Testament records of the original Lord's Supper. But the German equivalent *Verheissung und Zusage*, i.e. promise and pledge, denoted for Luther the Divine Word conveying to the worshippers the benefits of the Lord's death from His own hand. He who gave the promise, His dying bequest of saving bliss, is now present to ratify what He has graciously pledged Himself to bestow on human need and faith. 'The promises of God belong to the New Testament; nay, they are the New Testament,' which is a Word of promise as well as of commanding power. As receiving is believing, a promise is the true correlative to faith. Genuine worship puts the human soul in its right position as the recipient of God's good pleasure, and its spirit, at the Eucharist as elsewhere, is therefore one of adoring thankfulness, rapturous or quiet, to Him who is at once the Giver and the Gift; it fulfils the old word, 'Whoso offereth the sacrifice of praise glorifies Me'. For this reason Luther often preferred the term 'Eucharist' even to 'Communion' or 'Mass'.

IV

The glory of God as the Giver thus forms the supreme end of worship for Luther, not any notion of using God for ends of our own, however useful and social they may be. The primary consideration is what God has done and does for man in Christ, His sovereign grace.[1] It opens up into the love and service of our fellows indeed, for, as the worshipping congregation are all priests of God, the true

[1] This and other elements in the spirit of worship may be studied best in his important *Vermahnung* or *Counsel for Christians on Public Worship and Unity* (1525).

communicant is held to perform the two chief functions of
a priest, namely (*a*) in offering the sacrifice of praise, and
(*b*) in openly confessing by his presence at the Eucharist
that he believes in God, thus showing forth the Lord's
death and life; thereby, Luther holds, 'he is doing as
much as if he were preaching and instructing people how
to believe in Christ'. Such a true worshipper prays for
his fellow men and is quickened to take thought for their
interests. But the deeper pulse of worship is adoring
thankfulness to God, since that inspires the Christian to
stand suffering and do good service. Luther did not distinguish between glorifying God for what He is, for His
majesty and greatness, and thanking Him for benefits
received. These are held together in his concept of praise.
He extended the thought, very naturally, beyond actual
worship. 'He is glorified in us, as we receive and hold
every blessing, not as something won by our exertions
but as the outcome of His mercy, His promise, His gift';
the rhythm of daily life is God blessing man, and man
receiving the divine benefits with a glad, grateful heart.
But in the provisions for public worship such a spirit is
pre-eminent; the services outlined by Luther are alive
with praise. For it is common praise, even more than
common prayer, that not only raises the soul out of self-
centred piety but enables the individual to forget himself
and his self-conscious experience, as he joins in the corporate worship of the Lord. No contribution of Luther
to worship was more significant than his stimulus to congregational singing, and the best of his own hymns voiced
the praise of God with spontaneous power. Under his
guidance those who broke into the sunlight and fresh air
of Christianity during the first half of the sixteenth century, had songs on their lips.

(*a*) Indeed this characteristic of the service, especially
as regards the Eucharist, helps to correct the impression
made by some of his writings on theology, that the
emphasis upon a Christian's sense of sin is unduly empha-

sized. While forgiveness is fundamental to fellowship, the acute consciousness of personal wrongdoing does not cover all the experiences of the worshippers. Is every one haunted by guilt or in serious distress of soul? Surely a large variety of less intense needs and desires may move the devout to communion. Unless it is carefully qualified, the view that a Christian is all through life a penitent, appears to lend a somewhat dolorous appearance to the good life. But, particularly in his later writings and always in his regulations for worship, the place assigned to praise shows how far he was from carrying on a sombre medieval piety. Thus he gave the daring advice to continue singing the Hallelujah even during Lent and Holy Week, on the ground that 'Hallelujah is the voice of the Church which is as constant as the commemoration of Christ's passion and victory'. He would not have this cry of rejoicing silenced, as the Latin Church had ruled, at the pre-Easter season, any more than he would allow gloomy hymns to be used at funerals. This served in part to correct the danger of introspection which beset his stress upon the aching heart of the worshipper. There was indeed a risk, not always avoided, of such an insistence bringing back the very self-consciousness and individualism against which Luther himself had reacted in the Latin Mass, and of making the eucharistic service turn too much upon the individual's subjective emotions in receiving God's assurance of pardon and peace. So long as his synthesis of the Word, the Sacraments, and the Church was retained, this peril of the weaker pietism was less dangerous, however. And his insistence upon the objectivity of the Word did much to guard against it.

(b) The claim that the preached Word is essential to any sacrament or service also roused some criticism within as well as without his own communion. His stringent rule rested on the belief that preachers would be calling others to 'Come and see' the Lord, to whom they testified, recalling the stories and promises of His presence and moving hearers to reach out for what He had for them. Erasmus and other contemporaries furnish plenty of evidence to prove how much need there was for such preaching. Luther knew the risks of evangelical preaching degenerating into wordy harangues and rhetoric, but he was prepared to take the risks, so deeply did he feel the need of the objective Word as well as of the mind being informed and the conscience trained in such fellowship with God through worship. To a modern it seems as though, in the interests of reverence, the Eucharist might almost be left to preach itself, as a rule, the Word being only read to the devout. Luther hardly appreciated the value and virtue of silence in worship. Ideally the preaching he desiderated was a testimony to the living Lord. But, when that is replaced by irrelevant sermons, sentimental or argumentative, the worshipper longs to be left alone with his Lord, instead of being lectured. Historically the bracketing of the preached Word with the Communion Service in Reformation worship is intelligible; it was sound and fruitful in making the Eucharist a real Communion Service, safeguarded against superstition, so long as the sermon was a means to worship. But it easily becomes an end in itself. How easily, even Luther could not foresee. Yet he did protect his congregation against their preachers by providing a liturgy, where the worshippers could at least pray unmolested.

(c) In arranging the prayers of the service he was generally more successful, especially in the direction of greater simplicity. His own Litany was a thorough revision which amounts to a new work, a form of congregational prayer whose merits were soon recognized. He drew on liturgical books of his own monastic order and on missals with excellent judgement. Both in what he omitted and in what he composed, he exhibited a grasp of essentials and a rare power of devotional writing. It is well arranged, direct, and impressive, 'an admirable work, which need not fear comparison with what it was intended to displace'.[1] His collects for public worship are also strong and richly varied. Not that he was a trained liturgist, any more than were the early Tractarians in the England of last century. But like them he soon discovered that intense convictions about God, the Church, and worship, require to take shape in something more human than arguments on paper or preached sermons, if they are to be permanently effective. Hence the attention which he came to pay to the prayers of the sanctuary. It was not enough to expose false, adventitious worship; fresh forms had to be devised for expressing the genuine worship which was to be offered in spirit and in truth.

For all this labour Luther was not ill equipped. He was a scholar in philosophy and theology, who had practical experience of popular religion from the inside, and when he lifted the task of reforming the worship of his churches he was at the height of his powers. But to cut channels for public devotion is a fine art. One may have the art of translating the Word and of preaching it, without possessing this further talent. Luther sometimes saw what had to be done rather than how it should be done. Sometimes he is more himself in discussing worship; sometimes, though not so often, less than himself. Even those who may agree in whole or part with his essential interpretation of the faith may not consider that his efforts to express it in terms of worship are invariably happy or adequate. He himself would have been the first to understand such a position. But any one who takes the trouble to read Luther at first-hand before criticizing his supposed opinions, will probably allow that whatever he wrote about Christian worship was inspired by what he did believe, from experience and reflection, to be a genuine response of man's soul to the living God, to a God whom to know was, for the individual and for the Church, to worship. 'Habere Deum est colere Deum.'

JAMES MOFFATT.

[1] Dr. Brightman and Dr. Mackenzie, in *Liturgy and Worship* (p. 140).

ZWINGLI

THE Reformation-movement begun in Switzerland by Zwingli arose at the same time as the Lutheran movement in Germany, and in many respects strongly resembled it. On the main issues dividing the Reformers from Rome (such as the superiority of Scriptural to ecclesiastical authority, justification by faith, and the priesthood of all believers), Zwingli and Luther were at one. Nor—as recent research has proved—can we question the high esteem in which Zwingli held Luther as the pioneer of reform, or the far-reaching influence which Luther exercised on Zwingli's mind. At the same time there were considerable differences in the views held by the two men, and even in the emphasis they severally laid on beliefs they held in common. Zwingli at one time felt compelled to insist—and insisted doubtless with sincerity, though what partly moved him to do so was a desire to evade persecution under the Edict of Worms—that, while he revered Luther as a great servant of God, he had not learned the Christian evangel from him, had preached it before he heard of him, and refused to be classed among his disciples. As the disagreement between them developed, their consideration of each other's views became more superficial and unsympathetic; and as was to be expected in the case of one so obstinate and violent as Luther, there were on Luther's side no half-measures about the antagonism. He gave the Zwinglians (so Bucer said) only such love as a Christian owed his enemies, and fell ill with the fear that Zwingli himself might be lost.

Zwingli indeed was cast in a very un-Lutheran mould. True, during a serious illness in 1519, when he had been preaching his own Reformed version of the Gospel for three years, he underwent what was, according to some, a new conversion: he experienced the sinner's despair of himself and consciousness of salvation through faith in God's grace. Probably the form this experience took was determined by the effect of Luther's writings on his mind. Yet his temperamental attitude, after as well as before that crisis, presents a striking contrast with that of the German Reformer. Unlike Luther, he was constitutionally and by training a humanist, with a great admiration for the New Learning and for Erasmus: unlike Luther, he had no quarrel with philosophy, no suspicion of human reason, no specifically mystical leanings; his appreciation of the numinous was less sensitive and emotional, his personal experience of Divine pardon less revolutionary and passionate. He trusted the common sense and goodness of the ordinary man. He was consequently less emphatic than Luther regarding original sin, more sympathetic towards democracy, more concerned with social righteousness (as distinct from personal religion), more tolerant of views differing from his own, and so more disposed to believe in the salvability of the heathen. All this, along with a less reverential attitude towards ecclesiastical tradition, gave to his piety and his ideals of worship a character of their own, and enabled him to rectify in part such defects in the Protestant movement as sprang either from Luther's conservatism as an ex-monk, or from his other limitations. If, in consequence of his less revolutionary experience of conversion, the movement he led was less emotional than that headed by Luther, it was for that very reason more ethical; nor does it deserve to be described as an intellectual rather than a religious movement. On the other hand, Zwingli's literary and historical sense, clear analytic mind, and balanced judgement, brought to the service of Protestantism a contribution which it was beyond Luther's power to render.

Yet it would be a mistake to regard Zwingli as a theological liberal in the sense in which we use the words

to-day. Notwithstanding the boldness of his critical judgement and his debt to the humanism of Erasmus, he
remained at heart a Biblical Christian, with all a Biblical
Christian's conservatism.

The conservative type of his piety is seen, firstly, in his
attitude to Scripture, fresh familiarity with which was the
great source of his revolt against medieval observances.
Here we must remind ourselves that the acceptance of
the sanctity and Divine origin of the whole of canonical
Scripture was then common to all Christendom. It is
true that Luther's discovery, in certain parts of the Bible,
of the all-important doctrine of justification by faith led
him to under-value other parts, from which that doctrine
was absent; but even his characterization of the Epistle
of James as 'a right-strawy Epistle' rather illustrates his
slap-dash style of speech, than represents the Protestant
attitude generally, while his new opinions on points of
authorship did not really touch the question of inspiration. Nor again did Calvin's theory of the *testimonium
Spiritus Sancti internum*, and his scholarly attitude on textual
and historical criticism, materially affect his veneration
for the Bible as God's Word. No one, in fact, doubted
that, when you had got at the true text of Scripture, and
had pruned away possible small errors due to human
transmission, what was left was Divine and authoritative.
And Zwingli also, while mastering Hebrew and Greek
that he might study the sacred book in the original,
shared the belief of his contemporaries in its plenary
inspiration, and shared too the Reformers' acceptance of
its supreme authority as over against and independent of
the previously accepted authority of the Roman Church.

Zwingli's full acceptance of the Paulo-Lutheran doctrine of justification by faith and not works did not blind
him to the Christian's need of authoritative guidance as
to what God desires him to do, feel, and believe, i.e. to
his need of a Law. Like other exponents of this doctrine
of justification, when not arguing that precise point, he

tacitly assumed that man needs a system of moral precepts if he is not to slip into antinomianism and other
kinds of pious foolishness, and that the Scriptures contain
the substance of such a legislation. His view of justification by faith was therefore not quite identical with
Luther's, nor did he—as Luther tended to do—make this
doctrine the be-all and end-all of Scriptural teaching.
He treated the Bible as the beautiful and attractive Law
of God, to whom Christians owe obedience. Indeed, he
carried his veneration for its precepts so far that, whereas
Luther was prepared to allow in worship whatever, being
hallowed by custom, was not forbidden in Scripture,
Zwingli desired to rule out everything, whether customary or not, which Scripture did not expressly sanction.
His conservatism here was no doubt excessive, and his
acceptance of Scripture *en bloc* as the Divine Law and
his view of its authority as strictly ultimate (on the
lines generally approved by medieval Christendom) were
doubtless mistaken; but we cannot expect Reformers to
see clearly and at once all the implications of their first
steps in reformation. Zwingli's own sound moral instinct
protected him against the dangers of adhering too closely
to the implications of his Biblicism. Thus, on the question of Sunday-observance he took a latitudinarian view.
He 'derived', says G. Rietschel,[1] 'the solemn observance
of Sunday not from the Old Testament Law, but simply
from the common need of edification; and he viewed
work as among the "things indifferent", in regard to
which each person should preserve his own freedom, in
so far as it involved no offence to his neighbour'.

Another mark of Zwingli's Biblical conservatism is his
acceptance of Augustinian predestination, which went
back to certain expressions by means of which Paul had
proclaimed God's grace, and ultimately to the determinism characteristic of Semitic piety. Let the reader consult, in Johann Adam Moehler's *Symbolik*, the extracts

[1] *Lehrbuch der Liturgie*, i, p. 162.

there collected from the writings of Luther, Zwingli, Calvin, and Beza, wherein God's sole causality is taught in terms offensive not only to Moehler himself and the Tridentine Fathers before him, but to the modern Protestant also.

'One and the same deed therefore,' wrote Zwingli, 'for example, adultery or homicide, in so far as it is the work of God as author, mover, impeller, is not a guilty act; but in so far as it is the work of man, it is a guilty act and a crime. For He is not bound by law, but the man is by law even condemned.'
'He therefore moves the brigand to slay the innocent, even though the latter is unprepared for death.'
'What God does, He does in freedom, remote from every evil disposition, and therefore also without sin, so that David's adultery, which had God as its author, was no more a sin in God than when a bull mounts and impregnates a whole herd of cows.'

Views similar to these, if usually less bluntly stated, occur in the writings of the others named; and one can only marvel at the elasticity of otherwise Christian minds of later days, which were, mainly as a result of Calvin's influence, long able to entertain such beliefs about God and human morality. Protestant students of the Reformation would do well to recognize more frankly than they do the service rendered to truth and common sense by the Council of Trent, when it repudiated the more emphatic expressions of that quasi-Pauline determinism to which the great Reformers were so addicted. Doubtless for those who can overlook or ignore its appalling implications, such a doctrine has often been a comfort and an inspiration. But appalling implications cannot be indefinitely overlooked and ignored; and it is to-day a quite inadequate apology for a theory which denies man's freedom, asserts his responsibility, and represents God as moving him to sin, to adduce Luther's sense of God's grace, and Zwingli's and Calvin's concern for God's sovereignty. Beard wanted to trace 'the milder, more

rational, humaner spirit of the great reformer of Zürich'
in Arminianism; but the speculation rests only on an
appreciation of Zwingli's general liberality, not on his
actual teaching. The best we can say in his defence is
that finding determinism in the Bible, he felt obliged to
believe it, and thought he could defend it, and that he
found comfort and inspiration in it, but did not grasp its
inconsistency with human personality and responsibility.

When we turn to his views on worship, we find them
characterized by a love for simplicity and moral reality.
When once his eyes were open to the shakiness of Roman
authority and the weak points in the liturgy, he became
critical towards the whole medieval system. He was

scornful of the veneration and invocation of saints: he
maintained the right of Christians to eat meat during
Lent, and saw no reason why confession should be either
compulsory or made to a priest. Musician though he
was, he wished to dispense with all music and singing in
Church (here differing from Luther); but he laid stress
on the systematic reading of Scripture in worship (though
setting aside the traditional lectionary) and on the preaching of the Gospel-Word. His normal Sunday-service
began with prayer, followed by the Lord's Prayer; then
came the sermon, usually of an expository kind; after
that, a general confession of sin, with absolution; finally,
another prayer and a benediction. He carried his liturgical reforms through, not with a high hand, but only in so
far as he was allowed by the civic authorities, and—in
case of opposition—in so far as he could convince them
and his colleagues of the Scriptural soundness of his
views.
Under a system in which a central place was given to
personal experience of God's grace in Christ, a sense of
trust in and responsibility to Him, and the practical
implications of such a relationship for devotion and
conduct, the sacramental element necessarily took a

subordinate place in worship, as compared with prayer and the preaching of the Word. So it was with our Lord Himself in relation to Rabbinic Judaism, and so, too, with the Swiss Reformation in relation to traditional Catholicism.

Zwingli abandoned, for instance, the quasi-magical interpretation which it had become customary to give to Baptism as practised in the medieval Church. Catholic teaching had made of it a pure *opus operatum*, valid because it was declared to be divinely commanded, and supernaturally efficacious whenever it was performed with the intention of doing what the Church prescribed, be the officiating person priest or layman, Catholic or Protestant, Jew or infidel. Its effect was to secure for the baptized that grace which wiped away the stain of original sin inherited from Adam, and so, by removing this barrier to salvation, to make ultimate escape from hellfire at least possible. It was, of course, intended that the act should be performed trustfully and reverently and with a determination to educate the baptized child in Christian things; but all this made no difference to the efficacy or otherwise of the rite: efficacy was ensured simply by the use of water, the pronunciation of the Triune name, and the intention (readily presumed in cases of doubt) to do what the Church ordains. Is it really incorrect or unjust to describe such a view as 'magical'? Zwingli, with his more Scriptural appreciation of the personal nature of the faith implied by baptism, and his healthier views on original sin as *morbus* rather than *peccatum*, repudiated the Roman conception of the rite along with the usages associated therewith, denying that water or any other material thing could cleanse the human soul from the stain of sin, and substituted an interpretation of Baptism as a sacramental sign whereby the people of God were drawn together and held together in the one Christian faith. If (as was usually the case) the recipient was an infant, the sign was naturally representative, given and accepted vicariously by his god-parents on his behalf. Against the Anabaptists, who felt that they had Scriptural authority for confining baptism to conscious believers, Zwingli defended infant-baptism on the ground that it was the true Christian equivalent of Jewish circumcision.[1] While prepared to allow the validity of Baptism when performed by laymen or women, he naturally regarded the minister as the normal officiator, and the Church as the normal place for the performance of the office. Soon after his installation at Zürich, he introduced a form of service couched in the vernacular and including nothing unscriptural. It ran as follows: the priest said, 'In the name of God, Amen! Our help stands in the strength of the Lord, Who has made heaven and earth.' He asked the god-parents if they wished the child to be baptized in the baptism of Jesus Christ, and what was its name. A prayer followed, in which reference was made to the Flood and the Red Sea as foreshadowing Christian baptism, and a blessing on the baptized besought: 'Give the light of faith in his heart, whereby he may be incorporated in Thy Son, be buried with Him in death, in Him also arise in a new life, in which, following Him daily, he may bear his cross gladly, may cling to Him with true faith, firm hope, and fervent love, . . . and at the last day, at the universal judgement by Thy Son, appear unafraid: through the same our Lord Jesus Christ Thy Son, Who with Thee lives and reigns in the unity of the Holy Ghost, one God for all eternity. Amen.' The assistant then said, 'The Lord be with you', to which the answer was made, 'And with thy spirit': he read next with comments the story of Jesus blessing the children, took the child in his arms, and questioned the god-

[1] In *The Congregational Quarterly*, July 1935, p. 363, a passage in which the Anabaptist leader Hubmaier depreciates the baptism of infants, is inadvertently quoted from R. J. Smithson's recent book, *The Anabaptists* (p. 146 f.), as if it had been written by Zwingli. The words occur in a letter of Hubmaier's which is printed in Zwingli's *Opera*.

parents again as to their wish and as to the child's name.
He then baptized the child with the words: 'I baptize
thee into the Name of the Father and of the Son and
of the Holy Spirit.' Zwingli insisted on the Scriptural
formula '*into* the Name' (in distinction from the less
correct Lutheran formula '*in* the Name'), as recalling
more impressively the actual incorporation of the baptized into Christ. Then came the conclusion: 'May God
grant thee that, as thou art now dressed bodily in the
white garment, so at the Last Day thou mayest appear
before Him with a clean undisguised conscience! Amen.
The Lord be with you. Go hence in peace!'

We turn to Zwingli's much discussed and oft-deplored
views regarding the Lord's Supper.

Here, as elsewhere, he was under the influence of Erasmus. When he came to Zürich in 1519, he would have
liked to abolish the Mass and substitute a simple com-
memoration-service on evangelical lines. But usage was
too strong for him; and he was wise enough not to try to
force his personal views on an unwilling public. Modifications were, however, gradually introduced. In his two
Disputations at Zürich (January and October, 1523) he
maintained that the Supper was not a sacrifice, but a
commemoration of one. In August–September 1523 he
wrote *De Canone Missae Epichiresis*, in which he pleaded
for several changes.

'We do not move the Canon from its place,' he wrote, 'but in
the place of what we have hitherto used we put another, fully
aware how hardly we shall be spoken of—some will upbraid us
for audacity, others for impiety. Nor would they be wrong in
so doing, if the earlier Canon were free from blemish; but since
it was introduced into the churches not only with audacity, but
with the utmost rashness, and has first been convicted by us of
impiety, it is not audacity but virtue to have deserted error; it
is not impiety, but the true worship of God, to have overthrown
impiety. Nor do we here impose on any one a law, that he

should not be allowed to pray otherwise than we are going to pray; but we fully allow every man to pray freely in his own sense. Would indeed that our ancestors also had done so. . . . Let each man pray—as he chooses—according to the inspiration of the Divine Spirit.'

Zwingli excluded every item for which Scriptural authority could not be quoted. He excluded the invocation of saints, but admitted a little singing. The Gospels and Epistles were to be read, not in Latin, but in the vernacular German, and accompanied by explanations. He protested that Christ was not offered up afresh as a sacrifice: for *offerimus* he substituted *commemoramus*. Yet he spoke frequently, not only of God's word, but of Christ, and even of Christ's flesh and blood, as spiritual food and drink.

'As we believe that Thy Son, once offered for us, made reconciliation with the Father, so also do we firmly believe that He offers Himself to us under the species of bread and wine, that the memory of that generous act may never be abolished. . . . Grant that, while we eat His flesh and drink His blood . . ., we may overcome the hardships and afflictions of this world, with Him as leader and protector.'

In his *Instruction* to the clergy of the canton Zwingli pleaded for the commemorative view as against the sacrificial and otherwise faulty Roman doctrine and practice. In April 1525 he introduced a form of service according to his own heart, and in the *Action oder bruch* (= Brauch) *des nachtmals*, written a little earlier, he describes it. The service was held four times a year—at Easter, Pentecost, Harvest, and Christmas. Zwingli spoke as if now for the first time the people of God were able to celebrate rightly; but he disowned any desire to exclude too rigidly all forms (e.g. singing) other than those commended. He laid stress on the commemoration of and thanksgiving for the saving act of Christ in dying for men. He prescribed how, particularly at Easter, the younger folk, the middle-aged, and the old people were to

gather on Maundy Thursday, Good Friday, and Easter
Sunday respectively, and whereabouts in the Church
they were to be (males and females gathering separately).
The order of items (minor details apart) was as follows:
an opening prayer; the reading of 1 Cor. xi. 20–29; the
Gloria (chanted antiphonally); the reading of John vi.
47–63; the Nicene Creed (antiphonally); a short admonition; the Lord's Prayer; a further prayer; the reading of the words of institution; the distribution of the
elements; the reading of Psalm cxiii (antiphonally); the
final thanksgiving; doxology, Amen, and dismissal.

The Lutheran attitude to the Sacrament differed con-
siderably from Zwingli's. Luther inclined strongly towards the traditional Catholic view. He wished to reform
the Mass, not to abolish it. He laid less stress than
Zwingli on the communal character of the Supper. His
theory of 'Consubstantiation', regarding the physical presence of Christ's flesh and blood, strongly resembled the
orthodox Roman doctrine of Transubstantiation. He
rejected the Catholic idea of the necessity of an ordained
priest to work the miracle, whereby the physical presence
of the body and blood was ensured; but he compensated
for it by the notion that Christ's body was ubiquitous.
Zwingli also asserted that in the Supper the participant
does truly, sacramentally, and spiritually receive the
Lord's body and blood.[1] But at Marburg, in 1529 (at the
Colloquy arranged by Philip of Hesse), he pleaded that
general Biblical usage and the particular context showed
that the words 'This is My body . . .' were to be interpreted metaphorically, not literally. Luther, after arguing
for the contrary view, rejected the hand that Zwingli, with
tears in his eyes, held out to him, and refused to recognize
him and his party as fellow-members of the Church.

[1] Dr. C. A. Scott has shown that, prior to 1524 and after 1528, Zwingli
wrote in this sense (*Expositor*, vi. iii, pp. 161–71). He urges that Zwingli's
occasional insistence on the *purely* commemorative view was due to the
exigencies of controversy. Cf. Darwell Stone, *A History of the Doctrine of
the Holy Eucharist*, ii, pp. 38–43.

Calvin's position was intermediate between those of Luther and Zwingli. He rejected Luther's doctrine of 'Consubstantiation', and agreed with Zwingli in denying that the Supper was a sacrifice. On the other hand, he sympathized with Luther's desire to insist on the believer's real participation in the Lord's body and blood, and felt Zwingli's comparative lack of emphasis on this aspect so keenly as to describe his doctrine on one occasion as 'profane'. His own somewhat subtle theory was that the reality of the participation in the body and blood was guaranteed, not by their physical or corporeal presence, but by their dynamic effect on the soul of the participant. Yet on the whole he recognized that Zwingli's view owed its defect merely to the exigencies of controversy, and differed from his own in emphasis only. This being so, the customary modern depreciation of Zwingli's doctrine in favour of Calvin's supposedly more adequate teaching is largely unjustified.

We may go farther and plead that Zwingli's emphasis on the commemorative character of the Supper at least does better justice to its historical origins than does Calvin's. Any idea that bread and wine were in the future to be the mysterious vehicles of the Lord's presence would surely have been unintelligible to the Twelve, to whom Jesus intended His words to be intelligible. It is most improbable that, when (with the redemptive associations of the Passover-festival in mind) He distributed the bread and wine, He so much as thought of anything more subtle or mysterious than a simple commemorative symbol with the sacred potency belonging to it. The Aramaic original He must have used for 'This is My Body' would not even contain any word meaning 'is'; and therefore, although the Greek and English correctly express the meaning, no literalistic stress can rightly be laid on the actual word 'is'. If we can accept as historical the words 'Do this in remembrance of Me' (which are strangely absent from the Marco-Matthaean

story, and occur only in 1 Cor. xi. 24 f. and in the longer
—and inferior—of the two texts of Luke), Jesus was laying far more stress on commemorating than on being fed.
He was about to die for the new Israel: He would die
when the Paschal victims, which the members of the old
Israel were to consume together, were being killed. The
likeness of His death to a Paschal sacrifice of deliverance
from spiritual bondage could hardly escape notice. Yet
He passes round, not flesh, but bread. No emphasis is
laid in any of the narratives on bodily sustenance, or on
the idea of the Lord being spiritual food for His followers,
or on the promise of His continuing presence with them.
The emphasis is placed rather on the symbolic resem-
blance of His body to that of the Paschal victim and of
His blood to the sacrificial blood of the Covenant, and
on the memorial character of the rite. It is worth observing that, at the institution of the Supper, there was also
present to Jesus' mind one other thought—attested by
all three Synoptists, but only faintly reflected by Paul
(1 Cor. xi. 26)—viz. the symbolic anticipation of the
triumphant Messianic feast in the Kingdom of God
(Mark xiv. 25; Matt. xxvi. 29; Luke xxii. 16, 18). True,
the significance of this thought was not appreciated by
Zwingli; but it is equally ignored in all those traditional
interpretations which are so confidently employed for the
purpose of putting him in the wrong.

When once the Christian thinker has disentangled his
mind from such insoluble questions as those concerning
the precise differences between substance and presence,
and between the different kinds of presence (real, spiritual,
carnal, corporeal . . .), he is in a position to do better
justice than is usually done to Zwingli's commemorative
emphasis. People speak and write contemptuously of
'a *mere* commemoration', as if a real commemoration did
not of itself necessarily involve much more. *What* was it
that Zwingli wanted to commemorate? *Why* did he want
to commemorate it? *What* did he expect the conse-

quences of commemoration would be? Granted that the
Saviour is still able to be present with and minister to His
own (and who argues that Zwingli denied or forgot
that?),[1] all that is needed to make such presence and
ministration a reality is sufficient receptivity on the part
of the worshipper. The Lord's presence with Christians
in the Supper does not differ in kind from His presence
with them on other occasions, when their receptivity is
equally great. We recall that Brother Lawrence had so
schooled himself into this receptive attitude that he could
affirm: 'In the noise and clatter of my kitchen . . . I
possess God in as great tranquillity as if I were upon my
knees at the blessed Sacrament.' For most Christians,
however, deliberate commemoration of the Lord's redeeming death, with the aid of the Eucharistic symbolism
and in an atmosphere of Christian brotherhood, is the
needful and effective means of creating such receptivity
—the means *par excellence*, as compared with any other
specific Christian discipline.

It must be insisted that, in all Zwingli wrote about the
Supper, the question of Christ's *spiritual* presence with
His worshippers was never in dispute, belief in it being
common to all. What *was* in dispute was simply the
sense in which Christians might say, as Zwingli himself
repeatedly said, that in the Supper they do truly feed on
the body and blood of the Lord. His own answer was
that the feeding is spiritual, sacramental, or symbolic,
and consists essentially in trusting in the Christ who died
for us, and in being thereby reassured of God's gracious
favour and nourished and refreshed in our souls. Such
trust in the living and present Redeemer is the heart of
the whole matter. Why should Calvin's theory, which
agreed with Zwingli's in denying the local and corporeal
presence of Christ's body and blood, be so frequently
acclaimed as superior to it, simply because Calvin laid
more stress on the description of the rite as eating and

[1] Cf. Lindsay, *History of the Reformation*, ii, p. 55 f.

drinking, rather than trusting and being reassured? Zwingli would probably have shrunk from Calvin's concrete insistence on the presence of the body and blood, because he would have feared in it too close an approach to the quasi-pagan crudity of Roman literalism. But on the positive affirmation that mattered most, there was nothing to choose between the two great Swiss reformers.

One other matter calls for mention before we conclude our study of Zwinglian piety, and that is the close relationship which it fostered between Church and State. Luther, while retaining the medieval view that the State, like the Church, must be Christian, and that non-Christians had no right to the exercise of civic functions, was far more prepared than was either Zwingli or Calvin to contemplate such a separation of the functions of Church and State, and such a relation between them, as would make possible an actual oppression of the Church by the State.

'In contradistinction to this,' writes Troeltsch,[1] 'Calvinism is much more active and aggressive. . . . It organized itself in a newly-formed republic, the very existence of which was based on Calvinism, and its spirit is dominated by the extremely systematic and rational character of Calvin, the pupil of jurists and humanists, who had never been a monk like Luther.'

Zwingli, too, was a humanist who had never been a monk; and in favouring the closest relations between the Visible Church and the State (in his case, of course, always the Swiss city-state), he was Calvin's true predecessor. He accepted the traditional conceptions dominant in democratic and republican Switzerland of the religious interests and functions of the State. He argued with his opponents on Church-matters before the civic Council, and left it to the latter to decide what was to be done, while he took it for granted that it was the business of a Christian state to patronize and protect the Church and

---

[1] *Protestantism and Progress*, p. 71 f.

enforce its considered teachings. He held that the unpleasant duty of excommunication was exclusively the business of the State. He shared with Calvin the view that ordinary civic life was the proper sphere for the exhibition of Christian righteousness, and that the Church was the divinely appointed means of leavening or disciplining society, the source of her power for fulfilling this function being Christian worship as prescribed by God Himself in the New Testament Scriptures.

Zwingli was profoundly patriotic; and his patriotism, combined with his Christianity, led him at one time to oppose vehemently the hiring-out of Swiss soldiers as mercenary troops for the service of foreign powers: at another time, it permitted him to take part in the political affairs of his city, and even to acquiesce in the punishment of Anabaptists as guilty of disobeying the law of the land. It also made him willing to devise plans for the defence of Protestantism against the Emperor; and it was his consequent willingness to serve personally in any struggle on this issue which in point of fact led to his death: for when he was killed at the Battle of Kappel on 11 October 1531 (in which the forces of the Protestant cities of Switzerland were defeated by those of the Catholic Cantons), it was not merely as chaplain of the troops, but as an armed combatant.

Zwingli was under forty-eight when he fell at Kappel; and his early death not only put a serious check on the growth of his influence, but also prevented his own piety from coming to its full maturity. What he would have accomplished had he survived to old age, it is impossible to say. Beard observes that, in that case, Zwingli 'might have escaped heavy censure and much invidious comparison with Luther'—and, we may add, with Calvin also. But even as it was, his influence was considerable. His thirteen years at Zürich had made him the most powerful and formative agent in the development of Swiss Protestantism. An incidental manifestation of his prestige is seen in the fact that his communion-liturgy was retained, almost unchanged, in Zürich until 1675. When in 1532 Farel began his work in Geneva, and when Calvin first settled there in 1536, the ground for the Protestant advance in Switzerland generally was already prepared; and Farel's and Calvin's successes were in no small degree made possible by Zwingli's work. His influence, furthermore, working through Bucer in Strasbourg and Bullinger in Zürich, as well as through Calvin in Geneva, extended beyond the borders of Switzerland into Southern Germany, the Rhineland, the Netherlands (here partly owing to the connexion with Erasmus), France, Italy, and above all Great Britain. It does not fall within the scope of this essay to examine the changes undergone by Zwinglianism in being merged in and superseded by Calvinism. But the part it filled as the forerunner of Calvinism and as a leaven within Calvinism and within the Protestant movement generally was great and wholesome. Its greatness is illustrated by the fact that the so-called 'Reformed' type of Christianity (i.e. that deriving from the Swiss movement) was far more extensive and influential than the purely Lutheran, which never attained any very great hold outside Germany and the Scandinavian countries. Of modern Protestant bodies, probably Congregationalism owes the greatest debt to Zwingli's influence. The wholesomeness of the Zwinglian type of Christian piety and worship resulted from the generosity and nobility of its founder's character, from the broad healthy simplicity and reasonableness of his mind, and from the personal reality of his religious faith and devotion.

C. J. CADOUX.

CALVIN

I

FEW princes of the Church have been so unanimously disliked and abused in modern times as John Calvin. It is still fashionable for every right-minded (and ill-informed) modern man to be appalled at the memory of the great ecclesiastical statesman who saved evangelical religion in the day of reaction, and left his mark not only on the doctrines but also on the institutions of the Reformed Church in France, Holland, Scotland, England, and America.

That Hilaire Belloc's *Ballade of the Heresiarchs* should begin with his name is a compliment intelligible enough; Calvin has been Rome's one really dangerous opponent. Catholicism and Calvinism confront one another as two absolute types of Christianity, thorough-going logic leading the one to an infallible Pope, and the other to an infallible divine decree. The priestly hierarchy is to the one what the body of the elect is to the other, the constitutive reality of Christ's Church. Anglicanism, appealing to life rather than to logic, has steered a *via media* between the Scylla of Rome and the Charybdis of Geneva. Catholicism and Calvinism are uncompromising; the antithesis is complete. Indeed in the empirical stuff of history the extremes almost meet; Jesuits and Calvinists have not a little in common.

But Calvin is hardly a hero to modern Protestants, many of whom know him only as an unpleasant name. Is he not the father of a sour, inhuman, safely discredited Puritanism: did he not accept Augustine's inconsistent predestinarian theology and then make it self-consistent but incredible with a Frenchman's relentless logic: was he not responsible for the burning of Servetus at the stake; and Calvinistic worship, has it not been bare, austere, and dreary?

There is, as Fairbairn remarks, something imposing in the multitude and variety of aversions that converge on Calvin; yet they help the historian as little as do the notorious exaggerations of John Knox, a disciple whose enthusiasm for his master's achievement in Geneva led him to describe it as 'the maist perfyt schoole of Chryst that ever was in the erth since the dayis of the Apostillis'.

The purpose of this chapter must therefore be to offer a critical estimate of the genius of Genevan piety and worship, and with the work of Luther and Zwingli as a background, to discover its main differentia. And here liturgical forms are a valuable guide. For just as the cultus was one of the main preoccupations of the Reformers because the break with Rome showed itself in practice just there, so within Protestantism itself there is an intimate connexion between faith and the forms of worship which express it. Christian institutions, like all institutions, embody fundamental ideas.

II

The primary differentia of Calvinism as expressed in the classic notes of its theology and piety was an adoring sense of the transcendence and sole causality of God, before whose infinite majesty, incomprehensible essence, boundless power and eternal duration[1] man is utterly insignificant, save to illustrate the operation of God's grace in election and redemption. As is His majesty so is His mercy. This is Calvin's master-thought and characteristic emphasis, the key which unlocks everything in his thought and life.

Though all the Reformers assume the absolute sovereignty and foreknowledge of God, the servitude of man's will, the corruption and impotence of human nature,

[1] *Inst.* iii. 20, 40.

it is Calvin, thanks to what Troeltsch has called 'the doctrinaire logic peculiar to men of the second generation', who gives to these common presuppositions a new emphasis. For him, therefore, 'le premier poinct de la chrestienté est d'adorer Dieu droictement'.[1] Fundamental to and constitutive of worship is an adoring sense of the honour and obedience due to God ('qualis sit Deus et qualiter coli ab hominibus velit').[2] His dominant thought is not so much, as with Luther, justification by faith or the mode in which the guilty man may be made right with God; it is election or the fact of the absolute sovereignty of grace.

This difference of emphasis between Luther and Calvin comes out in the ideal of public worship set up by the latter; it is a difference which the hymn-books of the Lutheran and Reformed Churches have sufficiently illustrated. If the Lutheran emphasizes the consolations of grace, the Calvinist cannot forget its implicit demands. The prevailing note with the one is joy and peace in believing, the evangelical experience of the saved soul which sobs out its glad discovery *Simul peccator et justus*. With the other it is obedience and an austere heroism, that subdued glow and restrained passion which cries *Soli Deo gloria*. To the Lutheran, salvation is freedom through faith; to the Calvinist it is election to serve the glory of God. And therefore, while for the one the Scriptures are a *Trostbuch*, the crib wherein Christ is laid, for the other they are the divine Law, 'la sainte loy et parole évangélique de Dieu', confirmed as such to the conscience by the consentient witness of the Holy Spirit. Obedience is the great watchword ('omnis recta dei cognitio ab obedientia nascitur').[3]

Along with adoration and obedience went the related conception of God as Lawgiver. Though the Bible was interpreted by means of the *testimonium spiritus sancti internum*, it tended to become in fact an infallible legal code,

[1] Op. xi. 486.   [2] Op. xlviii. 326.   [3] Op. ii. 54.

challenging and judging every detail of personal life and current ecclesiastical practice. The place of the Decalogue in the Sunday Morning Service, together with the formal excommunication of all unworthy participants in the Lord's Supper (the fencing of tables), gave to the Calvinist cultus what Niebergall rightly calls *einen recht harten Charakter.*[1] It is significant that on the bare walls of many Calvinist churches in Holland the Mosaic tables of the Law stand out as the sole ornament. The Biblicism which was the ruling principle of the whole system too often degenerated into Bibliolatry, and its implicit logic was never more nakedly expressed than by Thomas Cartwright, the founder of Presbyterian Puritanism in Elizabethan England, whose comment on Deut. xiii was, 'If this be bloody and extreme, I am content to be counted so with the Holy Ghost.'

Calvinism is further differentiated from Lutheranism by the accent which it places on the conception of the Church as the whole company of the Elect, a conception which goes back through Hus and Wyclif to Augustine. Luther takes his stand on the purely religious assurance of the individual man that God in His sheer grace has redeemed him; in his own dark moments he chalks the words *Baptizatus sum* on the table before him. Calvin's thinking is collectivist throughout. Its accent falls not so much on the individual as on the company of the Predestined, the holy people of God which is the Church; its architectonic principle is High Churchmanship. In contrast with the individualism of Luther's piety stands Calvin's sense of the community chosen by God and for God. Successive editions of the *Institutio* make it clear that his predestinarian theology never results in the ruthless atomism which it seems logically to imply, but in the empirical church of believers where the Word of God is sincerely preached and heard, and where the Sacraments are administered according to the

[1] *Der evangelische Gottesdienst im Wandel der Zeiten* (1925), p. 51.

institution of Christ. Whatever the tremendous assertion
of the utter supremacy of God's grace might involve in
theory, its practical meaning and result was the Church
within which all might find salvation, a Society called by
redeeming love into communion with the risen Lord and
having all the privileges, powers, and responsibilities of
the Body of Christ. 'Satis clarum testimonium habemus
nos et inter Dei electos et ex ecclesia esse si Christo com-
municamus.'[1] That is, personal assurance of our salvation is grounded not in our knowledge of the inscrutable
decree of God (a frivolous and blasphemous notion) but
in the promise that God accepts as His children all who
are in believing fellowship with His Son. Calvinism is,
above all, Churchmanship; but only that faith in the
Church is worth anything which includes faith in one's
personal membership of it.

The bearing of such a doctrine of the Church on the
function of worship is clear. Worship is not primarily
designed to bring the consolations of grace to the sin-
laden soul, but to be a solemn offering of confession,
homage, and thanksgiving on the part of the whole congregation of the elect. They meet together to set forth
God's most worthy praise and to hear His most holy
Word. ('In gloriam Dei petimus . . . antequam ullam
pro nobis precem concipimus, praefamur ut eius voluntas
fiat.'[2]) Calvin always refused to derive religion from
human aspirations or needs, such eudaemonism being
the basis of religiosity rather than of religion. Answering
Cardinal Sadolet he says, 'It is unsound theology to
confine a man's thoughts so much to himself and not to
set before him as the prime motive of his existence zeal
to illustrate the glory of God. For we are born first of all
for God and not for ourselves.'[3]

It was this Genevan doctrine of grace in all its solemnity
and comfort which put iron into the blood of Huguenots
in France, Beggars in Holland, Puritans in England, and

[1] Op. i. 74.   [2] Op. i. 907, 936.   [3] Op. v. 391.

Covenanters in Scotland. That all is of God and for God was to these men and women no matter for metaphysical speculation; election meant a task for the will rather than a conundrum for the intellect; they lived (and died) by the profound religious assurance that the chief end of man is to know God and to enjoy Him for ever, and that 'totum mundum hoc fine condidisse ut gloriae suae theatrum foret'.[1]

III

The chief difference between Catholic and Protestant worship is seen in their respective emphasis on the Word and the Sacraments as the means of communion with God. In the medieval church the grace of the gospel is a 'thing', a divine stuff fused indissolubly with the sacramental act, and working in magically objective fashion on the soul of the communicant without any necessarily corresponding faith on his part.[2] To the Reformers (even though Luther and his followers later lapsed far in the old direction) grace is the attitude of God in Christ to sinners, which faith alone appropriates. Obviously the proper object of faith is this gracious attitude or will of God, and because the Word is His uttered will, grace is supremely mediated in the Word. It is mediated, not through the supernatural power which the sacrament of Orders confers on the action of the priest, but through the Holy Spirit which is ever the real agent of grace.

The Reformers therefore removed the Sacraments from the central position, explaining that God's promises in His Word and the believing trust of men were alone essential. Whereas the correlative ideas of *sacrificium* and *sacerdotium* formed the basis of medieval Catholicism, Protestantism proclaimed with Luther that 'Verbum

---

[1] *De aeterna Dei praedestinatione*, Op. viii. 294.
[2] If this is hardly fair to the purpose and intention of medieval Catholicism, it is true of its empirical operation.

et fides sunt correlativa'. The Sacraments, therefore, are *sigilla verbi*, signs accompanying, manifesting, and strengthening to us in our weakness, the Divine Word of promise. Indeed, there is never a sacrament without an antecedent promise, the sacrament being added as a kind of appendix with the view of confirming and sealing the promise. No expression of this could be sharper than Calvin's repeated assertion that it is only the weakness of our faith which makes these external helps necessary. He even asserts that grace, the treasure of the Church, may be completely enjoyed without them;[1] for example, the thief on the Cross when converted became the brother of believers though he never partook of the Lord's Supper.[2]

But this, like Augustine's 'crede et manducasti', so far from minimizing the importance of the Sacraments, links them inseparably with the will and purpose of God, and so places them in the setting of the Word. Baptism and the Supper are the needed 'Monstrance of the Evangel',[3] visible words speaking to the heart by the inward working of the Holy Spirit. Yet the Word alone explains these indispensable and divinely instituted signs; the Sacraments derive their value from the Word with which they are so closely connected that on being dissevered from it they lose their nature.[4] 'Rectam sacramenti administrationem non absque verbo constare.'[5]

Calvin was not the morose fanatic he is often alleged to have been; the principle of accommodation was strong in him, thanks to his humanist education and his sense of statesmanship. Yet the trenchant polemic against the principles and practice of medieval Catholicism, which pervades all his work, may not be minimized. Criticism of Catholic worship as essentially impure and unspiritual, and as the corrupt and presumptuous sub-

---

[1] *Inst.* iv. 14. 14; 16. 26. [2] *Inst.* iv. 16. 31.
[3] Professor Carnegie Simpson's phrase.
[4] *Tracts*, ii. 344. [5] *Op.* ii. 1041.

stitution of human devices for the norm revealed in Scripture, is the key to the understanding of his Puritanism, and of the notorious bareness of Calvinist worship in general.

His test of true religion is spiritual reality. The only acceptable worship of God is from the heart; and since this inward attitude alone determines real devotion to God and His will, worship becomes relatively independent of given forms; the outward is depreciated and dependence on it discouraged. Ceremonies may be useful for the stimulus and the expression of religion ('serviunt caeremoniae tanquam vel adminicula vel instrumenta'), but the moment they pass this limit they become hurtful.

Calvin's Scripturalism reinforces this general principle; he contends that Reformers are iconoclasts only because Catholics have been innovators. He attacks the cult of saints and relics and the use of images, not only as disguised idolatry and as the materializing of the Divine, but as innovations without any warrant in Scripture, the supreme example of such disobedient falsification of the Divine Law being the Mass: 'summum illud abominationum omnium caput.' Not only in his monumental *Institutio* but in his *Tracts* he conducts a brilliant and ruthless campaign over the whole field of current ecclesiastical practice, 'ut sublatis superstitionibus earumque instrumentis ad evangelii puritatem religio componeretur'.[1]

But the puritanism which denounced the symbolism of ornament and ceremonial in worship, casting out altarpiece and crucifix, candles and flowers, alb and chasuble, choir-singing and organ-music as a vain show veiling from men the tremendous issues of which they are in presence when they call upon the name of God, is often wrongly interpreted. It did not necessarily mean distrust of beauty and the arts for their own sake; though the old fiction that Calvinism was peculiarly inimical to

[1] Op. v. 319.

beauty, deliberately stifling all artistic development, dies hard.

The bareness of Calvinist worship which did sometimes become 'a pure fanaticism of baldness' is not to be so explained. Calvin himself anticipates and repudiates this explanation: 'Afin que personne ne nous calomnie en nous regardant comme par trop moroses . . . je ne dispute pas au sujet des cérémonies qui servent seulement au décor extérieur.'[1] Again: 'Quand on condamne l'idolatrie ce n'est pas pour abolir l'art de peindre et tailler.'[2] The fact is, as Dr. Oman points out, that the stark simplicity of Calvinist worship was not negative at all but was an attempt to solve one of the fundamental questions concerning freedom raised by the Reformation, namely, the relation of freedom to the world. Under the new sense of the significance of freedom a new import was given to the truth that the only acceptable worship is of the heart, and that the intrusion of the merely material attraction is a degradation of its pure service. The best worship penetrates to that region where the things of sense cannot accompany men; where, with nothing to speak to the senses, the Eternal God in purest spirit is present in His supersensible glory. The naked walls of a meeting-house remind men, in Pascal's words, that 'l'éloquence vraie se moque de l'éloquence'; and that 'to call on the name of God, to claim the presence of the Son of God, if men truly know and mean what they are doing, is in itself an act so tremendous and so full of comfort that any sensuous or artistic heightening of the effect is not so much a painting of the lily as a varnishing of sunlight'. (B. L. Manning.)

Moreover, this sense of bareness and coldness in Calvinist worship is a modern inference; in the sixteenth century it was largely mitigated if not eliminated by two new facts.[3]

[1] Quoted by Stern (cf. n. 3).   [2] Op. iv. 1195.
[3] Reasons of space compel the omission of a third material fact, Calvin's

The first was intelligibility and rationality which the
use of language 'understanded of the people' gave to
worship. This use of the vernacular, demand for which
appears as early as the age of Hus and the Lollards, is the
new fact common to Protestantism everywhere. It meant
an enormous gain in spiritual reality that the minister
faced the people, praying clearly and in the vernacular;
so that each member of the congregation might pray in
public as he would do in private, with the heart's attention. If 'Dieu veult déclarer sa vertu souveraine en ce
glayve spirituelle de sa parolle quand elle est annoncée
par les pasteurs',[1] the same principle must apply to the
whole of the liturgy in which this preached Word is
central. (Incidentally, it is notable that every detail of
the First Prayer Book of Edward VI, issued in 1549, was
in English; even the Kyrie eleison.)

In the worship of the Reformed Churches the congregation, in virtue of this new fact, once again takes the place
assigned to it in the New Testament; the Sacrifice of the
Mass becomes the Communion of the Lord's Supper.
The sense of the numinous, a non-rational awe before
the sacred mystery, gives place to the clear light of the
understanding which knows what it is doing while it
prays, and so relates the sense of the holy to the world of
moral realities, and makes reverence rational. Calvin puts
in a nutshell what might well serve as a shrewd criticism
of Rudolf Otto's work on The Holy: 'de dire que nous
puissions avoir dévotion, soit à prière, soit à cérémonie,
sans y rien entendre, c'est une grande moquerie.'[2]

The second fact counteracting the potential austerity
and dreariness of Calvinist worship was congregational
singing, an almost entirely new phenomenon which

wise moderation and his principle of accommodation. See Doumergue, ii.
479–524; Karl Holl, *Gesammelte Aufsätze*, iii. 254–84; and Ed. Stern, *La
Théorie du culte d'après Calvin*, which give useful illustrations of this far-
reaching principle.

[1] Calvin's letter to the Duke of Somerset, 1548.
[2] *La Forme des Prières: Epistre au Lecteur*, Op. vi. 166.

modern worship owes to Luther and Calvin; Zwingli, though more musical than either of them, did not encourage it. The great point of difference between the medieval and the modern hymn lies in the fact that the former was monastic, belonging almost exclusively to the clerks in the choir, and forming no part of the popular devotions; the latter belongs to the people. The singing of hymns or metrical psalms is the part of Protestant worship which is most distinctively congregational; if there is any Protestant counterpart of the medieval office hymn in the Latin Breviary it is perhaps the anthem sung by the modern church-choir.[1]

Farel had abolished singing from the Genevan service. Calvin, seeing its great importance and its intimate relation to prayer, reintroduced it, albeit limiting it strictly to the metrical psalm. His work was necessarily creative from the first since both words and melodies were lacking; but though he himself translated a certain number of psalms his gift to posterity lay in his use of Marot's work and in his active encouragement of the musicians Franc, Davantès, Bourgeois, and Goudimel, with the result that the two words *psaulmes français* express more succinctly than any others the characteristic note of Reformed worship throughout the world. It is sometimes forgotten by those who rightly praise Luther's contribution to congregational singing that the popularity and power of the metrical psalm early evoked an envious compliment from the Lutherans, who described it as *la sirène calviniste*. Tiele's description of Calvinism as the ugliest of all religions only serves to show that it was not intended for the natural man. Sir Walter Scott puts a juster reflection into the mouth of the young Englishman who accompanies Andrew Fairservice to the Kirk, in *Rob Roy*:

'All nature, as invoked by the Psalmist whose verses they chanted, seemed united in offering that solemn praise in which trembling is mixed with joy as she addresses her Maker. I had

[1] F. C. Burkitt, *Christian Worship*, p. 104.

heard the service of high mass in France, celebrated with all the éclat which the choicest music, the richest dresses, the most imposing ceremonies could confer on it; yet it fell short in effect of the simplicity of the Presbyterian worship. The devotion, in which every one took a share, seemed so superior to that which was recited by musicians as a lesson which they had learned by rote, that it gave the Scottish worship all the advantage of reality over acting.'

IV

The Reformation laid primary emphasis on the Word as the basis of faith and worship. Protestant worship recalls the Word-Service of the Synagogue rather than the Mystery-Service of the Temple and of Eastern and Western Catholicism; in it the preaching and hearing of the Word take the central place. 'To go to church' in Reformed Geneva was *aller au sermon*. Farel entitled his Genevan liturgy *La manière que l'on observe en la prédication, quand le peuple est assemblé pour ouyr la parolle de Dieu*, and Calvin himself speaks of participation in public worship as *fréquenter les sermons*.

To appreciate this momentous fact we have to see it against the background of its history; and even so, misinterpretation is easy unless we attend to other facts which are often overlooked.

The history of the Christian cultus is the history of a tension between its two great constitutive elements, a rivalry of opposites which dislike reconciliation, and slowly set up a state of unstable equilibrium until choice is made between them. On the one hand something is visibly done (Δρώμενον)—a sacred rite, a central act of sacrifice, imitative symbolism or communion. On the other hand something is audibly spoken (λεγόμενον)—common prayer, reading from a corpus of sacred writings, preaching. In the history of worship these two elements often appear as mutually incompatible, in the sense that one tends either to relegate the other to a position of secondary importance or to displace it almost altogether.

The ellipse with two focal centres is always trying to become a circle with only one. Liturgical law is like mechanical in that it seems to require the cultus to have only one centre of gravity. Either the Word is the mere accompaniment of the elaborate Rite, having little independent significance; or the Rite is a mere rudimentary survival, the Word being the primary and central reality.

In the worship of the primitive church λεγόμενον and Δρώμενον—common prayer, mutual edification and the sacred eucharistic act—stand together in the fullest inward harmony.

In the Catholic liturgies of East and West the Mystery, the complex and precisely regulated cultus act, slowly usurps the central place, while living congregational prayer retires into the background, the λεγόμενον becoming a stereotyped sacred formula uttered by the priest. The intimate bond between liturgy and worshippers is broken; worshippers 'assist' at a spectacle which virtually goes on without them, and ultimately does so in fact, with the emergence in the West of private masses. Moreover, while the two focal points of primitive Christian worship were the publishing of the Word and the Supper, the former was now pushed into the background and virtually lost, as the latter became a meritorious work before God (the sacrificial offering of Christ's very Body and Blood in the Host) and the supreme means of grace (conceived of as the mysteriously infused participation in the divine nature, embodied in the transubstantiated Bread). The climax of the Δρώμενον is hastened and enhanced as the Word part of the service is progressively abbreviated and belittled. If preaching plays any part in the Mass it occurs in the interpolated vernacular service called Prone; but this is not that evangelical preaching of the Word as the Reformers were to rediscover it.

Two facts dominate Protestant worship. First, the central place given to the sermon; second, the transforma-

tion of the Mass into the Communion of the Lord's
Supper. The resultant problem for Protestantism everywhere was the relation of these two facts to one another.
Could the Protestant Word-Service succeed any better
than the Catholic Mystery-Service in preserving its two
focal points within a liturgical unity? Three different
answers were given by Luther, Zwingli, and Calvin
respectively.

Luther, after casting out everything recalling its quasi-
magical and meritorious significance, used the scheme of
the Mass to construct a cultus uniting Preaching and
Communion into one indivisible whole. But what would
happen when no communicants were present? Their
presence, unnecessary at Mass, was plainly presupposed
at the Supper unless the old Catholic abuses were to
revive. Luther found that the average man, like his
medieval predecessor, shunned frequent Communion,
with the result that the Lord's Supper as the regular
climax of the Sunday morning liturgy fell necessarily
into abeyance; the service of worship was thus strictly
incomplete. Luther disliked drawing out the logical con-
sequences of this hard fact but he was ultimately compelled to treat the Lord's Supper as a separate and special
service; Christ's table was only spread when guests could
be expected. Luther accepted the concrete situation,
albeit reluctantly, because he regarded his whole reform,
even in matters liturgical, as *Volkspädagogik*; he abated his
idealism in the interests of the slow process of popular
education. Temporary acceptance of the second best
seemed to him preferable to the perfectionism and new
legalism of the Anabaptists.

Zwingli, unlike Luther, broke radically with the past,
and affected the same separation deliberately, in accordance with *a priori* principles. For him the Lord's Supper,
far from being, along with the Word, the objective basis
of the life of the Church, was only an occasional con-
fessional act; the congregation took part in it four times

a year. The centre of gravity in the Christian cultus had moved definitely from the Canon Actionis of a Mystery-Service to the Sermon of a Word-Service.

Calvin has been the victim of much misunderstanding in this matter. It cannot be stated too emphatically that all his life he resisted this destruction of the original liturgical unity of Christian worship. He regards the separation of Word and Sacrament into two distinct services as a vicious practice (*vitiosum esse morem nostrum*, Op. x *a*. 213). Far from separating the Supper from the preached Word in order to make a different service of it, he demands that it be attached thereto to form a natural climax and thus shows that he understands its true nature. He thought of worship as forming one whole, the strictly liturgical part being inseparable from the homiletic part, the one requiring and demanding the other. In his famous articles of 1537 he asks for a celebration at least once a week (*singulis ad minimum hebdomadibus*); in more than one eloquent letter and in the last, definitive edition of the *Institutio* he makes precisely the same demand and adds that the custom of having Communion once a year only is most certainly a diabolic invention (*diaboli inventum*). The complete Sunday liturgy service is to be a preaching service which shall include Communion at the Lord's Table.

Niebergall and Achelis seem strangely blind to this abundant evidence, which is, however, properly emphasized by Stern, Doumergue, and W. D. Maxwell.[1] The German scholars confuse Calvin's own position with that of Calvinism, the patent facts being that it was the opposition of the people and above all of the Genevan magistrates

---

[1] See his two important articles in the *Church Service Society Annual* (1930 and 1931), which, along with the researches of Büchsenschütz, Erichson, and others, illustrate in detail Calvin's well-known championship of ancient Catholic usage. Calvin's constant appeal to *quod in veteri ecclesia observatum* sometimes makes striking contrast with the prejudices and scruples of his contemporaries and his successors. See Macmillan's *Worship of the Scottish Reformed Church* (1931).

which forced him to put up with an arrangement of which he disapproved so strongly that he insisted on having a formal minute recorded in the registers of the Consistory that the limitation of the celebration to the three great festivals and to a Sunday in September was provisional only ('ut posteris facilior esset ac liberior correctio', Op. x*a*. 213). It was his life-long desire to restore the ancient practice of weekly communion for all the people, and to abolish the medieval custom of lay communion only once or twice a year. The fact that the actual practice by Calvinism has almost everywhere coincided with Zwingli's theory is not to be denied, of course; but it is significant that projects for cultus reform within Protestantism have nearly always attempted to return to the rejected theory of Calvin and to escape from the practice of Zwingli. Calvin, writes Doumergue, 'en effet est de tous les Réformateurs celui qui a le plus rejeté la division du culte en deux parties. . . . Le culte calviniste est un.' (ii. 504.)

We come now to the form of Calvin's liturgy. Thanks to the ruthless iconoclasm of his predecessor Farel, who had actually reduced public worship in Geneva to the naked minimum of a lesson and a sermon, Calvin had a *tabula rasa* on which to work out the service which has been the classic type in the Reformed churches for four centuries.

The service proper, which is conducted by the minister from the Communion Table, begins with the famous Confession of Sins which in one or other of its alternative forms is still substantially repeated by every Presbyterian church throughout the world. (Thus, Confession very properly precedes the Sermon. Calvin avoids Zwingli's mistake of beginning with the sermon and making it lead on to the Confession; the preaching of the gospel of forgiveness should obviously follow confession of sin rather than provoke it.) Scripture sentences of remission of sins, or the formula of Absolution follow: then, during the singing of a metrical psalm, the minister goes into the

pulpit. Free prayer or a collect for illumination follows,
asking for the grace of the Holy Spirit that the Word may
be faithfully published, and received with due humility
and obedience. A passage of Scripture is then read and
on this Text the sermon is preached. Calvin was an
enemy of read sermons and of long sermons; because of
his asthma his delivery was slow, but even so he preached
no longer than half an hour; the purpose of the sermon
was not only instruction but quickening; the human
heart must be *touché au vif*.

Returning to the Communion Table the minister leads
the people in the Great Prayer of Intercession, which
embraces the needs of all sorts and conditions of men and
includes the Lord's Prayer in the form of a long para-
phrase. The Apostles' Creed is sung by all and the
minister prepares the Elements. Without any interrup-
tion of the service, prayer is followed by the Words of
Institution and a serious exhortation which includes excommunication of the unworthy and the assurance 'qu'en
certaine foy nous recevions son corps et son sang'. Communion ends with the admonition not to linger by the
Bread and Wine but to lift the heart thither where Christ
is in the glory of His Father. After a hymn, a short
prayer of thanksgiving, and the Nunc dimittis, the Benediction ends the service.

'The Reformers did not go into the by-ways when they
compiled their services but followed the main stream
of Christian tradition. They simplified the old worship
but they remained Catholic. This cannot be too much
emphasized.' In these words Dr. Maxwell sums up
modern research on the origin of the Calvinist liturgy and
its place in the central liturgical tradition of Christendom.
Calvin's service is no creation *de novo*; it goes back to
Bucer and Diebold Schwartz in Strasbourg, whose service
is a translation and a simplification of the Mass, with
certain elements omitted. Evangelical throughout, it
nevertheless preserves liturgical continuity and is a true

Eucharist. There is a clearly traceable relationship all along the line from Schwartz's German Mass of 1524 to *La Forme de Strasburg* (Bucer), to *La Manyère de faire prières* (Strasburg, 1539), to *La Forme* (Calvin, 1542, 1545), to the Book of Geneva, and to the Book of Common Order.

Calvin's service is not derived from the medieval daily offices or choir services, nor is it parallel to Anglican Mattins, which go back through the seven daily offices to the Benedictine Rule. Moreover, Brightman was certainly in error in deriving it from the medieval service of Prone. Even on those Sunday mornings when the magistrates did not permit a celebration, it was still the *missa catechumenorum* of the early church or the *missa sicca* of the medieval. Just as the famous Confession of Sins springs from the Confiteor of the Mass, so the Great Prayer of Intercession is derived not from medieval Bidding prayers but from the Canon. Calvin's ordinary Sunday morning service, like that of John Knox, was thus a classical Ante-Communion. 'The Strasburg Sunday morning service', says Maxwell, 'was a Eucharist, celebrated in the vernacular and devoid of all medieval ceremonial, but still a true Eucharist just as the Eucharist of the primitive church was a true Eucharist; just as the vernacular Eucharist of the Anglican church to-day is a true Eucharist.'

Moreover, worship was conducted by the minister at the Communion Table, 'the focal centre of Christian worship from the earliest times. Acting in his prophetic capacity he ascends to the Pulpit; but acting in his priestly capacity, presenting the worshipping company's praise and prayer to God, he stands or kneels at the Holy Table, the earthly counterpart of the heavenly Mercy Seat. . . . The Holy Table, not the pulpit nor the prayer-desk, is the centre of the Christian fellowship with God and in God.'[1]

J. S. WHALE.

---

[1] Quotations from W. D. Maxwell, to whose articles this concluding section is closely indebted.

XI

THE PURITANS

NONCONFORMITY has a Puritan ancestry, Puritan in the narrower sense of that word. For if the distinctive marks of Puritanism are strictness of religious observance, an ascetic attitude towards life, and a scrupulous obedience to conscience, then there is a Catholic as well as a Protestant Puritanism, an Anglican as well as a Nonconformist Puritanism. These similarities among men in other respects dissimilar are patent enough to all but those who prefer to ignore them. But here we have to deal with the Puritanism which had its origin at Geneva and its master mind in John Calvin. Not that all English Puritanism of that order was Nonconformist, no more so than all eighteenth-century Evangelicalism was Methodist. Presbyterians and Congregationalists were sections of a larger body of Christians divided by strongly held and hotly disputed differences, but none the less agreed in much of their outlook on things visible and invisible. All were men of the Bible, the whole Bible, and nothing but the Bible. All were idealists seeking for nothing less than a revival of what John Owen (1616–83) called 'the old glorious beautiful face of Christianity'. All were militants, and in days when as yet the art was unknown of entering into and understanding the mind of those on the other side, intense in their hatreds. The world, the flesh, the devil, and the pope, these were the enemies.

It will be well at the outset to take note also of some other outstanding features of Puritan belief and practice in more immediate relation to our subject. Firstly of the sanctity of what they chose to call the Sabbath, or, alternatively, the Lord's Day. For this they contended with a determination that was little short of fanatical. The

accepted festivals and saints' days of the church year belonged to the hated Catholic tradition and were therefore
damned as superstitions. During the Interregnum (1643–
60) Parliament, as did governments before and after
them, appointed days of national humiliation and thanksgiving in accordance with current events, but the Sabbath retained its lonely splendour as the sole red-letter
day of the Puritan calendar.

Next something must be said of the prominence given to
'the ministry of the Word'. In this the English were at
one with the Reformed Churches of the Continent and
at variance with much of former Anglican practice. Indeed the Book of Common Prayer left, and still leaves,
the place of the sermon at worship in an equivocal position. In its exhortation at the opening of morning and
evening prayer the 'dearly beloved brethren' are called
to confession, thanksgiving, petition, and the hearing of
'God's most holy word', and not more. Richard Baxter
(1615–91) in his *Reformed Liturgy* (1661) proposed to
correct the oversight. In place of the exhortation he inserted an invocatory prayer with the petition 'may thy
word be spoken and heard by us as the word of God'.
A Christian congregation met to hear of God and that
from God.

Of their sincerity in this high valuation of preaching
ministers and people gave strenuous proof. In the hey-
day of Puritan ascendancy ministers preached not only
on Sundays but gave week-day lectures in their own and
neighbouring churches. A lecture on market-days was
common in country towns. There were also fasts and
thanksgiving days, national and private, and it is on
record that sometimes ministers preached as many as five
or six or even more sermons in a week. Their hearers
were equally unsparing of themselves in the attention
with which they listened, and that in days when dis-
courses, not only those preached by Puritans, were of
what seems to us insufferable length. Not only did they

listen but the more educated often took notes, even children being sometimes among 'the writers'.

Next as to the Puritans' manner of prayer. The form adopted was that known as extempore. Not that they were all opposed to liturgies as such. Geneva had its service book, clearly there was nothing incompatible with the reformed faith in such a usage. But Englishmen had another liturgical example before them, to wit the *Book of Common Prayer*, and about that compilation no Puritan could be in two minds. It was to him the incarnation of those relics of Catholicism which he most detested in the national church, of all that he most wished to see utterly and finally abolished. Under the influence of that violent reaction Puritan practice in public prayer was shaped. It was not an influence favourable to the adoption of a liturgy. A small number of London dissidents are known to have used the Genevan book about 1590, but it never secured any general popularity. The one attempt at uniformity of Puritan worship was made under parliamentary authority by the Westminster Assembly of Divines. It took the form of a *Directory* (1645), and did not go beyond making suggestions to ministers as to how best public worship might be conducted.

At the Savoy Conference (1661) the dispute was reopened, at least so far as the *Book of Common Prayer* was in question. Baxter with the other representatives of those who sought comprehension within the established church —Presbyterians they were commonly styled—laid before the bishops a full statement of the Puritan case. Their criticisms of the Anglican liturgy were many and detailed. The form of prayer they desired was after the manner of their own extempore utterances. Collects they condemned for their brevity and their repeated invocations and conclusions. Responses and the alternate reading of the psalms by clerk and people were censured as 'causing a confused murmur in the congregation' to the detriment of both intelligibility and edification. According to Scripture audible expression was for the minister; to the congregation it belonged 'only with silence and reverence to attend thereunto and to declare their consent in the close by saying Amen'. This involved recasting the Litany in the form of one long prayer. A plea was entered against the prohibition of free prayer, that gift 'being one special qualification for the work of the ministry bestowed by Christ in order to the edification of his church, and to be exercised for the profit and benefit thereof according to its various and emergent necessity'.

Baxter, intrepid as always, seized the opportunity to draw up an alternative service book 'with forms taken out of the word of God'. His brethren questioned his wisdom on the ground that he was likely to offend the Independents and others who objected to any liturgy as such. But he persisted and produced what he named the *Reformed Liturgy*. It was drawn up on quite other lines than the *Book of Common Prayer*. That he had not Cranmer's consummate mastery of liturgical phrasing need hardly be said. Nor did he compose any prayer of such merit as the General Thanksgiving, the work of Edward Reynolds (1599–1676), one of his colleagues at the Savoy, already bishop-designate of Norwich. Baxter's achievement was none the less a notable one, of which neither he nor those associated with him had any cause to be ashamed. Yet it remained a dead letter. The bishops refused to countenance such an alternative form of service, and if the Puritans could not use it within the Church they had no desire to use it when once they were thrust out of the Church into Nonconformity.

What circumstances decided for some Dissenters conviction decided for others. The Independents and those akin to them objected to liturgies on principle. The use of any prescribed form they accounted as contrary to the very nature of prayer, dependent, as they held it to be, upon the prompting of the Spirit. Henry Barrowe (d. 1593) defined prayer as 'a confident demanding which faith maketh through the Holy Ghost according to the will of God, for their present wants and estate of their hearts or church, . . . a pouring forth of the heart unto the Lord'. A set form of words drawn up by others, long ago it might be, was no vehicle for expressing the wants of a congregation of believers met in the Spirit. Under divine quickening they knew their own wants, and their only need was for the appointed minister to give utterance to what was in all their hearts, to be, in Puritan phraseology, their mouth to God.

Such was the orthodox Congregational doctrine, sound in theory but in practice found liable to grave drawbacks. These became increasingly apparent as the years passed. In the cool and critical atmosphere of the eighteenth century the need was felt, especially among younger ministers, for some modification in established custom. They were fortunate in being able to enlist the help of the most gifted Congregational minister of that or any other time. Isaac Watts (1674–1748), to whom they went, undertook to give them instruction in the conduct of public worship, and afterwards published the substance of his teaching as *A Guide to Prayer* (1715). No better treatment of its subject has ever appeared in print. Its author showed himself well aware that the old controversy did not stand where it had done; that if it was possible to make a fetish of the *Book of Common Prayer* it was equally possible to make a fetish of opposition to it or anything like it; that the day had passed when either minister or congregation could maintain a spirit of devotion through prayers of an hour or more in length; and that some of the expressions sanctified by tradition had become grotesque. He did not spare ministers who were in the habit of using odd phrases or odd vocal mannerisms, or those who 'ran great lengths in a doctrinal way'. The language used in public prayer, Watts contended, should be 'grave and decent, which is a medium between magnificence and meanness', and delivered in the tone 'with which we usually speak in grave and serious conversation, especially upon pathetical and affecting subjects'. He urged ministers when leading the worship of their people not to rely on 'sudden motions and suggestions', but to prepare for their high task by meditation, reading, and holy conversation. Let them mark the difference between conceived or free prayer and the extempore utterance of the moment, which was more properly expressed in ejaculatory form. They would do well to draw up a scheme of prayer for a year's use, with freedom to make such modifications from time to time as they might feel desirable. Thus they would make their ministrations what they ought to be, and what they had hitherto so largely failed to be, 'a piece of holy skill'.

Some more detailed illustrations of Puritan and Nonconformist worship must now be given. Let it be remembered that our survey covers some two centuries and that within its scope are the early Separatists of Elizabethan times, the brief Puritan ascendancy in the middle of the seventeenth century, the rise of Nonconformity proper after the Act of Uniformity (1662), with the ensuing days of persecution under Charles II and his brother, followed by the period of Toleration down to the outbreak of the Evangelical Revival in the reign of George II. It is not possible to find equally vivid descriptions of worship for all dates and sections of our survey. Nor is it to be supposed that as things were at its close so they were at its beginning, or vice versa. There were changes, but these were not so much in outward form as in the underlying spirit; in any case they were negligible in comparison with the changes of more recent days.

From depositions given against them in 1588 we have this account of the religious observances of some early Barrowists:

'In the somer tyme they mett together in the feilds a mile or more about London. There they sit down upon a bank and divers of them expound out of the bible so long as they are there assembled. In the winter they assemble themselves by 5 of the clock in the morning to that house where they make their Conventicle for that Sabbath day men and women together. There they continue in their kind of prayer and exposition of Scripture all that day. They dine together, after dinner make collection to pay for their diet and what money is left some one of them carrieth it to the prisons where any of their sect be committed. In their prayer one speaketh and the rest do groan or sob or sigh, as if they would ring out tears. Their prayer is extemporal. In their conventicles they use not the Lord's Prayer, nor of any form of set prayer.'[1]

The next passage is taken from Samuel Clarke's *Lives* (1662) and describes the activities of a notable Puritan minister, Thomas Wilson (1601–52) of Maidstone, on any Sunday between, let us say, 1645 and 1652. After studying on Saturday night till twelve, he usually rose at two or three, about seven called his family together, and then read, expounded, or prayed with them till between eight and nine.

'About Nine a Clock he went to church, and commonly began with singing two Staves of a Psalm; after which he prayed briefly for God's Assistance in, and for God's Blessing upon his own holy Ordinances; then he read some part of the Old Testament, and expounded (sometimes three, or four, or more verses, as more or less matters was contained in them) for the space of an hour.... Having ended his Exposition, he spent about an hour in the Pulpit.... In the Afternoon at Church he did as in the Morning, only his Exposition then was upon some part of the New Testament.'

After morning service

'when he came home to his Family, he constantly went to Prayer with them before Dinner.... Then, usually eating little or no Dinner, he went into his Study till his Family had dined: And then coming down he spent some time with them in singing, and other Religious Exercises.... After the publick Duties were ended, many of his Neighbours came to his House, where he called his Family together, required of them, and of others

---

[1] Burrage, *Early Dissenters*, ii. 27.

present, an account of his Sermons preached that day; and most of those that were present would tell him somewhat; one what the Text was, another the Division of it, another the Doctrine, another the Reasons, and others the Explanations and Uses, methodically as he had delivered them, all whom he would help and encourage. . . . After Repetition he sung a Psalm, and concluded with Prayer, and so went to Mr. Swinnock's to Supper, who had been his quondam Patron. And by that time they had supped, there would be a hundred, or more, gathered together to Mr. Swinock's House, to join with him in the conclusion of the day. . . .'

Our remaining illustrations are taken from the diary of Robert Kirk (1644–92), a Scottish episcopal minister who visited London in 1689, shortly after the accession of William and Mary and the passing of the Toleration Act. An enthusiastic sermon-taster, Kirk sampled religion in all the varieties the metropolis could then provide, and noted his impressions. He frequently heard Baxter at Charterhouse Yard, and thus describes one of the services he attended there:

'His clerk first sung a Psalm, reading the line. Then the reader read 3 Ps., Isaiah 5 and Matt. 22, after he had given an extempore prayer. Then the minister, reading the papers of the sick and troubled in mind and [those] intending a journey, he prayed and preached a sermon on popery. . . . He repeated the Lord's Prayer at the end of his last prayer. The most of the men were discovered during the whole time of sermon, yet some few kept on their hats when the Scriptures were a reading.'

On another occasion Kirk notes that Matthew Sylvester, Baxter's colleague, 'with reading of Scriptures repeated the belief (and at the article of hell, said: He descended into the unseen state), and out of Exod. 21 read the ten Commandments'. Another of Kirk's visits was to Dr. Bates's (1625–99) meeting-house at Hackney.

'He had no reader nor Scripture read. He had a little green pulpit with a flowered velvet cushion on it. He prayed not for the King or Queen nor Church; he reflected on none. He used not the Lord's Prayer and prayed not for the success of convocation as Mr. Baxter did. He prayed to deliver Ireland from anti-Christian tyranny and superstition. He prayed for the Parliament, directed by the name of the Great Council of the land. All the men and women there kneeled or stood at prayer. He read not sermon from his notes. He, as all regular clergy, had all intercession and thanksgiving in his first prayer.'

Next for Kirk's impression of an Independent preacher, George Cockain (1620–91), whose congregation gathered in a meeting-house of two rooms, a hall and a little parlour. The preacher

'had no Psalms before or after sermon. The people heard sermon with heads covered, and stood at prayer. . . . Sermon began in the afternoon at half-past one. The preacher prayed not for the Protestant Churches, nor English, nor any Churchmen, only barely for the King and High Council without naming the Queen. He did plead vehemently with God for a young man at the grave's mouth, the only hope and visible standing of his father's family, saying: "Lord, 'tis rare to find a good man, more a young good man. Thou sparest 10,000ds of debauched youths, may not this one dry but tender and fruitful branch escape the blast of thy displeasure. Save his soul. Spare his body. Sanctify all to the parents seeing thou dost it, not theirs nor ours, but thy will be done." He had not the blessing at the end. The minister vested in a black coat.'[1]

From these examples it is possible to gather the form which Puritan and Nonconformist public worship commonly took. Within generally defined limits there was no doubt a good deal of diversity of practice. It is worthy of note, for instance, that John Cotton (1584–1652), one of the *émigrés* to New England, where he was chief among the Congregational ministers of his day, records some additional features in the services there held. In his *True Constitution of a Particular Visible Church* (1642) he sets it down that worship should follow the apostolic injunction that 'first of all supplications, prayers, inter-

---

[1] D. Maclean, *London at Worship, 1689–90.*

cessions and giving of thanks be made for all men'. As among the English Separatists so in New England a place was given to 'prophesying', and if time allowed it was open to the elders to call on any others of the brethren present, whether of the same church or of any other, to speak a word of exhortation. It was also open for 'any, young or old, save onely for women, to aske questions at the mouth of the Prophets'. Neal, in his *History of the Puritans*, states that the English Brownists also gave opportunity to questioners. From Cotton we further learn that in New England churches the deacons, who sat below the elders on raised seats facing the congregation, at Sunday afternoon service after prayer and preaching 'do call upon the people, that as God hath prospered them and made their hearts willing, there is now time left for contribution. Presently the people from the highest to the lowest in sundry churches do arise; the first pew first, the next next, and so the rest in order, and present before the Lord their holy offerings.'

In the administration of the Lord's Supper also there was some diversity of practice, more particularly as between Congregationalists and Presbyterians. Under judicial examination in 1593 a member of the earliest known Congregational church in London deposed that their manner of celebration was,

'That five loaves or more were set upon the table. That the pastor did break the bread and then delivered it to some of them, and the deacons delivered it to the rest; some of the congregation sitting and some standing about the table. And that the Pastor delivered the cup unto one, and he to another, till they had all drunken: using the words at the delivery thereof according as it is set down in the 11th Cos. 24.'[1]

In some Independent churches the supper was celebrated every Sunday, but Cotton notes that in New England the observance was a monthly one. He goes on to describe the communicants, at least as many as possible, sitting

[1] Burrage, op. cit., ii. 32.

round the table and in that attitude receiving the bread
and wine 'according as Christ administered it to his disciples, who also made a symbolical use of it to teach the
church their majority over their ministers in some cases,
and their judicial authority as co-sessors with him at the
last judgement'. The minister having blessed and broken
the bread bade the people take and eat it as the body of
Christ broken for them. He then took it himself and gave
it to all those sitting at the table, and from the table it
was reached by the deacons to the people sitting in the
next seats about them. So afterwards with the cup. Of
Presbyterian usage we owe our most vivid picture to the
diary of Samuel Sewall, a New England visitor. It belongs to the year 1689, the scene was the meeting-house
in Little St. Helen's, London, and the administering
minister, Samuel Annesley (1621–96).

'The Doctor went all over the meeting first to see who was
there [a reference to the fencing of the tables], then spake something of the Sermon, then read the words of Institution, then
prayed and eat and drunk himself, then gave to every one with
his own Hand, dropping pertinent Expressions. In our Pue
said—Now our Spikenard should give its smell; and said to me,
Remember the Death of Christ. The Wine was in quart Glass
Bottles. The Deacon followed the Doctor and when his Cup
was empty filled it again; as at our Pue all had drunk but I, he
filled the Cup and then gave it to me, said as he gave it—must
be ready in new Obedience and stick at nothing for Christ.'[1]

It is to the celebration of the Lord's Supper that we
owe one of the most notable changes of those times, the
introduction of the singing of hymns. Psalm-singing there
had been from the first, though not without misgiving in
some quarters. Was it, for instance, possible in a mixed
congregation to obey the apostolic injunction to sing with
grace in the heart when the congregation might include
the graceless? This was a question much canvassed among
early Dissenters. Bunyan (1628–88) decided it in the nega-

[1] *Massachusetts Hist. Soc. Colls.*, V. 253.

tive, but generally the vote was cast in favour of singing, within strictly defined limits. Nothing but the psalms of scripture were permissible, none of what Barrowe called 'the apocryphal erroneous ballads in time-song' used in the Church of England, a reference presumably to the *Benedicite* and perhaps to more. The Barrowists indeed are credited with eschewing even metrical versions, and singing the psalms as they found them in their Bibles without regard to time or probably to tune. The vocal result of this is difficult to imagine. But Puritans generally used metrical versions of the Psalter, of which there were several in circulation. Here we may notice that of Henry Ainsworth (1571–1622), minister of the Congregational church at Amsterdam, at which city there was published in 1612 his *Book of Psalms Englished both in Prose and Metre*. This was several times reprinted, and used in New England until 1692. As his title indicates, Ainsworth gave both a prose and verse translation of each psalm, and accompanied these with explanatory notes. Of tunes he remarked, 'I find none set of God, so that each people is to use the most grave, devout and comfortable manner of singing that they know.' For their help he inserted with his versions some thirty tunes then current in England or on the Continent. Of these he gave the air only, there being then a sound instinct, for which bad reasons were often advanced, that part-singing was out of place in a congregation.

For many years the psalms retained their monopoly. But there were occasions when they left something to be desired, and particularly was this so after the sacrament, when, following the example of the Master and his first disciples, the worshippers joined in song. Watts confessed to some weariness of ringing the changes on two or three psalms whose suitability for such moments had become something of a recognized convention. But he was not the first to innovate on the established tradition. That honour belongs to Benjamin Keach (1640–1704), minister of a Particular Baptist church in London, who in 1673, to the scandal of a large party in his denomination, introduced among his own congregation the custom of singing a hymn, one of his own numerous compilations, after the sacrament. Some thirty years later Watts, with qualifications of a vastly higher order, introduced the same change into Congregational churches. Among his early compositions was a book of twenty-five sacramental hymns. This contained 'When I survey the wondrous cross', the masterpiece which entitles its author to the first place among English hymn-writers. To the same sacramental inspiration was due another hymn, worthy to be placed only second to Watts's, Philip Doddridge's (1702–51) 'My God, and is thy table spread'.

It remains to say something of private or out-of-church devotional practice. The Puritans set little store by sacred buildings, many of them indeed rejected the idea of such consecration as superstitious. From New England they largely adopted as most to their minds the term 'meeting-house', and this retained its place in Nonconformist nomenclature until the Methodists popularized the word 'chapel'. Public worship had its appointed times and places; on other occasions, whether as a conscious revival or not, they followed the early Christian example of the 'church in the house'. In many seventeenth-century homes there was a daily religious observance which in its fullness and regularity suggests a comparison with monastic discipline. But it was monastic with the notable difference that it was associated with family life. The institution of the family was given a new significance by the men of the Reformed Faith. The covenant is for you and for your children, so ran the Scripture used at baptism, and this carried with it further implications of family solidarity in Christ. The head of the household was held answerable for the spiritual welfare of all beneath his roof. If he lived up to his responsibilities twice in the day he conducted what was known as 'family duty'. That these

ministrations were long and might be sadly irksome to
the younger of those present may readily be supposed.
Oliver Heywood (1630–1702), the famous Yorkshire divine, records his children's playing at prayers, and his
giving them 'seasonable correction which brought them
into an exact complyance in the outward man', and this
must have happened only too often in many homes.
Sunday in particular was the day for household religion.
Baxter in his *Reformed Pastor* lays it down that the master
of the house should then have all those under his charge
go through the catechism and should examine them on
the sermons they had heard. If this was beyond him he
and his family should resort to the house of some godly
neighbour possessed of the capacity which he lacked.
Profitable books, such as some 'smaller moving sermons',
might be read with benefit on such occasions in addition
to the Bible. It is safe to suppose that even in godly
Kidderminster lay practice lagged behind clerical exhortation, but Baxter's directions indicate what must have
been customary among the more religious of his parish-
ioners. Sermons of the kind he specifies were certainly
much in demand. For example, a volume entitled *The
Great Assize*, by one Samuel Smith (1584–1665), was reprinted thirty-nine times within seventy or eighty years,
and attained its forty-seventh edition in 1757; other pub-
lications of his also enjoyed a remarkable popularity.

In addition to 'family duty' the Puritans were in the
habit of holding 'private days', so called to distinguish
them from 'public days' appointed by government in
connexion with national events. A few friends, or in some
cases those present might number fifty or more, met
together perhaps to pray for the recovery of some one
sick of body or soul in the house where they were gathered,
or of some one at a distance thus afflicted. On such an
occasion eight hours or so were spent in prayer and
preaching. It was no uncommon thing for one of the
ministers present to pray for three hours. All this was

usually done fasting, 'private day' and 'private fast' being more or less interchangeable terms, unless the gathering was one for thanksgiving. Fixed days and seasons of abstinence as practised among Catholics the Puritans condemned, but on special days of prayer when some evil threatened nation, church, or individual, they held fasting to be an appropriate mark of humiliation.

Of the readiness with which men and women joined in prayer for one otherwise quite unknown to them Henry Newcome (1627–95) gives a striking example in his diary. News reached him at Manchester in 1659 that a girl at Cambridge had promised her soul to the devil. The next day there happened to be a meeting of the presbytery, and at six in the morning, before the business of the session began, Newcome got together a few of his friends, who spent three hours with him in prayer for the girl's deliverance. Subsequently they held a private day on her behalf. At Cambridge he records there were some who sat up all night praying for her. 'It was a University then', he comments, 'when so many Masters of Arts and Fellows of Colleges could be found to keep a night to such a purpose.' Another illustration of the value the Puritans attached to prayer is to be found in a letter addressed to Cromwell in 1650 by that great enthusiast Major-General Harrison:

'My Lord, lett waiting upon Jehovah bee the greatest and most considerable busines you have every daie; reckon it soe, more then to eate, sleep, or councell together. Run aside sometimes from your companie, and gett a word with the Lord. Why should not yow have three or four pretious soules allwaies standing at your elbow, with whom you might now and then turne into a corner? I have found refreshment and mercie in such a waie.'[1]

Of the intense reality of Puritan piety there can be no question, but it was not of that kind which makes a permanent contribution to the practice of the devout life.

[1] *Original Letters*, ed. J. Nickolls, p. 10.

From among all its literary output only the *Pilgrim's Progress*, and in a lesser degree the *Saints' Everlasting Rest*, have retained their power of appeal for subsequent generations, and neither of these is a book of devotion in the stricter sense. There is something amateurish about Puritan attempts in that field, a deficiency explicable in part by the forms in which they expressed their spiritual needs, explicable further by the ecclesiastical cleavage which cut them off from the sifted experience of centuries embodied in Catholic piety. None the less attempts were made. Manuals were issued for the use of communicants. Books were published on prayer and the religious life. Deserving of special mention is a volume often reprinted, in its abbreviated form known under the title of the *Practice of Christianity*. This was the work of Richard Rogers (1550–1618), not a Nonconformist but a Puritan dissident of the established church, its design being to set forth the directions discoverable in Scripture for living the Christian life.

For the inner and more individual side of Puritan piety we must consult the diaries that have come down to us. That there are such records is in itself significant. The Puritan advocated the value of keeping a day-book and contributed not a little to the development of that particular form of self-revelation. Into its pages, happily for posterity, he often put a good deal of information about his family, his friends, and other local personages and their doings, but it was primarily an account of God's dealings with his soul and that soul's relations with God. To ministers—and the fullest diaries that have been preserved are clerical—Richard Rogers wrote, 'it were meet for them to take a view of their weeks worke at the end of it, to keepe a register of Gods speciall mercies and deliverances, and another of his chastisements and afflictions; and how they goe under them, and profit by them'. The diary was to be used as a book of private devotion, read and re-read, it might be with the marginal comments of later experience. Here are to be found covenants, vows, and self-dedications, providing matter for subsequent self-examination. Notable also is the store set on religious emotion, on being 'well-stirred up' when preaching, perhaps even to tears, on 'meltings', 'enlargements', 'quickenings'. Yet if the Puritan loved to enjoy his religion his characteristic word for his devotions is 'duty', indicative that with or without enjoyment they remained his obligatory task.

A. G. MATTHEWS.

PART III

CONTEMPORARY STUDIES

XII

PSYCHOLOGICAL CONSIDERATIONS

SOON after the ancient monogram of the Lord had been placed in Mansfield College Chapel at that point where the eyes of the congregation most naturally focus, a man was heard to ask, 'What is that funny piece of three-ply wood doing there?' We may safely assume that it had never occurred to him, when, looking up as he entered the main entrance to the College, he saw the words DEUS LOCUTUS EST NOBIS IN FILIO, to enquire, 'What are those queer markings in the stone?' Nor, if one day as he passed the Chapel his ears had caught the strains of

> O Jesus, King most wonderful,
> Thou conqueror renowned,

would he have murmured to himself, 'Whatever is the reason of those silly vibrations?' He would respond to the hymn, he would at least believe that there was something to respond to in the motto, but in the monogram—the shorthand epitome of both motto and hymn—he saw nothing but a piece of meaningless matter.

'When the sun rises do you not see a round disk of fire something like a guinea?' Blake supposed himself to be asked; and his reply was, 'Oh! no, no! I see an innumerable company of the heavenly host, crying, "Holy, holy, holy, is the Lord God Almighty!"'

The Word of God is mediated to us through 'phenomena'—through presentations to the senses, chiefly the visual and the auditory. Let us take the monogram ☧ as an example of a phenomenon possessing this mediating power when conditions are suitable. By using it for illustration we may be able the more easily to set in relief a psychological problem which public worship inevitably presents.

A man, whose mind and heart are open to the meaning of the symbol, stands in the archway of the screen looking down the Chapel. His eye takes in vaguely the proportions of the building, the chairs, the pulpit, the table, the lectern, the stalls, the Reformers in their stone niches, and the coloured record of saints, apostles, prophets, martyrs; but it quickly comes to rest on the small central pattern of wood which is the key to the whole scene, and there is a sudden lift in his heart, a catch of the breath: Χριστός, ὁ Κύριος Ἰησοῦς Χριστός, Son of Man, Son of God, Prince of Peace, Prince of Glory, Shepherd, Brother, Friend, Saviour, Lord Jesus—what names, what pictures, surge into the mind, what memories of gracious dealings in the soul. What unutterable meaning had that symbol when they scratched those rude initials in the catacombs, and what tones and overtones have been added to it for him who stands in the archway of the screen, and, letting his eye wander again for a moment, sees Prisca, Monica, Francis, Hus, Luther, Wesley, Livingstone, and a throng besides, men and women who, if we asked them whence their victory came, could make a full reply by tracing two letters of the Greek alphabet.

For the person we have been envisaging the Word of God was conveyed to his spirit through the medium of that wooden symbol. God spoke, and His servant heard, because he was attuned to the transmitting medium. Recognizing the voice as the voice of God, the hearer probably made a movement of the spirit Godwards. That movement might find outward expression, as by a falling on the knees or a whispered hallelujah or an uttered vow, or it might have no manifestation perceptible to the senses, and consist of a purely internal act of self-dedication or a breathless silence of adoration with no conscious self-reference at all. If these things happened, that is, if

God was recognized as speaking and was responded to, then a condition of prayer which is communion had been attained.

In this relatively simple example we are already faced with a psychological situation of considerable complexity. We have assumed in the illustration that the 'phenomenon'—the monogram—did in fact serve as a medium for the Word of God, and that the Word was heard and was responded to as of God. But it is evident that the transition made by the worshipper, from the significant phenomenon through to its inexhaustible meaning and on to the recognition of that meaning as being the present word of the living God to him, was a psychological progress by no means inevitable. Indeed, it implied a prior cultivation of the inner life of an advanced kind. Had he been at a primitive mental stage, he might have reached no further than the symbol, so that the monogram would be for him simply an impersonal holy thing—a *tabu* object. It is not very probable, however, that a visitor to Mansfield would be held up by a sacred symbol in that way. If it had significance for him, it would be significant because of that for which it stood; he would appreciate it for what it expressed to him. Yet, even though he penetrated through to its meaning, if he reached no further than appreciation, the symbol would not have served its purpose. The apprehended meaning might kindle great emotional fervour, the historical imagination might be stirred, there might be a thrilled contemplation of the heroic and triumphant world which had flashed upon the inward eye, but worship and communion would not have been achieved.

There is always in public worship this *tertium quid*—the 'phenomenon'—which is the sensible medium of God's Word, and which, while conducive to the communion of the worshipper with God when rightly used, is in danger of becoming an obstacle to communion by reason of the interest it arouses and the emotional satisfaction which may be derived from resting in it, and in that for which it stands, without moving on to a direct to and fro commerce with God.

This statement may be challenged. Protestant worship, an objector may say, is spiritual. Where it is most true to itself it goes furthest in the elimination of these 'phenomena'. That is why Puritans are uneasy about externals —crosses, monograms, and so forth. These outward things are liable to keep the mind in the realm of the temporal and spatial, and to distract the worshipper from God.

We delude ourselves, however, if we think it is really possible to eliminate this third element, which, while it may be a medium of the Divine Word, may also be a positive hindrance to communion.

Let us take two illustrations which will be regarded by some as exhibiting a progressive 'spiritualization' of means of worship.

In many chapels, on the wall behind the central pulpit is inscribed a text. This piece of writing, again, is, or may be, a medium of the Word of God. Obviously it is a 'phenomenon' no less than the emblem which we discussed at first. What is perhaps not so quickly seen is that the appreciation of the meaning of the verbal symbol may stand in the way of direct communion with God just as may the appreciation of the emblem. The contemplation of truth about God or of His dealings with men requires one posture of mind, responsive listening to Him requires another. The movement from the one to the other is not inevitable, and, without much practice, it is not easy. Many who go to church hardly seem to realize that it requires to be made, or, if they feel the need of it, they are troubled because they find it difficult of accomplishment.

Precisely the same psychological difficulty arises in the hearing of the preached Word. A sermon is, like the text and the emblem, a 'phenomenon', a sensible medium of the Word of God. Here the Word is mediated by a living personality, and in the measure that the preacher is quickened by the Holy Spirit, the sermon becomes a vital demonstration of God.

Yet, just because inspired human utterance is able, perhaps more effectively than any other medium, to evoke emotional response to the Word of God, the sermon is a 'phenomenon' which is in especial danger of being enjoyed for itself in suchwise that the hearer is held up at the stage of appreciation, and does not pass on to direct worship, to direct communion with God. We recognize this in our disparaging references to those who gush about 'the *beautiful* sermon we had this morning'. Do we recognize, on the other hand, how exceedingly difficult it is for the untrained worshipper to make that transition from appreciation to communion, and by an act of will to pass beyond the preacher and the feelings aroused by his message to God and His direct word of promise to, and of demand upon, the individual soul? A little self-examination and a little reflection on the inherent difficulty of the psychological operation to be performed might increase our charity.

Thus far we have considered the 'phenomenon' (sign, word, speech, action, &c.) as the medium of God's Word to us. It may also be, of course, the medium through which our word to God is expressed. Clearly, however, the function of the medium is not identical in the two cases. In the former it is a means of making us aware of something, in the latter it is not a means of making God aware of anything, but of fixing our attention, directing our thought, and stimulating the outward-going movement of the spirit towards God.

Here, too, it is easy for the mind so to concentrate on the 'phenomenon' as to be unable to attend to God. This is true whether the medium be the spoken or the written word or a combination of the two. In public prayer there are special difficulties of mental concentration to consider, but, even if they have been so far overcome that the worshipper has followed what has been uttered, he may yet stop short at the point where he feels 'What a beautiful prayer', without having appropriated the content as his own in real prayer.

One reason for the strong hold which extemporary prayer has on Free Churchmen is that it is, or at the very least sounds like, the spontaneous speech of a man to God. It is the vivid exhibition of one actually communing with God.[1] The minister is felt to be occupied in an activity which is 'real' and natural. God is there, and the minister is speaking to Him—speaking in the name of the congregation, and speaking in the terms one would naturally use if proper regard is given to Him who is being addressed, to the year and the day and the place of speaking, and to the political, social, economic, and spiritual circumstances of those who are being represented. When some one speaks thus to God in a manner which sounds perfectly genuine, the attention of a listener tends to be directed towards God as One who is 'real' and who is hearing. This accent upon the living God facilitates the process whereby the listener passes beyond mere listening to active communion himself.

This note of 'reality' in extemporary prayer derives from the minister's sincerity of utterance in his speaking to God. That he should shut his eyes and speak 'out of his head' is not an essential condition, though it may be the most appropriate practice for individual ministers.[2]

The chief drawback to such extemporary prayer is that it is a very difficult medium for common prayer. If it helps the worshipper to pass beyond the 'phenomenon' to God, it does not make easy his carrying the content of the prayer to God. The mental agility required to grasp the thread of another man's thought as it moves on

[1] Cf. the woman's remark quoted by K. L. Parry (p. 235).
[2] For a further discussion of *ex tempore* prayer see the writer's *Our Approach to God*, pp. 226–34.

in a prayer of any continuance, to make it one's own, and to direct it to God, is considerable. It is hardly surprising if (as we know from testimony) very many folk have long since given up the attempt in despair. We have here a main cause of the fatal passivity which is so distressing a characteristic of our congregations to-day.

One of the most urgent needs of a large number of our churches is the recovery of active corporate worship. Yet he who begins to discuss what practical steps may be taken to inaugurate this recovery is at once accused of being unspiritual and a small-minded person who occupies himself with frills. All that is needed, we are told, is a new baptism of the Holy Spirit. Given that, and the most suitable mode of Service will emerge of itself; without it, any amount of tinkering with form and method is futile. This assertion has, of course, an admixture of truth in it. No serious Christian would be tempted to forget that a spiritual revival must be the work of the Holy Spirit. But to make Him an excuse for refusal to think and to take action upon thought is nothing less than dishonouring to God. And does the doctrine of the Holy Spirit preclude the possibility that He Himself is preparing the way for revival by moving men to thought and experiment?

Public prayer provides a good illustration of the issue. To the intelligent it presents a group of psychological problems. Here is one. The difficulty of concentrated listening is undeniably very great. To follow a prayer by ear requires concentrated listening. How should the prayers be conducted so that they may be most easily followed by the inevitably slow-moving mind of the congregation?[1] That is a question in the domain of psychology.

---

[1] For great sections of the Church, of course, this is an unnecessary question. It is not intended, they would say, that the prayers uttered by the minister should be followed in detail by the congregation. The present chapter, however, assumes that the ideal of Free Church worship is *common* prayer. For the writer's defence of this assumption see *Our Approach to God*, pp. 133–41.

The answer to it will be found only after open-eyed, unprejudiced, painstaking investigation. It is not intellectually honest to appeal emotionally to the activity of the Holy Spirit in lieu of taking the mental trouble which the solution of the problem demands. But if and when the answer has been found, we are not at the end of our difficulties. No one in his senses supposes that once the prayers have been made such that they can be followed, it will automatically ensue that they will be followed; yet the accomplishment is not the less necessary because it is very modest.

In public worship, then, a difficult and delicate psychological adjustment is required to be made by the worshipper, owing to the fact that the spiritual activity of a to and fro commerce between God and the human soul has to be externalized in sensible expression. He needs to set his attention in two directions simultaneously: towards the invisible God, and towards the sensible phenomenon. Or, if the phenomenon is conceived more as a window through which the worshipper glimpses God, then we shall have to say that the direction is the same, but that the attention has to be set simultaneously on two different distances; because the window analogy breaks down when we are trying to describe the double concentration involved. If one is looking at a view through a window he does not need to pay attention to the composition and texture of the window; but in public worship the translucence of the 'phenomenon' is largely dependent upon the attention which has been given to it.[1]

[1] Spatial metaphors are unavoidable. It may be objected that the writer is treating God as an object amongst other objects, and that this is philosophically illegitimate. He would reply that the structure of the human mind is such that it must translate God into 'concrete' terms in order to apprehend Him at all. We seem bound to employ spatial metaphors if we are to describe the psychological processes consequent upon this psychological necessity. They are seriously misleading only if we forget that they are metaphors.

The mental adjustment required is, however, further complicated by the need for the adaptation of the individual mind to the assembled brethren. If the worship is to attain vitality and richness as a corporate activity, there must be a deliberate self-identification of the worshipper with his fellows. It is no wonder that Services seem unprofitable when we are looking simply for the expression or the satisfaction of our own moods and sentiments. To be what they should be, their range of thought and sentiment will be far wider than that of any single member of the congregation. Embraced in the fellowship there is not only the merchant rejoicing over the acquisition of his pearl of great price, but also the publican crying in his heart, 'Lord, have mercy upon me a sinner'. We do not know what the common worship of the Church is until by an effort of the imagination and the will we link ourselves with the publican in his need and the merchant in his exultation, let our own temper of mind be what it may.

Truly corporate worship demands, then, a triple orientation of the mind: towards God, towards the 'phenomena', and towards the brethren. When we consider it analytically we may well be disposed to deem it beyond the capacity of man. It is not that; but it is difficult, and is only to be achieved when through habit a man is able to make broad the field of his awareness, and with little or no effort to contain within it two of the directional goals while he gives closer attention to the third. If this requires a very narrow concentration, then, indeed, it is impossible for the field of awareness to contain the other two.

An illustration will, perhaps, make clearer the truth we are trying to indicate.

Let us consider a pianist who is reading a piece of music entirely 'unseen'. His purpose is to convey to the ear as perfect an embodiment in sound of the composer's musical conception as the conditions will allow. Since we are concerned to use this situation simply as an illustration, it will be enough if we abstract from the complex mental operations he needs to perform three important *agenda*. (1) He must endeavour to play the right notes; (2) he must seek to interpret the composer's purpose in terms of time, rhythm, accent, volume, balance, &c.; and (3) he must listen to what he is playing—to his own audible effects. These three demands apply continuously throughout the piece, and thus they have to be fulfilled simultaneously.

Provided the piece is not of unusual technical obscurity and difficulty, the trained musician will give a tolerably competent, if not artistically finished, rendering of it. His knowledge of chords and progressions will be such that he will take in at a glance whole stretches of the notation without having to make a conscious analysis of their component parts; his familiarity with the spirit of the composer, or at least with the school or the period to which he belongs, will guide him in his almost effortless interpretation; and he will be so free from the necessity of narrow concentration on these things that he will be able to listen to his effects, and adjust his muscular control of the keyboard to the advice of his critical ear. He accomplishes his task at the cost of close mental concentration. This concentration is, however, upon a wide field, and it is maintained by means of 'diffused attention', the focus of which ranges over the whole field and never sets one part in such high relief that other parts are completely hidden by its shadow.

So much for the trained musician. Now observe the beginner. Every note on the page in front of him needs careful attention. Chords have to be spelt out, intervals calculated, parts accurately distributed. The score, his fingers, and the keys make full demands upon his powers of concentration. If his imagination is stirred by some hint of the significance of the piece, and he attempts a little interpretation, his blunders increase in direct proportion to his enthusiasm; and as for listening to the noise he is making, it is a condition of his persistence that he is mercifully unable to do so.

We have taken two extremes. There are, of course, innumerable grades of capacity between them. The point to notice, however, is that where, because of novelty, one of the three requisite operations demands exclusive attention, there (unless the need is for attention of minimal duration) the player is prevented from achieving his purpose successfully. This illustrates a principle of general application to situations which require a wide field of attention.

Now extemporary prayer turns public worship into what from one point of view may be regarded as an exercise in 'unseens'. 'Unseens' (the reader will remember) may be of differing degrees of unfamiliarity and difficulty.

Corporate prayer requires diffused attention, the focus of which (never a sharp focus) is upon the less familiar element in the field of awareness, wherever the factor of unfamiliarity is present. Normally, then, in 'free' worship the worshipper needs so to have trained his imagination that he can without effort hold within the grip of his awareness both God, the Object of his worship, and the people of God, his fellow worshippers, while he is free to set the focus of his attention upon the discursive movements of the *sensibilia* which give content to the praise and prayer and mould the assembly into a unity of mind and heart. Extemporary prayer as it is often practised, however, proceeds at such a speed and is so full of the unanticipated that all (and, indeed, for most folk more than all) a man's powers of concentration are needed for the mere following of it. It need not be made so difficult as that; but let us be quite clear that, where it is, it kills corporate worship.

There are those who think it expedient that there should be more familiar acquaintance with the *sensibilia* in order that the focus of attention may be centred more

frequently on God. They would not do away with either
spontaneity or variety, but they hold that a familiar
liturgical element, when rightly conducted, releases the
mind for worship, and gives greater vitality to the non-
liturgical elements, because it has helped to habituate
the movement of the focus of attention over the whole
field. Monotonous repetition, they would add, Sunday
by Sunday, year in and year out, is not a necessary condition of familiarity. A worshipping church is capable
of acquiring an increasing treasury of 'Uses', which are
familiar without being stale, and flexible without being
strange.

We have been thinking of prayer with its accent upon
the outward-going movement of the spirit towards God.
But the aim of Christian prayer is communion; and this
implies (if, as we must, we keep our spatial imagery) the
rhythm of a to and fro movement between the worshipper
and God. On the worshipper's part even in prayer there
should thus be receptivity as well as activity. This is a
further factor in the psychological complexity of corporate
worship. Intelligent speaking and intelligent listening
require different dispositions of the mind. In conversation face to face change from one to the other is easy,
because the presence and voice (or presence and silence)
of our interlocutor provide the external conditions which
by habitual association automatically dispose the mind
in the requisite fashion. But to speak to one who is not
apprehensible by any of the senses, and to listen even
while we are speaking—this is an accomplishment not to
be achieved without much cultivation.

It will be noticed that this task of listening while speaking (or, at all events, of listening to God while listening
to, and associating ourself with, some one speaking to
Him) belongs to corporate prayer as distinct from private prayer. In private prayer we can be as silent as
we will—our themes, our pace, our activities and passivi-

ties, can obey the dictates of our spiritual judgement. If we are to participate in corporate worship, on the other hand, we must be willing to follow a pattern. That pattern should be such as will help to promote the supple movements of the mind which corporate worship and communion demand. For example, the spoken prayers will be worded not only so as to express what the assembly desires to say to God, but also so as to call up a clear concept of Him who is being addressed, and, by signifying His nature relative to our need, to adumbrate the very answer of God to the cry of our souls. Those who object to the constant reference to God's attributes in public prayer, on the ground that He is not a vain potentate to be flattered by names and titles and complimentary phrases, do not seem to realize that this attributive language is employed for our sakes, not for His. In private prayer it may not be necessary; in public prayer it is a device so helpful to human frailty that we cannot doubt it meets with the Divine indulgence. The truth is that, if we are to distinguish between more and less important parts of a spoken prayer, the part which helps to intensify our awareness of God is of far more consequence than that which defines our petition, and the indulgence we need for addressing God in worshipful terms is simply a particular application of the general forbearance which we require by reason of our humanity.

We turn to consider the fundamental psychological problems of the preacher. As Mr. Shillito shows (pp. 218 ff.), the true purpose of a sermon is to be declaratory of the Word of God, revelatory of God Himself. Who is sufficient? There are not many Isaiahs or Jeremiahs in a generation. To achieve his proper aim the preacher must be inspired. Inspiration is an activity of the Holy Spirit, and it does not therefore come within the province of psychology for explanation. Something, however, can be said about its conditions.

Significant for the preacher is the New Testament assertion that the coming of the Holy Spirit was not until
Christ's Ascension. The full power of God was made
available for human souls by the Incarnation—by the
life and death of the incarnate Lord. For us psycho-
physical beings the spiritual has always to be mediated.
The Divine Spirit within must work in and through the
'given' in experience. Amos sees a basket of summer
fruit, and because he is Amos, the vision is transfigured
into a word of God. Shall we say that he derived his
inspiration from the basket of fruit? Yes, *in a secondary
sense*, certainly. But the inspiration itself was the Spirit
of God conveying His Word to Amos through the basket
of fruit. The Word is transmitted through a medium to
a person of 'sensitivity'.

Now the 'given' which constitutes the Christian Gospel
is the Christ. He is the Word which the preacher is called
upon to declare. In the Scriptures we have transmitted
to us through the centuries writings stamped with His
impress. They bear witness to Him, they bear witness
about Him. They are the source of inspiration *par excellence*, because amongst possibly mediating phenomena
they stand in a unique relation to the historically incarnate Lord which makes them intrinsically adapted to
be media of the Spirit's utterance to the human soul.
They are not themselves the Word in the sense that
Christ is the Word. If they were, then the Church would
need lectors only, not preachers. They are, however, the
condition of our adequate inspiration.

The importance of the Scriptures for the preacher is not
due simply to their being the work of 'inspired' men. The
writings of many poets in many ages have been 'inspired',
and, if inspiration were the one qualification for entry,
the canon might be expanded indefinitely. No, the Bible
is of outstanding importance because it concentrates
upon, and preserves the direct impress of, the Son of God
who went about a man among men and who died the

death of a malefactor and rose again, and because, in consequence of this, it is a medium of inspiration through which the Spirit can awaken man to the profoundest insights. Veiled within writings addressed to the special conditions of particular localities at particular times in history is the eternal Word which had been revealed in human life subject to the conditions of time and space. A man must be a prophet or a poet to discover a 'Thus saith the Lord' in a basket of summer fruit; he need only be a simple Christian of quiet mind and honest intention to hear some message of the Divine voice speaking through the human medium of the sacred writings. That message, being timeless, is for all time, and is therefore something applicable to the special temporal conditions of any generation.

As has been said, inspiration, being the work of the Holy Spirit, cannot itself be the object of psychological investigation. Nevertheless, psychological factors are involved in the process of receiving inspiration, and these are, or should be, as susceptible of analysis as any other mental states or events. Since the Scriptures are the most fruitful proximate source of the preacher's inspiration, what requires to be considered from a psychological point of view is his mode of approach to them.

Here we can do little more than draw attention to what will be commonplaces to most readers.

The preacher's object is to hear a 'Thus saith the Lord' to him and to the people to whom he ministers. Consequently his primary intellectual enterprise is to discover the eternal truth embodied in the historically conditioned writing in front of him, and to perceive the concrete application of that truth to the particular social and spiritual circumstances of a group of people who are in actual process of 'making history'. He is, in short, called upon to meditate on his text in a systematic way. He will study it in its literary context and in its historical setting; he will bring his imagination into as full play as possible; he will look for the essential meaning of which the text is the embodiment, and consider to what practical conclusions it points; and he will cast about for images which will convey effectively the message to his hearers.

These things are, doubtless, commonplaces, and scarcely need more than mention. What we would emphasize is the purpose for which the meditation is undertaken. It is that the minister may receive from on high a Word to proclaim. That means that while the phases of his meditation may have much in common with the processes he would go through if he were preparing a lecture, yet his psychological orientation will be wholly different; it means also that he will not be treating his text simply as an instrument for provoking and corroborating his own personal witness to what God has done for him. He will avoid intellectualism on the one hand, and pietism on the other. Not, of course, that either argument or personal testimony should necessarily be excluded from the sermon; but neither may be central, if the Word is to be preached. The minister's task is to listen for the Word, and to proclaim it. The marrow of his sermon should therefore be 'Thus saith the Lord'. It is only stating this truth in another form when Dr. Will says that the purpose of preaching is not to develop thoughts about God, but to reveal the presence of God Himself;[1] for the Word is more than a proposition, it is a living Personal Reality.

Of the psychology of the effective conveyance of the Divine message we cannot treat at length here. The essential conditions of useful preaching are, however, only two, and they can be stated very briefly. (1) The preacher requires to have a mind intent on God and his flock, and not on himself; and (2) he requires an intimate pastoral knowledge of his people.

(1) The temper of mind which fulfils the first condition

[1] *Le Culte*, ii. 119, note.

may perhaps be apprehended by any one who dwells in thought on the following words:

'Let the preacher labour to be heard gladly, intelligently, obediently. And let him not question that he can do this better by the piety of his prayers than by the fluency of his speech.[1] By praying for himself and for them he is going to address, let him be a bedesman or ever he be a teacher: and approaching devoutly, before he put forth a speaking tongue, let him lift up to God a thirsty soul, that so he may give out what from Him he hath drunk in, and empty out what he hath first replenished.'[2]

(2) The importance of the second condition needs no demonstration—at least to those who have learnt anything from the psychological investigations of the last thirty years.

When we said that the marrow of a sermon should be 'Thus saith the Lord', we did not, of course, mean that the minister's task is to deliver himself of oracular assertions to be 'taken or left' by his congregation. (They would certainly be left.) His task is to deliver a message from God to particular individual persons. The message is a message for all, but it has to be conveyed to each.

We should distinguish here between *bringing home* the message to individuals and *applying* it to individuals. The latter is not the work of the pulpit. To attempt it is to commit the unpardonable discourtesy of preaching at individual members of the congregation, and at the same time to fail in duty to the whole. The former, on the contrary, is the very purpose of preaching. If it is to be achieved, the preacher must know his people—their idiosyncrasies, their prejudices, their inhibitions, their emotional environment, their intellectual 'universe of discourse', their moral conflicts and moral blindnesses, in

---

[1] The discerning will not read this as a contradiction of what is said about the importance of words by E. Shillito, pp. 211–16.

[2] *The Preces Privatae* of Lancelot Andrewes, ed. Brightman (Methuen, 1903), p. 257. A quotation, it seems, from St. Fulgentius, Bishop of Ruspe in Numidia, early sixth century.

short, their 'psychology'. He needs thus the psychological insight of the wise pastor, and not the psychological arts of the manipulator of crowds.

The conclusion of the matter is this: the psychology of effective preaching is the psychology of the man who has entered deeply into the meaning of the two commandments which our Lord said summed up the whole law and the prophets, and who, entering in, has obeyed.

E. ROMILLY MICKLEM.

XIII

THE PREACHING OF THE WORD

WHEN Mansfield College was being planned, Dale wrote a letter to Fairbairn in great agitation; he had heard that it was proposed to put the pulpit at the corner of the platform. To put the preacher to speak cross-wise, so that the 'altar' might be visible, was in Dale's eyes 'to dishonour the function of preaching'. He let the matter drop when he was told that only from the corner could the voice be heard, but he found it a miserable humiliation that the chapel should not 'be fit for its main purpose'. 'I wonder what would be said of architect and building committee, if after they had erected a concert hall, a fiddler could be heard only when he stood in a corner.'

These words are quoted not because of their bearing on the place of the pulpit in the Chapel. Long experience has shown that from that corner there has been great preaching. What is important is the revelation which they give of the mind of Dale, who is justly honoured among the founders of the College. Dale himself belonged to the company of the great historic preachers. 'His thought took shape in the spoken discourse, but then it was discourse that recalled the heroic age of the English sermon.'[1] Such a man was resolved that from the very first in the new college in Oxford the preaching of the Word should be magnified. As he saw the vision of Mansfield, he saw it as a house of sound learning and piety, from which there should go forth men who in wonder and awe should preach the Word. He dreaded greatly lest at any time such an office should be despised or set in a lower place. Because it can be so great a calling, it can also be, if it is not taken seriously, a vain,

[1] Fairbairn on 'Dale as a Theologian', *Life of Dale*, p. 696.

pretentious, and idle profession. From the beginning Mansfield was committed to a lofty ideal of the preacher's office.

Fairbairn no less than Dale believed in preaching. No one who heard him in the fullness of his powers will ever forget his own sermons. It was as if the whole man was in action. He remains in memory as a perfect example of a man gripped, and in intellect and conscience and heart held fast by a Word, which had been given to him. Such a man could not concede a secondary place to preaching. 'The order of the apostles was an order of preachers; and ever since the power of God has lived in His Spirit and in the Word. The force that created and has ever moved the Church has been the preacher, not the priest.' For Fairbairn the speaker was the man 'possessed of God who speaks of the God Who possesses him. . . . The man who can send forth winged words bearing the quickening truth of God.' This meant, indeed, an exalted ideal of preaching. But in the history of Mansfield there has never been and must never be a lowering of the pitch in this matter. The office of the preacher is a perilous and impossible calling, but there is no escape from it by the reduction of the demand. It is impossible but in this respect it is in keeping with the Christian Revelation.

If in 1886 there was a place for the preaching of the Word, there is no less a place in 1936. It is still true that by the Word the Church is made and on the strength of it the Church lives. Without it the Society has nothing to define its purpose or justify its separate existence. And the Word if it is to have free course must have its preachers.

But if such things are true they imply a definite interpretation of the Church. This word is used loosely, and needs to be defined much more strictly if it is to have any practical value. For Churchmen to take such a word, and make it extensive enough to cover anything which they wish included at any given moment, is to expose themselves to the impatience and contempt of serious thinkers. For every such idle word men will account at the Day of Judgement. It is also true that for its many idle words the Church is already in judgement. The Word, the Church, the Preaching must be related to each other. They must be consistent with each other, belonging to the same Pattern.

There is no preaching of the Word if the Church is chiefly a Society for the study of religion. Such a society is an excellent thing, and may well have a valuable place in the network of societies. But it cannot have any room for what is meant in historic and apostolic usage by preaching.

Nor has the preacher his former part to play in a Church which exists simply to carry out certain reforms in human relationships. A Society of people of goodwill, who are against Slavery or War or Bad Housing, will need orators to awaken the nation to these horrors. They must have public assemblies for the declaration of their plans. Their Society will need officers and directors. They should indeed appeal to the mind of Christian people. To say that they are not Churches does not mean that they are unworthy of the support of Christian men. It only means that they are not entitled to take over this distinctive name, and they offer no place for the preaching of the Word. It is necessary in the interest of economy in thinking to attach some more distinctive meaning to the Church. It may become so wide that there is little of it in any given spot. When that is done it is a familiar experience to find that the office of the preacher is made to correspond to the reduced meaning of the Church. There is still preaching, but it is not what has hitherto been meant by the preaching of the Word. Ethical lecturers or advocates of social reforms are not unfairly treated when they are refused the title of 'preacher'.

The Church is not a Society for the preservation of an

ancient symbol, or *cultus*, which has become detached from its original meaning. It was in the mind of certain Catholic Modernists in the beginning of this century to keep the *cultus* of the Church though they were prepared to relinquish the historic Christian doctrines, for the sake of which the *cultus* was first practised. But though the Catholic Church somewhat roughly condemned them, and grouped with them others who were in reality far removed from them, the Church was right in its claim that it could not allow its *cultus* to be accepted and celebrated by those who had ceased to believe its Word. The Church cannot keep this Word unless it is prepared to set it forth in preaching. If the heart of the matter can be set forth without words, then it must be added that the Word is not what it was at the first nor what it has been wherever it has come with power into human life.

If the Church is such that it needs the preaching of the Word, some things follow for the guidance of the preacher.

The preacher is like other men, a seeker; but he is not a preacher of the holy gospel by virtue of that; he is not a leader in an expedition of discovery; he is where he is, because something has been given to him. If the distinction must be made, he is a Finder rather than a Seeker.

This goes along with a large and frankly owned area of undiscovered truth; it is his to confess frankly as St. Paul did many times 'concerning this matter I do not know' or 'I have only my own evidence to give'. But it has never been the practice of the Christian Church in any of its many varieties of faith and doctrine to choose its ministers because of the ignorance which they share with others, but because of something which is given to them. 'This grace' has been given to them to minister the Word.

The conditions are such that no man can take any credit for this ministry. If he lives in a realm of grace, then all boasting is excluded, and he can honestly preach as one who has received something in trust. He will be dishonest if out of a false humility he steps down so that he is undistinguished from others, when God, not for the sake of giving honour to His preacher, but for the sake of His holy Kingdom, has distinguished him.

A Jeremiah cannot forget that he has been made ' . . . a defenced city, and an iron pillar, and brasen walls'. It is a degradation to the word which a preacher delivers if he despises his own calling. The preacher is not humble when he refuses to stand apart from other men; he is yielding to a false timidity, to the 'craven fear of being great'.

And those who hear him know this. They have a right to ask certain questions. To what spiritual country does the man belong when he preaches? Out of what world does he come when we see him in the pulpit? His ministry may deal with a thousand matters; he will not think it his duty always to propound a scheme of redemption, or suppose that he has not preached the Word unless he has dealt directly with the nature of the divine redemption. But if he is a man whose native air is now that of a redeemed world of which he is the witness and herald, then he will be free to deal with many things, some of them in comparison secondary, for whatever be his subject, the hearer will always hear the undertones.

'To preach Christ is to feed the soul, to justify it, to set it free, and to save it if it believes the preaching.'[1] To accept this calling is the first condition of preaching.

But the preacher who does this is on one side of his work a craftsman whose material is words, and he cannot do all that he is called to do if he is a poorer craftsman than he need be. Preaching is an art of which the necessary material is words. It is a subdivision of rhetoric, and it must therefore be studied as the instrument which was used by Demosthenes and Cicero and Burke. Because it is concerned with sacred themes it does not cease to be an art

[1] Luther, *The Liberty of the Christian Man.*

by means of which the human spirit takes material and impresses itself upon it. The speaker who preaches Christ is still an artist dealing with words no less than a sculptor with his marble. To set in contrast the high spiritual purpose of the servant of God with the skill of the artist is misleading. There is no end served by saying that the artistic element is only secondary. Things may be secondary and yet important. The profound insight of Pascal is the main thing; but because of his mastery of his own tongue he has won a hearing for his word, which he might have missed. Bunyan says that he might have stepped into a 'higher style'; if he had, he would have stepped down into a lower place; for his art was unconsciously but perfectly mastered. Pascal himself had no doubt in his own mind that the artistic care and skill of the writer counted for much. Two tennis players use the same ball; but one places it better than the other. It is possible, Pascal added, to write well even upon theology.

The preacher cannot escape from the call to be an artist in words. With his use of his voice and of gestures, both important matters, this chapter does not deal; in addition to all such means, there is the handling of words, of which something must be said. To this, far too little attention may be given by the preacher. Some preachers even take a pride in their neglect of their instrument. In the same breath they speak of their calling to preach the Word, and their neglect of the words which are their instrument, as though there were no relation between the two. There can even be found in some preachers a belief in the literal inspiration of the Word written, along with a contempt for all the ways whereby through words a way is opened into the hearts of men. This can only be because there is a confusion between the true and the false meanings of rhetoric. If by rhetoric we meant the handling of words so that their full value may be in exercise, then it is not a luxury, still less an unworthy attainment to choose and to arrange words with pre-

cision and beauty; it is as much needed by the preacher
as the knowledge of his medium is by the sculptor or the
architect.

The preaching of the Word is one variety of art. No
less than the poet, the preacher takes words and impresses
a certain meaning upon them. But since his instrument
is something so common that it has lost for most men any
association of mystery, he may find himself in a peculiar
danger. Marble, canvas, the strings of a violin, do not
lose their mystery. Few men study such instruments; the
rest of us look on and wonder. But all of us are using all
the time the only material which the preacher has for his
art. It is his hard and perilous task to take the words
which everybody uses, and shape them to divine uses. It
is so easy to speak; he may think that he needs no discipline in this art. He will certainly treat with the scorn
which they deserve all affected literary tricks. He will
not form a pulpit vocabulary, nor will he adorn his
sermon by some of the hard-worked verses from certain
sacred poets, as a man might put a reproduction of a
Master in a prosaic book of chronicles. What are sometimes called 'literary' sermons fail to become literature
though they cease to be preaching. There should be no
vocabulary reserved for the pulpit.

What is needed is a recovery of the sacredness of words.
The preacher must enter into the mystery of his instrument; and because it is a universal instrument, it does
not become less needful to study it, and to handle it with
mastery and reverence.

Since the discovery of printing, words have lost much
of their mystery. This is true of the spoken no less than
of the written and the acted word. We only smile at the
'childishness' of Christina Rossetti, who could not bear to
see a paper with words printed on it blown about in a
London square, since she feared that the Divine Name
might be written upon it. There is a suspicion of magic
in this, but there is also a lively sense of the reverence due

to words. Perhaps the belief in magic had for its purpose
to prepare for that reverence. Magic itself is the crude
first attempt of man to deal with an admitted mystery.
It may be to the true study of rhetoric what astrology
was to astronomy.

Christina Rossetti was nearer than others to the mind
of the ancient seers and prophets. For them words were
always a solemn and significant thing. They never became cheapened in the commerce of the mind. The
coinage was never debased. The word never became an
idle formula. When the Hebrew prophet said 'The word
of the Lord came to me', it was to him an overwhelming
and even heart-shattering experience. When he said
Thus saith the Lord, he was repeating no idle formula. The
Word was like a fire that burned the prairies; a hammer
that broke the rock into pieces.

When Plato spoke of the Word in the *Phaedo*, a passage
which must always be ranked with the prophecies of the
Incarnation, he used 'Word' with a sense of its profound
mystery and power. He makes Simmias say in the *Phaedo*:[1]

'Failing this, that is to say, if a man can neither find the truth
by the exercise of his own faculties, nor learn it through the help
of another, then having chosen that which is at all events the
best and most irrefragable of Human Doctrines, he ought to
embark thereon, like a mariner going to sea on a raft (in
default of any better conveyance), and sail through life's voyage,
that is to say, unless it were possible to proceed on one's way
more securely and with less danger on some firmer vessel or on
some Divine Doctrine.'

What is the best way of all? It is to have some Divine
Word to direct our way. The mariner on his voyage in
search for truth should 'cling to the most stable human
teaching, unless he can procure a firmer vessel, *some
divine word*'. When we speak of using words in our preaching we must try to make our way backward to the mind
of man who could use such phrases while still the mystery

[1] Translation in Geddes.

which rested upon words had not faded away, and a Divine revelation could still be expressed by the analogy of a spoken Word.

We have to dismiss all the assumptions in such phrases as 'these are only words', or 'we do not want words but deeds'. Such a contrast would have been idle in the mind of Plato or Isaiah. And it is by their range of vision and by their usage we must estimate the resources of the instrument used in preaching. The Church will make itself contemptible if it sets apart a place in its worship for the use of a certain instrument, and at the same time by its carelessness and frivolity disparages it. It cannot be denied that there is a contempt for preaching which is well founded. The preacher may rise to the height of his calling, but because his peak is so high, the fall from it plunges him into abysmal depths. There would seem to be a growing demand that the preacher should respect his calling, and should set his standard by the most solemn usage. To preach may be little more than the weaving of pretty designs; or it may be the impression upon words and the conveyance through words of the Eternal Word and the Present Action of the Holy God.

We do not use 'mere words'. There are no 'mere words'. What there is in spoken language is a power quicker than a two-edged sword; 'pressing to the dividing of soul and marrow.' Where the word comes with its true resources, something happens.

Whatever may be the Divine Word committed to the preacher, at least there must be an appropriateness for the service of that Word in the instrument of language. If the Unseen Lord would communicate something to men, He must use this way already open into the spirit of man. The City of Mansoul is approached along the same roads whether it is Immanuel who comes, or Diabolus, or Another. But if we speak in this way we do not explain the mystery of the Divine Word on the analogy of the word of man to man, as though that were perfectly plain. That too is mysterious. It is only our blind familiarity which makes us lose the infinitely mysterious element in the spoken or written words, whereby the things incommunicable are communicated, and words unspeakable are spoken.

The oldest of all sounds from the creatures of this earth are the croakings of frogs on a spring evening; but the mystery of language is not dissolved by the discovery of such primitive beginnings; it is wiser to consider words as a mystery, pointing to something waiting to be revealed. Words are reserved for the Eternal Word. In a real sense the preacher has for his task to offer an instrument, patiently and painfully made ready for its predestined use.

In preaching, then, we are administering a Sacrament. The preacher has not the same preparation to make as the priest. But it is not a less serious task to handle words in the name of God than to offer to men the Bread and Wine. For the preacher there is no set arrangement of his material upon which he can invoke the blessing of the Eternal Spirit. His material can only be made ready by long preparations; he must know some of the agony of the artist who finds his instrument hard and intractable; he is all the time under the control of his Lord, both when he speaks, and in the solitude in which he makes ready. It is not a matter for pure enjoyment, though there are moments of exaltation for which it would be worth while to go through many deserts. But often the preacher making ready for this sacrament would give anything to escape. But there is no escape.

The man who is under this compulsion is not driven by weekly gusts—Sunday comes; he must prophesy! There is a steady incessant Power that keeps him to his task. The Gospel is more to him than the vision of beauty is to the artist or the inspiration of his theme to the musician; it must find expression. At all costs *it must out*. Men of the great school of preaching do not always preach because they like it but there is a fire shut up in their bones and they cannot contain. That is why the preacher must toil at his preparations, and master his material.

It is foolish to underrate such a study of the instrument. There have been and are many preachers who preach Christ greatly though they have little knowledge of the mysterious powers of language. But if the records of the pulpit are studied, it will be seen that the greatest of preachers were men who read largely, and had a familiarity with the past masters of their instrument. There is no sufficient plea to be offered by the man who uses words in a coarse and slipshod way. He is like a graceless priest who treats with flippancy the elements which are holy to him. Something might come on the wings of words, and it does not come because he has been false to his calling. Something incommunicable might be carried in this way; things audible might become signs of things which ear has not heard, but the priest of this sacrament has been false to his trust.

The very existence of literature is a witness to this sacramental character of words. When does a piece of writing or speech become literature? It may be a plain statement of fact, such as that on a certain day a football match took place in which one side scored three goals and the other two. This would not be called literature. But Virgil could describe a boat-race in such a way that it is eternal poetry. What makes the difference between the one use of words and the other?

This must be found in the sacramental character which we find in pure literature. There the expression is not separable from that something else which we can receive as we hear it or read it, for the words are not a clothing for the idea but its incarnation.

For the preacher there can be no limit to the research which he makes into the meaning of the Word. The greater part of his study will be out of sight; but the

F f

power of his preaching will be determined by the depth of his spiritual life:

> the gods approve
> The depth and not the tumult of man's soul.

But when we leave the instrument and think of the Word, there are some certain, almost self-evident truths which must be held by all who *preach* the Word.

Preaching must be a sacrament wherein God deals with man as a reasoning being. Its prelude should be: 'Stand upon thy feet like a man and I will speak with thee.' Language has provided for man magical incantations, which are common still in many religions; but there can be no room for magic of this kind in preaching. St. Paul contrasts prophecy with the 'speaking with tongues', and leaves no doubt of his own preference. For him and for all preachers it is true that an appeal must be made to the understanding.

ἀλλ' ἐν ἐκκλησίᾳ θέλω πέντε λόγους τῷ νοΐ μου λαλῆσαι, ἵνα καὶ ἄλλους κατηχήσω, ἢ μυρίους λόγους ἐν γλώσσῃ

1 Cor. xiv. 19.

So far as the preacher is concerned all the devices by means of which certain evangelists work up emotion through the repetition of choruses and perfervid formulas designed to produce a hysterical reaction, are to be classed with 'tongues'; and there are other more immediate temptations of the same order. They do not belong to the instruments which the preacher can lawfully use.

The place given to preaching in the Christian Church implies that there is something communicable from God to man, and to man not in his subconscious life, but to man as a reasoning being. The God about Whom and for Whom the preacher speaks can speak to man; He remains still the God Who hides Himself, but He is at the same time the God Who can reason with man, and take him into His confidence, no longer as a servant but as a friend. The preacher finds his call impossible if he has to confess that God and man cannot have a common language. It will always be the solemn task of the preacher to teach his people that God dwells in the thick darkness; but that truth will not stand alone. The preacher speaks because God has spoken. The God for Whom he speaks, *can* speak.

Preaching rests upon the 'mystery' of the Gospel. Its chief theme is the revelation of God, once dark, now made manifest. To St. Paul it came as a perpetual ground of wonder, that he had been given this grace to proclaim such a mystery. The proper subject of preaching is revelation. The true preacher does not stand in the pulpit to proclaim his own discoveries; he has had something given to him. He is not a being free to lecture upon his own explanation of the universe; or to share with his hearers in the books he has read, or even the newspapers. He belongs to a Church which has been created and sustained by a Word revealed. There will always be about the preacher, whatever his subject may be, the air of one who has listened and heard the voice and has 'some of the voice's greatness'.

> The lion hath roared, who will not fear?
> The Lord God hath spoken; who can but prophesy?

The Christian Revelation was communicated by the first Apostles in their preaching. They had varied ways of describing the Reality which had come to them. They preached Jesus as Lord; the Word of the Cross, the Gospel of the Resurrection; and always as truth communicable from them to other men. The confidence of the primitive Church in the sufficiency of language to bring home to strangers and aliens the truth of Christ is a significant fact. It was a safeguard against superstition, which is always one of the dangers besetting religion. The truth of religion, which is *preached*, comes at once under the head of a communication capable of being set forth by one man to other men.

Yet the Word to the preacher means something which can only be received by the hearers, who will assent to it by faith and surrender to its claims. Clearly when the Apostles preached Christ, they received from some of their hearers more than an intellectual interest, or even assent. Something happened. If they had only reported historical facts, then an acceptance of them would have been a sufficient answer. If they had offered counsel for virtuous behaviour, then the promise of a reformation in character would have been the fitting answer. But they would have failed in their task if, when they communicated what they knew as the Word, something did not happen, far more revolutionary than an intellectual assent, or a promise of amendment of life. Something happened in the spirit of the man who listened and believed; there was an encounter between the hearer and the Living God. The witness borne to the Resurrection released the powers of the endless life within that man. The preaching of the Cross meant for such a man the day of judgement, in which he was revealed to himself and pardoned. The preaching of the Word meant the coming into action within certain lives of that Lord Whose Word was like a fire and like a hammer that breaks the rocks into pieces.

It is claimed that in the sacramental life of the Church the Incarnation is prolonged. It can also be claimed that in the preaching of the Church, where it is preaching of the apostolic kind, the life of the Word made Flesh is manifested and released, and in that sense prolonged and fulfilled.

One of the preachers who were often heard in Mansfield College Chapel, Dr. P. T. Forsyth, wrote of such a prolongation is this noble passage:

'Or, I read the story of the father who beseeches Christ to heal his son. I hear the answer of the Lord, "I will come down and heal him". "Him!" That means me. The words are life to my distempered soul. I care little for them (when I need them

most) as a historic incident of the long past, an element in the
discussion of miracles. They do not serve their divinest purpose
till they come to me as they came to that father. They come
with a promise here and now. I see the heavens open, and the
Redeemer at the Right Hand of God. I hear a great voice from
heaven and these words are the words of the Saviour Himself
to me, "I will come down and heal him". And upon them He
rises from His eternal throne, He takes His way through a ready
lane of angels, archangels, the high heavenly host and the
glorious fellowship of the saints. They part at His coming, for
they know where He would go. These congenial souls do not
keep Him, and these native scenes do not detain Him. But on
the wings of that word He moves from the midst of complete
obedience, spiritual love, holy intelligence, ceaseless worship
and perfect praise. He is restless amid all that in search of me—
me sick, falling, lost, despicable, desperate. He comes, He finds,
He heals me on the wings of these words.'

That is an expression in exalted language of the work
in the soul which the preaching of the Word *can* do. The
Word preached makes a crisis for the hearer, and in that
moment through listening to the words of a man, who
has himself been surrendered to God, he becomes himself
the scene of another visitation from the Redeeming God.
Something happens. The Gospel becomes a contemporary document. The Word lives and glows.

But it does not follow that this frees the preacher from
any necessity to preach doctrine. If preaching is a
reasoned presentation of the Christian Gospel, everywhere it must have a basis of doctrine. That will not be
discussed as it might be in academies, but it is impossible
for a man to preach something which he calls the Word,
and at the same time to make no ordered confession of
his faith. No preacher who knows the mind of men as
it is to-day will be deceived by the plea that doctrine is
no longer needed. When the critics add that they need
only the simple self-evident truth of the Fatherhood of
God and the Brotherhood of Man, there is reason to
doubt their insight. Belief in the Fatherhood of God and

the Brotherhood of Man, taken by itself, is the most difficult of all creeds.

It is possible for doctrine to be so preached that it
becomes of thrilling interest. It is always the joy and
strength of a preacher to live and move within a frame-
work of Christian truth, which he accepts, and his hearers
come to understand. If he preaches Christ as a Living
Lord and Redeemer, he is always prepared to confess
what manner of Being He must be if such claims are
made for Him. He does not leave it an open question
what he thinks of Him. That is always the presupposition of every argument and every appeal.

Such a Word, received and reverenced, studied and
explored in prayer and solitude, will save the preacher
from many perils. He does not preach himself, and he is
not, therefore, at the mercy of his own moods, or even of
his experience. He is not compelled to preach only what
he has himself made his own perfectly; he can turn the
eyes of his people to Christ, Whose riches are unsearch-
able. He is releasing a power of which he knows something, of which neither he nor any man can know all.

Such a Word gives to him the joy of working within
limitations. There is room in his life for both discipline
and adventure. The comprehensiveness of the Word
is made known only to those who accept its apparent
limitations. To preach the Word is to be set free from
the multiplicity of themes, in which the preacher may be
lost. He is not commissioned to discuss all things that are
admirable. He is not an exponent of *all* excellent causes.
He need not think himself a prophet in general to his
age. In every rightly ordered society there is a distinctive task for each man. The novelist does not preach.
The preacher does not do the work of a novelist or an
essayist or an economist. He lives to preach the Word
which, if it is not preached by him, will not be preached
at all.

To preach the Word is to be delivered from the danger of

giving incomplete and unrelated messages, with nothing to unite them except perhaps their exposition by an attractive speaker. It is clear that in the days to come the more serious members of any community will demand that a preacher must speak to their condition. If they want entertainment they can go elsewhere. If they go to Church they will go more and more to learn what can be known of God. And they will not be satisfied with preaching which gives an account of Him; they will seek for preaching on the wings of which God Himself draws near. Whatever changes may come, there will always be a place for such preaching of such a Word.

The style of preaching will vary; the response to it is always the same. This is how Thomas Olivers, one of the first Methodist preachers, was converted by a sermon of George Whitefield:

'The text was "Is not this a brand plucked out of the fire?" When this sermon began I was certainly a dreadful enemy to God and to all that is good, and one of the most profligate and abandoned young men living; but by the time it was ended I was become a new creature. For, in the first place, I was deeply convinced of the great goodness of God towards me all my life, particularly in that He had given His Son to die for me. I had also a far clearer view of all my sins, particularly my base ingratitude to Him. These discoveries quite broke my heart.'[1]

There is no reason to doubt that given the same conditions the same things may happen. The necessary conditions do not include the style of Whitefield nor all the Calvinistic doctrines which he held. They do include a great honour and reverence given to preaching; and they do include a belief in the living power of Christ to act as he did in the soul of Thomas Olivers.

Preaching is in many eyes a despised and poor thing. But through the foolishness of preaching, God has revealed Himself to men. These are poor temporal means, to use M. Maritain's words. The Cross is in them.

[1] Wesley's *Veterans*, i. 205.

'In the last resort, let us consider the spiritual man *par excellence*. What were the temporal means of Wisdom incarnate? He preached in villages. He wrote no books—that again was a means of action too heavily weighed with matter. He founded no newspapers or reviews. His sole weapon was the poverty of preaching. He prepared no speeches, gave no addresses. He opened His mouth and the clamour of wisdom, the freshness of Heaven passed over men's hearts.'[1]

If when he preaches, something of that freshness of Heaven passes over men's hearts, if on the wings of his words the Lord Christ draws near, still the same to-day as yesterday, if the words on which, not without toil and agony, he has impressed what he has heard and seen, glow with the radiance of the Holy Spirit, then he can count himself blessed in his calling.

> If through my perjur'd lips Thy voice may speak,
>   If through a sinner Thou canst save from sin,
> Go forth, my Saviour, through my words to seek
>   And bring Thy lost ones in.
>
> I offer Thee my hands with recent scars—
>   Raw with the scars deep-cut by gyves of sin,
> Ply them in prison'd souls to break the bars
>   And by me, Lord, pass in.
>   E. SHILLITO.

[1] Maritain, *Religion and Culture*, p. 51.

XIV

PRAYER AND PRAISE

PREVIOUS writers in this volume have dealt with Catholic and Puritan types of worship. We are concerned in this chapter with Prayer and Praise in modern worship, but more particularly in Churches of the Independent or Congregational order. For an understanding of the usage of modern Congregationalism, however, we must take notice of another religious movement, the Evangelical Revival, which began with John Wesley, but which in some of its later developments showed a wide divergence from the mind and spirit of its founder. We cannot understand the development of Congregationalism during the last hundred years unless we do full justice to the fact of its double origin. It was the fruit of seventeenth-century Puritanism, but it came to new life and vigour under the influence of the Evangelical Revival of the eighteenth century. It implies no ingratitude to the influence of the Evangelical Movement, which quickened all the Churches of this country, to say that in many ways it took us away from our main Puritan tradition; not least was its influence seen upon our tradition of worship.

There were two main practices of Puritan Independency which were determinative of its mode of worship, and the Evangelical Revival had a marked effect upon both. One was Calvinism, which it shared with the Presbyterians, and the other was the idea of a gathered Church.

The theology of the seventeenth-century Independents was Calvinistic, and even when it moved away from some of the rigid doctrines of Calvinism, it never lost the austerity of Calvinism, and its worship was characterized by dignity and reverence.

The criticism is sometimes made of our free form of worship that it is too subjective. The 'Minister's Prayer',

as it is sometimes called, is inclined to be too expressive
of his own religious feelings. It is said in favour of a
liturgy that it saves us from the moods of the Minister.
The Churches of Calvinistic descent had no objection in
principle to the use of a liturgy, nor has modern Congregationalism. Mr. Matthews has pointed out[1] that the
Puritans did not object in principle to a liturgy, it was the
Book of Common Prayer to which they objected, as containing the relics of Catholicism. The early Independents
did, it is true, object in principle to all liturgical forms.
Dr. John Owen, in particular, condemned all liturgies as
'false worship, used to defeat Christ's promise of gifts and
God's Spirit'. But it must not be forgotten that the ejected
Ministers of 1662, who were the fathers of modern Congregationalism, were many of them of Richard Baxter's
way of thinking on this matter. The later antipathy to
a liturgy is largely explained by Dr. John Watson: 'If a
man declines to use a Liturgy and you lop his ears and
slit his nose to encourage him, human nature is so constituted that he is apt to grow more obstinate, and to
conceive a quite unreasonable prejudice against the
book.'[2]

It is significant that with the kindlier feelings towards
the Anglican Church which happily characterizes the
Free Churches to-day, modern Congregationalism has
shown a tendency to adopt liturgical forms. Upon that
we must say more later, but the point to be emphasized
here is that although the Independents came to reject a
liturgy, they cannot justly be accused of subjectivism.
Their Calvinism saved them from that. They never
forgot that the object of worship was Almighty God, and
they humbled themselves beneath His mighty hand. No
one had a greater sense of the Majesty and Glory of God.
We may agree with Dr. Dale that 'John Wesley rendered
immense service by the vigour with which he asserted the
moral freedom of man as against the Calvinistic Doctrine

[1] pp. 174-77.   [2] *The Cure of Souls*, p. 206.

of the Divine decrees',[1] but with the later development
of Evangelicalism there did appear a subjective element
from which perhaps we are not wholly free to-day.

The difference we are trying to indicate (it is a difference
of emphasis rather than of ultimate principle, between
the Puritan and the Evangelical tradition) can be traced
in the two words which are characteristic of each: Personal Religion and Experimental Religion. The essence
of Puritanism was Personal Religion. But this does not
mean that Religion is a matter of private opinion and
feeling, 'believing what you like'; it means the personal
verification and appropriation of the historic faith. No
doubt this is what experimental religion meant to John
Wesley, but there is a type of 'experimental religion'
which is in danger of subjectivism. Free prayer under
such conditions is in danger of becoming subjective and
autobiographical. But such a tendency is quite alien to
the Puritan tradition.

The same influence can be traced even more conspicu-
ously in Church Praise and Hymnody. Watts's Hymns
took the place of the old Metrical Psalms which were
liturgical in character. That is, their object was to set
forth the praises of God. Only he was anxious that the
God that should be praised was the God and Father of
our Lord Jesus Christ, and not the God of the Old Testament. He also wrote hymns to illustrate and drive home
the point of the sermon. But they never lost the objective
note, and they are filled with a deep sense of the Majesty
of God. Watts spoke of his hymns as 'Evangelic', by
which he meant that they set forth the truths of the
Gospel. But the 'Evangelical' hymn is of a different type.
The great hymns of John and Charles Wesley have enriched the hymnody of Christendom for all time, and
yet there was a real danger in the 'experimental' type
of hymn. As Dr. Benson says: 'From the liturgical point
of view the hymn of experience seems to violate the

[1] *The Evangelical Revival*, p. 22.

traditions and to create a new standard of Church Praise. Instead of a congregation uttering its corporate praise with a common voice, we have a gathering of individuals conducting their private devotions in audible unison.'[1]

A still graver danger was incurred by the enthusiasm of the Revivalists. The Hymn came to be regarded as a direct instrument for the conversion of sinners. It must always be a supreme task of the Church to convert sinners, and we dare not veto any successful method of moving men to repentance and extolling the redeeming mercy of God. But the object of a Hymn is to praise God and to magnify His Holy Name. There may be a use for evangelistic hymns of this type in Revival services, but in public worship hymns should be addressed to God and not to men.

Here then lies the answer to those who criticize our free form of worship as lending itself to individualism and subjectivism. It is a real danger. But in so far as we have yielded to it we have not been true to our Puritan tradition, and it is not inherent in our method of worship.

The other great principle which has determined our form of worship is that of a gathered Church. Here again the influence of the Evangelical Revival has made itself felt, for good certainly, but not entirely for good. A 'gathered Church' is not quite the same thing as a Church of 'converted' people in the strict Evangelical sense. The sense in which the word 'gathered' is here used is defined in the Savoy Declaration: 'The Lord Jesus Christ calleth out of the world into communion with Himself them that are given unto Him by His Father.'

There has always been a certain tension between the Calvinistic doctrine of Divine Election, which is here presupposed, and the idea of a 'gathered Church' to which professors are 'elected' by vote of a Church Meeting. It was not until Congregationalism had freed itself

[1] *The English Hymn*, p. 250.

from the Calvinistic doctrine of divine decrees that the way was open for the more spiritual conception of a gathered Church of which Dr. Dale is the classic exponent. 'The polity of the Congregational Churches require in the most distinct and emphatic manner the possession of the supernatural life as the supreme, and, as I think, the only indispensable condition of Church Membership. They receive members only on the declaration of their personal faith in Christ.'[1]

Thus the idea of a local gathered Church is that of the Church Universal, the whole body of the redeemed, emerging, becoming manifest, in one place. It is not a voluntary association, but a fellowship of believers. 'The formation of the Church rests not upon the will or consent or belief of men, whether as individuals or as societies, but upon the creative will of God.'[2] Now this is different in principle from the idea of a voluntary association of men and women who have a common religious 'experience', and who come together to express their religious feelings and to impart them to others. It is no condemnation of that type of religious gathering to say that it is essentially different from the idea of a 'gathered Church', which is determinative of the worship of Puritan Independency. We cannot exaggerate the importance of that principle as determining our mode of worship.

'Perhaps', says Dr. Forsyth, 'the exclusive use of free prayer descends to us from a time when the worshipping congregation was almost identical with the Church of believers, who had a real spiritual experience, and whose soul of faith the minister found it easy to enter through his own. Whereas now the Church is but the minority of the congregation, and a form so sympathetic as free prayer cannot do its mighty work because of unbelief.'[3]

Historically that is undeniably true. Our form of worship belongs to the idea of a gathered Church. It is

---

[1] *Essays and Addresses*, p. 123.   [2] Joint Lambeth Report.
[3] Preface to *Intercessary Services*, p. 4.

assumed that the people who gather are devout Christians who come together to perform the highest act of the Christian life, the worship of Almighty God.

> 'Make our best spices flow abroad
> To entertain our Saviour God,'

sings Isaac Watts, in one of his most beautiful hymns, of which only the first line is usually quoted and that for contempt. Nor must it be forgotten that they came prepared. There was family prayer every day, and not least on Sunday morning. They did not come to Church from an atmosphere of worldliness and look to a beautiful building and an entrancing liturgy to move them to more concerning cares, and help them to feel the reality of things unseen.

They did not even come, as we sometimes hear suggested in a Vestry prayer, to gain strength and inspiration for the coming days. It is often said that worship is a preparation for life. It would perhaps be truer to say that life is a preparation for worship.

'Our worship is a means to an end. That end is a life lived in the spirit of Christ by mankind as a whole, in time and in eternity. Our worship is achieving its purpose in so far as it succeeds in inspiring mankind to consecrate all its manifold activities to the glory of God. . . . It is because so much that passes for Public Worship no longer seems to have this dynamic influence in consecrating and enriching life that it is so widely neglected, simply because it is not worth while.'[1]

There is a great deal of truth in that, but it needs to be qualified. If it is said that worship is a means to an end, there is a danger lest the character of worship be determined by the ends of life. But it may be that it is the end that needs to be considered. It is not enough to ask: 'Will this service help me to live my daily life in the coming days?' May it not be that the obvious gap between life and worship is a condemnation of the life? Is it not the

---

[1] The Bishop of Southwark, *The Spirit in Life and Worship*, p. 287.

function of worship to give us a foretaste of that life which is life indeed, of which our earthly days are at best but a foreshadowing?

When Keats says 'Beauty is truth, truth is beauty', he probably means that Beauty is all that matters. To the artist that may be true, but Art is not the whole of life. But when the artist says 'Beauty is all', and consecrates his whole being to the creation of Beauty, that is worship. The scientist 'worships truth' when he says 'Nothing matters but truth; truth alone is divine', and sacrifices everything for truth. When the moralist says 'Goodness is all that matters', and dedicates himself to the good life, he worships goodness. Now Christian worship is the acknowledgement that the God revealed in Jesus Christ is the fountain light of all our seeing, the beginning and the end of all creation. In the act of worship we strain our frail mortality to the utmost to realize the fullness of our life in God. It should indeed cast its sanctifying light on the life of every day, but life itself can have no higher goal than to prepare us for that supreme act of worship.

But Dr. Forsyth's statement raises two questions upon which something should be said. Is it true that people of less mature religious experience are helped in their worship by a more liturgical and perhaps ornate type of service? And is it true that our traditional type of worship is permanently the best suited for a fellowship of believers?

In *Liturgy and Worship* F. H. Brabant writes:

'If we all arrived there,' i.e. at Church, 'feeling and thinking as we ought, no doubt our services would be simply the expression in speech and action of the inner state of our souls, with all the spontaneous directness of children. But we do not, most of us, arrive like that. We come stained and weary from a life that is largely unnatural, longing for something to lift us into an atmosphere of spiritual peace. . . . That is why the liturgy expresses not only what we feel, it also teaches us what we ought to feel. Worship has not only an expressive function but also a suggestive or impressive one.'[1]

That is a very important point. Father Dolling defended the rather elaborate ritual he used in the East End of London from the standpoint of its 'impressive function' in relation to the drab and colourless lives of the East End people. Here, undoubtedly, a vital difference emerges between the Catholic and the Puritan. The latter would rely upon preaching, but he would make it colourful and impressive, and perhaps there is not so much difference as used to be supposed between the ear and the eye as the medium of impression. But we are concerned here with the worship of a gathered Church. Even so, the 'impressive function' of worship must not be ignored. Is there not something to be said for the impressive power of a worshipping congregation? 'Thou art holy, O Thou that art enthroned upon the praises of Israel' (Ps. xxii. 3). The Psalmist seems to look back for spiritual refreshment to the reality of God 'enthroned upon the praises of Israel'. Dr. Dale's famous description of a Church Meeting is almost too well known to quote:

'To be at a Church Meeting, apart from any prayer that is offered, and hymn that is sung, any words that are spoken, is for me one of the chief means of grace. To know that I am surrounded by men and women who dwell in God, who have received the Holy Ghost, with whom I am to share the eternal righteousness and eternal salvation of the great life to come, this is blessedness. I breathe a Divine air. . . . I rejoice in the joy of Christ over those whom He has delivered from eternal death, and lifted into the light and glory of God.'[2]

'A means of grace'—there is the impressive function of worship. No doubt such an experience as Dale describes implies a rich spiritual life and understanding, but it remains true, in its measure, that to be in the midst of

---

[1] *Liturgy and Worship*, p. 13.
[2] Address to the Congregational Union, printed in *Constructive Congregational Ideals*, D. Macfadyen, p. 136.

a sanctified people who are manifestly engaged in the worship of God, is deeply impressive.

But the more important question remains. When the Church of God is assembled, in fellowship with all the saints to offer its praises and its prayers to God, is there any principle upon which we can judge the merits of various types of worship?

'I have often been puzzled', says Dr. Oman, 'about what makes a service worship. It does not depend either upon having a liturgy or wanting it. It does not depend on the sincerity or even the piety of the minister. More and more I come to think that it depends on worshipping with the congregation, and not merely conducting their worship.'[1]

It is this combination of the congregational and the individual element in public worship which constitutes its peculiar problem and difficulty, as E. R. Micklem has shown (pp. 193–201). 'The things man most needs from God he can least bear to ask in the hearing of men; the things the whole congregation needs may meet the case of no single man.'[2]

The duty of the minister is to lead the prayers of the congregation. Dr. P. Dearmer says, 'We should all, of course, flock to hear Milton praying extempore, if he were to come to life again, but there are many mute inglorious Miltons whom we would rather not hear.' But we do not flock to Church to 'hear a minister pray'. It is the congregation that prays. How can it best do so?

The most perfect example of congregational prayer is surely when all the people unite to say the Lord's Prayer together. Is it any less the prayer of the congregation when it is intoned by a choir? The reason for the intoning is clear. In a large congregation the difficulty of all keeping together and the discordance of many voices is apt to produce a confusion of sound which is distracting. Indeed, it was on that ground that the early Independents

---

[1] *Office of the Ministry*, p. 11.   [2] A. M. Fairbairn, *Studies*, p. 273.

objected to the saying of the Lord's Prayer and responsive prayers. They cause a 'confused murmur in the
congregation'.[1] Many people would claim that they can
make the prayer their own more easily when it is sung
or intoned. We cannot say, surely, that one method is
more 'spiritual' than the other. The essential thing is
that it should be done with sincerity and reverence, and
that the congregation should perform the mental act of
praying. To the writer, personally, no way of saying the
Lord's Prayer is so truly worshipful as to say it together,
with orderly reverence, but it is a question of personal
judgement, not of principle. The same applies to the
General Confession and the General Thanksgiving. These
also, whether recited by the whole congregation or intoned, are perfect examples of congregational prayer.
When the minister reads a collect, the conditions are
similar. The advantage of a collect is that it is familiar,
and in the case of most of the collects of the Prayer Book,
it combines the collective and the individual, in a way
in which perhaps only long usage can do.

A litany aims at the same result in a different way.
Here the congregation makes the prayer their own by an
audible response. But to be successful a litany must be
familiar. It is very difficult to concentrate the attention
on a printed page, and at the same time to make the
mental act of prayer.

Here a word should be said of the difference between an
historical liturgy and some modern 'home-made' liturgy
of which so many have appeared in recent times. An
ancient liturgy has something of that precious quality of
Holy Scripture of which Newman so finely says: 'It is far
higher and wider than our need; and its language veils
our feelings while it gives expression to them.' Above
all, we have here, in the words of Dr. Percy Dearmer,
'the accumulated wisdom and beauty of the Christian
Church, the garnered excellence of the saints'. A modern

---

[1] *Exceptions against the Book of Common Prayer*, 1661.

liturgy incurs the danger of all attempts to make the best of both worlds.

We must now consider the advantages of 'free prayer'. Its dangers are apparent. To hear a man pray eloquently may be a more pleasing experience and more moving than to hear a beautiful prayer well read, but there is no advantage of one over the other from the standpoint of the congregation praying. The advantage of free prayer lies in the essential nature of prayer as communion with God. The difference lies in the relative emphasis that is given to the content of the prayer and the act of communion with God. A devout woman said to the writer about a certain minister: 'So-and-so talks to God when he prays. You can't often say that in these days.' But that surely is the essence of prayer. The severest criticism of extempore prayer is that it is so often addressed to the congregation. To be able to lead a whole congregation to the throne of grace is the greatest gift in the ministry of prayer. But though it is a gift, it can be cultivated. The actual mode of preparation does not seem to involve any principle. The only adequate preparation is of the man himself.

The exact meaning of 'extempore' is rather an academic question. The essence of extempore prayer is that it arises out of that particular moment. There is a sense in which the moment cannot be anticipated. It does not exist until it arises. It is a great gift to be able to lead a congregation in prayer, at the very moment at which they have arrived, in the course of a service. But we are to pray not only 'with the spirit' but 'with the understanding also' (1 Cor. xiv. 15), and some men's understanding moves more slowly than others. There seems to be no principle involved in the preparation of the form of a prayer beforehand. There are only two fundamental conditions. The minister must know his people and be one with them in all their cares and joys, and he must know God. Granted these conditions, people of the

Congregational way would probably testify that they are helped most to pray by a praying minister, and while liturgical forms have their advantage, especially as regards the content of the prayer, they sacrifice that immediacy and directness of spiritual communion which is the essence of prayer.

We may be allowed to quote the beautiful words of Dr. Thomas Jones, the 'Poet-preacher', at whose feet Robert Browning loved to sit in Bedford Chapel:

'There should be perfect liberty in these things. The man who has to engage often in public devotions will sometimes need the help which the words of others afford. . . . As there are spring tides in the sea, when the waves pass their old boundaries and break high upon the shore, so there are uprisings of the soul which pass the limits of all liturgies, litanies, and prescribed forms of prayer and worship. The river is grander in its own native freedom than when it is confined by the art of man; it winds around the foundations of the mountains, foams among the rocks, leaps over the precipice, lingers on the plain, murmurs under the overhanging branches of the forest trees, and everywhere finds out and forms its own channel. There is a staid, grave, correct beauty in liturgies, but nobler and more natural are the free utterances of the earnest soul when our joys and sorrows, hopes and fears, trust, love, gratitude, are allowed to form their own course, and flow according to a divine law. Therefore I say, in the mode of worship let there be freedom. "God is a spirit, and they that worship Him must worship Him in spirit and in truth".'

A further word may be said about the relation of spontaneity to form. Canon Barry has written recently:

'As an art worship must be formal. There is nothing in the least incompatible between formal art and spontaneity. Some of the most perfectly spontaneous and lyrical conceptions of art have been worked through rigidly conventional forms. It is therefore a quite false ideal—as the Free Churches have begun to find out—to hope that by making worship informal we should thereby make it more spontaneous.'[1]

[1] F. R. Barry, *The Relevance of the Church*, p. 136.

There is surely some confusion here. The accusation of 'informality' is not usually brought against the Free Churches. It is more often said that we are just as rigidly formal as the Church of England, and that we do not use the freedom of which we boast. But the formality of a Free Church Service is precisely similar to the formality of a Sonata or a Sonnet. It is a form which leaves room for spontaneity. May it not be that the Sonata form has been so much favoured by musicians just because it is that form which leaves room for spontaneity? It does not follow that we are permanently tied to our traditional Order of Service, but it is not the fixed form but the stereotyped content of the Book of Common Prayer which seems to us to leave no room for spontaneity.

The influence of the Evangelical Revival has also made itself felt in the externals of worship.

'About the external incidents of worship the men of the Revival were very indifferent. One place was as good to worship God in as another; any old hay-loft, a farm-house kitchen, a carpenter's shop was as sacred as any cathedral. When they built chapels it was their only anxiety to get as large a chapel as they could for their money. . . . To the Revival the building is nothing and the heart of the worshipper everything.'[1]

But it was not of choice but of necessity that the Puritans worshipped in barns and warehouses. When it became possible to build Chapels of their own, they were too impoverished to erect costly buildings.

'The Nonconformists of the eighteenth century had no tradition to fall back upon in Church Architecture. They built in the usual fashion of their day. If they had been rich enough there is no reason to doubt that they would have been willing to employ Wren, Hawkesmoor or Gibbs, and would have accepted similar buildings to those erected for the State Church, with modifications as to the chancel plan.'[2]

[1] R. W. Dale, *The Evangelical Revival*, p. 27 f.
[2] A. L. Drummond, *The Church Architecture of Protestantism*, p. 43.

Dr. Drummond gives instances to prove that when Independency was strong and prosperous enough it was not indifferent to taste in the erection of a 'Meeting House', which denoted a trysting-place for the Christian and his God. 'It was plain, no doubt, but plain in the same way as the Holy of Holies in the Jewish Temple was unadorned—the abiding place of the Presence.'[1]

The typical Evangelical attitude to the sacredness of a building is expressed in William Cowper's beautiful hymn:

> Jesus, where'er Thy people meet,
> There they behold Thy mercy-seat;
> Where'er they seek Thee, Thou art found,
> And every place is hallowed ground.
>
> For Thou, within no walls confined,
> Inhabitest the humble mind;
>
> .   .   .   .
>
> Here may we prove the power of prayer,
> And bring all heaven before our eyes.

We do not always remember where the last line comes from.

> But let my due feet never fail
> To walk the studious cloisters pale,
> And love the high embowèd roof,
> With antic pillars massy proof,
> And storied windows richly dight,
> Casting a dim religious light.
> There let the pealing organ blow,
> To the full-voiced quire below,
> In service high and anthem clear,
> As may with sweetness, through mine ear,
> Dissolve me into ecstacies,
> And bring all heaven before mine eyes.

Was the Evangelical Cowper deliberately answering the Puritan author of *Il Penseroso*? The recent movement towards more worshipful churches among Congrega-

[1] A. L. Drummond, op. cit., p. 45.

tionalists is no departure from Puritan tradition. But
unfortunately it was not inspired in the first place by a
conscious revival of true Puritanism, but by the Anglican
Revival of the Oxford Movement. For example, there
may be architectural reasons for placing the pulpit at the
side, though its origin would seem to be the acoustical
difficulty of preaching in a Gothic Church built for the
celebration of Mass. The symbolism of our Puritan tradition would be better expressed by the pulpit being behind
the Communion Table, for ours is a ministry of the Word
and the Sacraments. The question cannot be fully discussed here, but reference may be made to the important
chapter on 'The significance of function in Church Architecture' in Dr. Drummond's book.

Praise is usually associated with the worship of song.
This is not strictly true, for prayer includes praise as well
as petition, and some hymns are rather prayers than songs
of praise. But the chief function of a hymn is to sing the
praises of God. Here also the problem is twofold, to com-
bine the praise of a congregation with the personal experience of each individual. But the more personal
elements of praise are better left to the prayer of thanksgiving. Song is the more natural expression of collective
praise. It is supremely in the hymn of praise that we
unite with the universal Church, in heaven and on earth,
to magnify the grace and glory of God.

Praise is the supreme act of worship. Both the impressive and the expressive functions of worship reach their
culmination in praise. For in praise we express with
heart and mind and soul the excellence and glory of God.
'Let all that is within me bless his holy name.' In praise,
too, we set forth the majesty and love of God. 'I will give
thee thanks in the great congregation.' Praise is also the
way of communion with God. 'Let us come before his
presence with thanksgiving.' We are here bidden to
rise from our dull cares and earthbound thoughts on
the wings of praise. Moreover, the very act of praise

implies a conception of God. It is the most characteristic Christian act of worship. 'The craving to be appreciated', it has been said, 'is the deepest principle in human nature.' It is more, it is a divine principle. If God is love, He takes pleasure in the praises of His beloved. Praise, then, must be an essential note in all our worship. Every service is a Eucharist, and not least the Holy Supper when we call to remembrance God's unspeakable gift. But in ordinary worship the hymn is the medium of praise.

After extempore prayer the Congregational hymn is the most characteristic feature of Free Church worship. The Congregational Churches have a grand tradition of hymnody, but we have also felt the influence of all the movements affecting hymnody in the last century. The influence of the Evangelical type of hymn has been noticed. The literary hymn has enriched our books with some beautiful songs of worship, but it has a danger. There has been a tendency to look for subjects which lend themselves to poetic treatment. A conscious literary motive is apt to detract from the supreme object of the hymn, to set forth the glory of God. The publication of *Hymns Ancient and Modern* marked an epoch in the history of English hymnody. We owe it largely to Dr. Allon that the antipathy that was felt toward many aspects of the Oxford Movement was not allowed to deprive us of many beautiful hymns. But it was unfortunate that we yielded so easily to the fascination of the sentimental Victorian tune which it did so much to popularize. The revolt is now in full swing, and it is led by Anglicans. It is interesting to observe that they are reviving the grand old Psalter tunes which we too easily surrendered to 'dwell in the miasma of the languishing and sentimental hymn-tunes which so often disfigure our services'.[1]

Recent Free Church hymn-books show an immense improvement. But the bane of Hymnology is still the

[1] R. Vaughan Williams, Preface to the *English Hymnal*.

denominational hymn-book. It divides us when we ought
to be most united and often creates a vested interest in
mediocrity and worse. Nothing but the best should be
tolerated in the worship of praise.

A minister once wrote to the late Poet Laureate to ask
permission to include hymns from the *Yattendon Hymnal*
in a collection of the 'hundred best hymns'. Dr. Bridges
granted permission but added: 'There are not a hundred
best hymns in the English language. There are not a
hundred good ones.' That is to set a very high standard.
But as Bishop Paget once said: 'Many hard and foolish
and untrue things might be left unsaid if men would only
wait until they could say them in good English.' And
how many false religious ideas would never have gained
currency if men had waited till they could be expressed
in a good hymn. The popularity of community singing
to-day should convince us of how great an opportunity
we have lost through our neglect to maintain our tradition of congregational singing. There are those who,
realizing the power of music to touch the heart of the
multitude, would have us exclude from our services all
but the most popular hymns and tunes. But our aim
should be to capture this interest in corporate singing
for the most exalted conceptions of the beings and ways
of God.

A word must be said in conclusion upon the greatest
factor of all in the conduct of Public Worship—the personal factor. 'Anybody can make sermons,' Dr. Selbie
once said, 'but it takes a saint of God to lead the worship
of the people.' The most beautiful liturgy can be spoilt
by the way in which it is delivered. But with the free
forms of service commonly used in the Free Churches the
personal factor becomes supremely important. We are
reminded of Principal Shairp's famous description of
Newman at St. Mary's: 'The look and bearing of the
preacher were as of one who dwelt apart, who, though he
knew his age well, did not live in it. From the seclusion

of study, and abstinence, and prayer, from habitual dwelling with the unseen, he seemed to come forth that one day of the week to speak to others of the things he had seen and known.'[1] One has a grave misgiving that the life of a busy minister in these days, with all the administrative work of a Church, and countless committees to attend, leaves him with little time to steep his mind in the language of devotion, and for that constant waiting upon God which is essential if he is to be the bearer of 'authentic tidings of eternity', and to lead his people into the secret place of the Most High.

If it be true, in the words of E. R. Micklem, that 'in order that she shall accomplish anything the Church must live, and her life depends on her worship',[2] then no part of a minister's training, and no part of his work, is so important as the preparation to lead the worship of his people.

But that must not be our last word. The minister may not be all that we could desire. It still remains the greatest experience that life offers, to take our place in the Church of the living God, to join our humble petitions with the prayers of the Saints, and to unite in the hymn of Creation, that Song of Honour which Ralph Hodgson heard when he 'climbed the hill as light fell short':

> I heard it all, I heard the whole
> Harmonious hymn of being roll
> Up through the chapel of my soul
>   And at the altar die,
> And in the awful quiet then
> Myself I heard, Amen, Amen,
>   Amen, I heard me cry!

K. L. PARRY.

[1] W. Ward, *Life of Newman*, i. 65.
[2] *Our Approach to God*, p. 11.

XV

THE SACRAMENTS

THIS chapter is designed to restate the historic Congregational doctrine of the Sacraments. Many in these days cannot understand Baptism nor give any meaning to the Eucharist beyond a shadowy 'Zwinglianism', which, as Dr. Cadoux has shown (pp. 145–51), is far from Zwingli's intention. The reason for this is that they have almost lost the capacity for conceiving that sole and sovereign and original activity of God in the work of our salvation which is the very foundation of our Calvinism as it is of that Catholicism which is the Mother of all western Christianity. Stress tends to fall upon *our* faith, *our* prayers, *our* dedication of a child. Naturally, therefore, it seems superstitious to suppose that Baptism regenerates or that we receive the Lord in Communion. But it belongs to our tradition and to the truth of the Gospel to lay all the stress upon the action of the living God. It is God who calls and regenerates, He who comes and gives Himself to us. His action is first and last; our worship is but *Antwort* to His *Wort*, an answer to His Word. *or gabe and aufgabe.*

I

'Verbum, inquam, et solum verbum, est vehiculum gratiae'; so Luther. The Word, and the Word alone, is the vehicle of grace. This is the fundamental principle of the Protestant doctrine of the Sacraments as of the Church. The Sacraments convey grace because they are modes of the Word, *verba visibilia*, as St. Augustine calls them. Except in historic Protestantism the Sacraments have been degraded either to a mere symbolism or to an impersonal operation. Protestantism stands equally opposed to Romanism on the one side and to what is sometimes styled 'Modernism' on the other, and to both for the same reason that in them the Sacrament is disjoined from the Word.

A Sacrament is 'externum symbolum, quo benevolentiae erga nos suae promissiones conscientiis nostris Dominus obsignat ad sustinendam fidei nostrae imbecillitatem, et nos vicissim pietatem erga eum nostram tam coram eo et angelis quam apud homines testamur'—'an outward sign wherewith the Lord sealeth to our consciences the promises of His good will toward us, to sustain the weakness of our faith; and we, again, on our behalfs do testify our godliness toward Him as well before Him and the angels as before men'.[1]

First, what is vital in the Sacrament is not man's 'experience' but God's action—God's action, not the priest's. The Sacrament, wrote P. T. Forsyth, 'is an *opus operatum*. More, it is an act of the Church more than of the individual. Further still, it is an act created by the eternal Act of Christ which made and makes the Church. At the last it is the act of Christ present in the Church, which does not so much live as Christ lives in it. It is Christ's act offering himself to men rather than the act of the Church offering Christ to God.' — *as Jeremias claimed.*

Second, a sacrament is a seal attached to a promise. Apart from the apprehension of a promise, a sacrament, as Calvin says, is as void and empty as a seal hanging on a parchment that has nothing written on it.

Third, by 'symbol' or 'sign' we mean more than illustration. The Sacraments 'are more than souvenirs, keepsakes. They are bequests. They are conveyances' (Forsyth). They are the acts of God in His Church, whereby that *opus operatum* of Christ, never to be repeated, is, as it were, extended and brought home to believers. His Majesty King Edward was hailed as king immediately upon the death of his royal father, but this will not render his later coronation otiose. The coronation is the ratifica-

[1] Calvin, *Inst.* iv. 14. 1.

tion, sealing, and formal conveyance of the sovereignty.
The promises of our God stand sure apart from all sacraments and rites. As there may be pledging of troth without kiss or ring, so there may be Christian life without
sacraments, but the despising of sacraments is no mark of
true spirituality.

Fourth, Protestantism proclaims, not a Gospel of sacraments, but sacraments of the Gospel. Where there is no
proclamation of the Word, there can be no sacrament.
By the Word is not meant some mumbled formula of
consecration nor the preaching of any religious or social
message which may have commended itself to the presiding minister. The Word is the Gospel of the grace of
God in Christ to which the Scriptures testify. This Word
is powerful, as St. Augustine says, not because it is spoken
but because it is believed (*non quia dicitur, sed quia creditur*).
The Sacraments belong to the administration of the
Spirit; the power of their working is an operation of the
Spirit. They are not the products of faith, but they are
not operative apart from faith. They are concerned with
grace itself proclaimed in the Word, accepted by faith,
and sealed in Sacrament.

Fifth, the Sacraments derive their whole meaning from
the redeeming Work of Christ. It is action which they
symbolize and convey. The essence of the Sacrament,
therefore, is action, not species. 'In so far as our action is
symbolical', says Forsyth, 'it is symbolical of Christ's Act,
not of his essence.' Again, 'the conveyance is not through
the element, but through the act'. The efficacy of Baptism is not in water but in washing, of the Communion
not in bread but in bread *broken*. The elements are as
integral to the Sacrament as the words to the sentence,
but as it is the whole sentence alone which is effectual as
conveying meaning, so it is the Word (and not the
elements) that conveys grace in the Sacrament.

Sixth, what man does is secondary but not therefore
unimportant. 'The Sacraments are part of the confession.'

They are the creed, the Christian faith, set forth in action, as preaching is the Christian faith set forth in word. In the Sacrament the Church declares its faith in the redeeming Act of God in Christ Who gave Himself for us and to us and washes us from our sins 'in His precious blood'. The Sacrament is *sacrificium laudis in confessione Nominis*, a sacrifice of praise in the confession of His Name. Apart from the Word declared and believed there is neither Church nor Sacrament.

Seventh, the difference between the operations of Word and Sacrament, says Forsyth, is 'psychological rather than ontological'. That is, if we ask whether Sacraments are necessary in the Christian dispensation, the answer is that they are necessary for the Church, but not necessary for individual salvation. Our salvation rests upon the promise of God. This promise is ratified and sealed in the Sacrament, but it is neither created nor conditioned by the Sacrament. Sacraments are necessary to the Church because we are embodied spirits and not angels.

II

'Baptismus signum est initiationis, quo in ecclesiae co-optamur societatem ut Christo insiti inter filios Dei censeamur'—'Baptism is a sign of the entering wherewith we are received into fellowship of the Church, that, being grafted into Christ, we may be reckoned among the children of God.'[1]

Baptism is the sacrament of regeneration, of the new birth; it marks the distinction between the Church and the world, the end of the journey to Christ, the beginning of the life in Christ. From the earliest days Baptism has been the door into the Church. That the rite is necessary for salvation Calvin explicitly denies (iv. 15. 20) on the ground that Christ's promise is of itself sufficient to effect its work. Our assurance of salvation rests upon the

[1] Calvin, *Inst.* iv. 15. 1.

eternal counsel of God, not upon a rite of which man is
the instrument. None the less, to refuse Baptism on the
ground that it is not necessary for salvation would seem
to be of pride or irresponsibility.

Man is regenerate by the Word of God, not by the
Sacrament. There is no mysterious potency in consecrated water or in consecrated bread; regeneration is not
effected through a formula but through faith; it is by the
blood of Christ (that is, by the crucified and risen Lord),
not by the water of Baptism that we are cleansed.

It is the Word of God, and the Word alone, that conveys
grace, but Baptism is a mode of the Word. Baptism,
therefore, conveys grace, the grace of regeneration, not as
if the rite in itself were anything, but because it declares
and seals the Word. Baptism, says Calvin, 'is like to a
certain sealed charter whereby he confirmeth unto us
that all our sins are so defaced, cancelled, and blotted out,
that they may never come in his sight, nor be rehearsed,
nor be imputed'.[1] The prodigal in the far country may
receive a message that his father will forgive him or has
forgiven him. On his return it is the father's kiss that
ratifies and seals the promise, nor would it occur to the
prodigal to deny that the kiss is a vehicle of grace. In the
gospel the message of washing and sanctifying is brought
to us; the message is sealed in Baptism.

The Baptism of adults is neglected where the Church
has either forgotten the significance of Baptism or has
departed from the Word. In Baptism the baptized person
confesses Christ, but if this be the primary significance
of the rite, the symbolism of washing is singularly in-
appropriate; a verbal statement or some ritual in which
the subject should be the agent would be proper. But
no one can baptize himself. Christ is the sole agent
through His Church. He ratifies and seals the promise
of forgiveness. By a formal, declaratory, and effective
act the old man is put off and the new man in Christ

[1] *Inst.* iv. 15. 1.

assumed; buried in Baptism we rise to the new life in Christ.

Baptism has no meaning apart from the Gospel of redemption. If there is no final and decisive difference between the man who is in Christ and the man who is not, between the believer and the unbeliever or the half-believer, if Christ has not performed a redeeming Act whereby we who believe are translated out of darkness into light and made the sons of God, Baptism is simply an inept survival of happier days and saving faith.

Christ washes away sin in Baptism as He becomes our life in the Communion. Baptism, says Calvin, 'indeed promiseth us that our Pharaoh is drowned and the mortification of sin, yet not so that it is no more, or may no more trouble us, but only that it may not overcome us'.[1] The significance of our Baptism lies in this, that Christ acting through His Body, the Church, has solemnly engaged Himself that He will never leave us nor forsake us, and has sealed His engagement by an act which symbolizes the cleansing of His redeeming death and brings it to each of us with a singular and private application.

III

The New Testament affords no positive and indisputable evidence that children were baptized in the Apostolic age. The justification of infant Baptism is ultimately theological rather than historical. The practice is congruous with the theology of the Word and the meaning of Sacraments. 'A Baptism *unto* the confession of the Church faith', says Forsyth, 'may be as true to the Gospel Grace as a Baptism *upon* it, and less individualist.'

Baptism is pre-eminently the Sacrament of the prevenient grace of God, of the historic, finished work of Christ. It declares that while we were yet sinners, or before ever we were born or thought of, Christ died for

[1] *Inst.* iv. 15. 11.

us. Christ died for us, and out of His work arose the Church. Out of and into the fellowship of the Church are all the children of believers born. They may have as yet neither sin nor faith of their own; it will be necessary for them later of their own consent to take up their inheritance in Christ and His Church, but their inheritance it is, as in fact it is not the inheritance of the heathen. Some men are born free, some attain freedom at a great price; the children of the Church are born free. No one may say without blasphemy that God loves some children more than others or deny that Christ has died for all, but the Baptism of infants corresponds with spiritual facts, that the children of the Church are born into the Christian inheritance, and that the promises of God to Christians are not to them only but to their seed after them.

Says Calvin:

'The children of the faithful are not therefore baptized, that they may then first be made the children of God, which before were strangers from the Church, but rather that they may be therefore received by a solemn sign into the Church, because by the benefit of the promise they did already belong to the Body of Christ.'

And again,

'For God's sign communicated to a child doth as it were by an imprinted seal confirm the promise given to the godly parent and declareth that it is ratified, that the Lord will be God not only to him but also to his seed, and will continually show His good will and grace not to him only but also to his posterity even to the thousand generation. . . . Therefore let them that embrace the promises of God's mercy to be extended to their children think that it is their duty to offer them to the Church to be signed with the sign of mercy, and thereby to encourage themselves to a more assured confidence, because they do with present eye behold the covenant of the Lord graven in the bodies of their children.'

[1] *Inst.* iv. 16. 9.

Baptism is not a Dedication Service, nor can it be replaced by any such. At a Dedication Service it is the parents who are the agents, at a Baptism it is Christ through His Church; at a Dedication Service it is the parents who declare what they will do, at a Baptism it is Christ Who through His representative, the minister, takes the child in His arms and declares what He has done and will do for the child; at a Dedication Service it is the parents who promise, at a Baptism it is Christ. Baptism has no efficacy apart from faith. In infant Baptism the faith is that of the Church, not of the child. 'The Baptism of the child', says Forsyth, 'is not its regeneration except in title, but it is a real act of the Church and of Christ in the Church.' The suggestion that the faith of the Church is not strictly relevant to the Baptism of the child belongs to the kind of effete individualism which might argue that the prayers of parents are of no significance for their children, since there is no mechanical force in prayer. But Baptism, where it keeps its evangelical meaning, is for the children of the faithful only. It is meaningless unless the child is received into, and to be brought up in, the household of faith. It is to be later fulfilled in confirmation or admission to full membership on declaration of personal faith; and the rite may not be properly administered except within the circle of the Church.[1]

IV

Calvin's doctrine, like that of those who stand in his succession, is that the Supper is no mere symbolism or memorial rite; there is in it an effectual working of the

---

[1] There are Congregational scholars who, following Dale and accepting in general the doctrine of the Sacraments here set forth, maintain that Baptism as the sign that Christ has died for all mankind may not properly be withheld from any child. On the other side, it is contended that Baptism is the door into the Church, and that apart from the fellowship of the Church it must tend to be regarded either as an 'empty' sign or as operative apart from faith.

Spirit whereby the promise is fulfilled. In other words, the Supper is a true Sacrament wherein God Himself is the agent through His Church. Thus, as Forsyth says, 'Prayer is a gift and sacrifice that we make; Sacrament is a gift and sacrifice that God makes. . . . In prayer we go to God; in Sacrament He comes to us.'

The Supper is, in particular, relative to the new covenant between God and man in Christ. 'After a certain manner it reneweth, or rather continueth (*renovat vel potius continuat*), the covenant which He hath once stablished with his blood, so oft as He reacheth unto us that holy blood to be tasted of' (Calvin). Again, 'the breaking of the bread is a sign, not the thing itself. But, this being admitted, yet we shall rightly gather of the deliverance of the sign, that the thing itself is delivered. For unless a man will call God a deceiver, he can never be so bold to say He setteth before us an empty sign.'

The Supper refers to the Act of Christ in our Redemption, and it is in action, not in species, that the Sacrament consists. 'Christ speaketh not to the bread, that it may be made His body,' says Calvin, 'but commandeth His disciples to eat.' The elements are set apart for their sacred purpose, but beyond this there is no potency or change or sanctity in them. The Supper is a Sacrament of the Word. This may be illustrated from the composition and playing of music: there is first the music in the composer's mind, second there is the music actualized in sound, third there is the musical score whereby the music may be realized for each generation afresh throughout all time. The illustration, if imperfect, will serve its purpose. We may conceive God's divine purpose of Redemption, the co-eternal Word, as corresponding with the music in the composer's mind; the Word made flesh corresponds with the music uttered by the musician; the Sacrament answers to the reading of the score whereby for all time the wonder is extended and renewed. Or, again, 'a spoken word', says Forsyth, 'is the symbol or

vehicle of a thought it conveys; but it is also the thought
itself in action. The visible letters of the word only
enable us to handle it.' Thus, as the letters are to the
word, so are the bread and wine to the act in the Supper;
and as the spoken word to the active thought, so is
Christ's symbolic act here to His real and final Act upon
the Cross. In the Supper the sacrifice on Calvary is as it
were extended into time and applied to the heart of each
believer; it is the seal and ratification of the Gospel. It is
Christ who consecrates and Christ who seals.

For those who had been present at the Last Supper 'the
breaking of bread' had a peculiar significance and pathos
which it cannot have for us. On the other hand, there is
a wealth of meaning in the rite for us which was beyond
their grasp; for we know, as they could not, the long history of the Church of Christ throughout the centuries.
The story of the Church does not add to the Word of God
but it enriches, explains, and illuminates the Scriptures.
Implicit in the New Testament are several moments
which properly find their place in the administration of
the rite. There is first the backward look to the Last
Supper and to Calvary—'in memory of Me'; there is,
second, the forward look to 'the bridal Supper of the
Lamb' in the perfected Kingdom—'till He come'; there
is, third, the feeding upon Christ by faith—'take, eat,
this is My body'; there is, fourth, the Church as the Body
of Christ—'as My Father hath sent Me, so send I you';
fifth, the rite is Eucharist, the Church's thanksgiving in
the confession of the Redeemer's Name, *sacrificium laudis*;
it is *sacrificium propitiatorium* only as it may mystically
be regarded as an extension of the Passion into time.
Above and before all there is the Real Presence of the
Lord Himself as surely as on that last betrayal night,
sealing His promise to believers and giving Himself unto
His own.

V

As regards the mode of the administration we have two clear principles.

First, 'rectam Sacramenti administrationem non absque verbo constare'—'the true ministration of the Sacrament standeth not without the Word'. This does not necessarily imply that there can be no celebration of Baptism or the Supper without preaching, but that except in a community where the Word is faithfully preached and heartily accepted there can be no true Christian Sacraments. In the rites of themselves there is no efficacy; it is not the water which regenerates nor the bread which is Christ. The Word, and the Word alone, is the vehicle of grace. The Sacraments are the seals; where there is no promise made and accepted, the seal is meaningless.

Second, the administration of the Sacraments shall conform to Holy Scripture as the standard and rule of faith. Says John Knox, 'in this congregation should be distributed the mystical and Last Supper of Jesus Christ, without superstition or any more ceremonies than he himself used, and his apostles after him, in distribution thereof'.

Upon this principle three comments may be made:

1. It is not to be maintained that any and every elaboration of ceremonial is inconsistent with true Christianity, but our tradition and principle holds fast to Scripture and regards arbitrary elaboration as undesirable and dangerous.

2. Scripture itself is to be spiritually and not legalistically interpreted. It is to be understood that the disciples at the Last Supper and the crowds at the feeding of the Five Thousand received the bread reclining; it is surely permissible for us to sit or even to kneel, but the sitting posture adopted by us in preference to kneeling is not due to slovenly want of thought, but to the awful sense that in

spite of all unworthiness we are called to sit at the Table of the Lord. Again, Baptism, at least of adults, was originally by immersion; but it is not to be thought that this is required by the Spirit under totally different conditions of society and climate.

3. In so far as Scripture is our norm, we may as little diminish as increase the ritual acts there indicated. As the minister in infant Baptism takes the child into his arms in the Name of Christ, so also must he *take* the cup into his hands and *break* the bread. Hence in those congregations where 'individual' cups are used, the chalice also should be placed upon the Table, and the bread should not be so cut up before the Service that there is none for the minister to break. This solemn taking of the cup and breaking of the bread is not only in accordance with Scripture but is consonant with our testimony that the sacrament consists in action, not in species.

It has been much disputed in the past amongst Congregationalists whether the Sacraments may be administered by the laity. Stress is properly laid upon the universal priesthood of all believers; but the true Congregational principle seems clear that except in cases of necessity it is the minister who should celebrate the Christian sacraments; for our God is a God of order, not of anarchy. Ministers have been called out of the Church under the guidance of the Holy Spirit in virtue of the spiritual gifts entrusted to them; they are ordained to be ministers of the Word and Sacraments. As a matter of order, therefore (not of validity), laymen should not administer the Sacraments unless under exceptional circumstances the Spirit should so direct.

Baptism and the Supper are Sacraments of the Church. There is, therefore, as little place for private Baptisms as for private Masses. There are, however, two apparent, but only apparent, exceptions to this rule. If for any sufficient reason, as for instance grave illness, the child cannot be conveniently brought to the Church, the minister should baptize the child at home in the presence of one or two other Church members as representing the whole Church. A minister who repudiates the Roman doctrine of baptismal regeneration must not therefore decline to baptize a dying child. The Baptism does not cause to die safely a child that otherwise were lost, but it is right and eminently fitting that the parents should be comforted by the solemn rite whereby the Church in Christ's Name and on His behalf declares and seals His promises of protection and salvation to their child so soon to be taken from their sight. Again, it is often fitting that in cases of extremity and serious illness the minister should carry of the bread and wine of the Communion Service to the sick, or, where this is inconvenient, should celebrate the Supper in the sick-room itself. But in the former case this is rather a local extension of the Church celebration than a private Communion Service, and in the latter there should, if possible, be one or two others present to represent the Church.

In conclusion, we may understand the Sacraments of the Word if we conceive that at them the Church passes out of the space and time of ordinary mortal experience into a heavenly space and time. 'The Lord's Table is the Lord's Table, and that Table is not made of wood or stones, nor is it many Tables. There is only one Upper Room. There is only one Lord Jesus Christ, Who hands to His disciples the bread, saying, "This is My Body".'[1] According to the ancient use the minister at the Sacrament cries, 'Up with your hearts!' and the people respond, 'We lift them up unto the Lord'. From that moment it is conceived that the heavens are opened, and the Church on earth gathers with the Church in heaven—'therefore with angels and archangels and all the company of heaven we laud and magnify thy glorious Name'. So, too,

[1] E. R. Micklem, *Our Approach to God*, p. 247.

time is, as it were, rolled up, and that which in ordinary human experience we know as successive is seen in the eternal simultaneity of heaven. From the blood of Abel shed at the foundation of the world, through the sacrifice of Abraham on Mt. Moriah to the holy Nativity of Jesus Christ, Immanuel, His sacred Passion, His Resurrection in victory, His triumphs in the Church, His coming again in power and great glory—the whole drama of Redemption is, as it were, present together before our eyes as visibly occurrent, and the promise of our own inheritance is sealed by the Lord Himself upon our wondering hearts.

N. MICKLEM.

INDEX

PRINTED IN
GREAT BRITAIN
AT THE
UNIVERSITY PRESS
OXFORD
BY
JOHN JOHNSON
PRINTER
TO THE
UNIVERSITY